THE POUND CAKE COOK BOOK

FRAN C. WHEELER

Copyright © 2008 Fran C. Wheeler

All rights reserved.

ISBN: 1-4196-9712-9

ISBN-13: 9781419697128

Visit www.booksurge.com to order additional copies.

THE POUND CAKE COOK BOOK

ACKNOWLEDGMENTS

I grew up thinking that grandmothers made pound cakes. Mothers and aunts and other adults might make cookies or even birthday cakes, but only grandmothers made pound cakes. A good pound cake always was my father's favorite dessert, so there would often be a pound cake on hand for Sunday dinner or other special occasions. We all looked forward to family reunions when everybody's grandmother would vie to see whose pound cake was the best -- as judged by which cake platter was empty at the end of the day.

Through college and graduate school, my only serious encounters with pound cakes were at these family gatherings. My father would search for a cake that had fallen or was a little "sad," while I would get us a cup (or two) of Great Aunt Ethel's boiled custard -- there was no doubt about our favorite part of the meal.

When I began compiling our family history in the late 1970's, I came to realize that great aunts and grandmothers would not be there forever to provide these classic desserts that we all loved so well. I had been capturing their stories, but their recipes, too, were a part of our family legacy. And so it started -- a recipe here and there, with no real plans except to save them for posterity -- just a shoebox full of note cards and clippings.

After starting to work at the SC Department of Health and Environmental Control, I crossed paths with several excellent cooks who led me further into pound cake cookery. Each of them helped convince me that mere mortals (not just grandmothers) could find success with a pound cake recipe. From Harriette Duncan, Mike Jarrett, Mary Senn and Margaret Senn, I gained enough courage to try the old recipes and to experiment with new ones. Of course, there were some failures along the way, but even these weren't all bad since my father especially enjoyed the cakes that fell and the crew at my office would eat absolutely anything! Their motto was: If it can be sliced, it will be eaten.

Over the past twenty-five years, I have continued to collect more and more recipes -- from church socials, from family picnics, from community cookbooks, from friends and relatives. In this part of the country, *everybody* has a favorite pound cake recipe and is willing and eager to share it. The shoe box was filled to overflowing and frequent requests for recipes eventually led to this compilation, <u>The Pound Cake Cook Book.</u>

Many folks helped to collect, test, and taste pound cakes of every size, shape, flavor and color. It would be impossible to acknowledge everyone who has been a part of this project, but a few folks deserve a special mention. Thanks to Mary Senn and Frances Wheeler for recipes, advice and inspiration; to both of my parents for proof-reading the manuscript; to all of my extended family for their willingness to taste test recipes; to Patti Sullivan, Linda Bennett and Betty Fowler for assistance with typing; and to Margaret Senn for her encouragement, patience and assistance with just about everything.

TABLE OF CONTENTS

Introduction i
Tips for Perfect Pound Cakes Every Time iii
Pound Cake Problem-Solving v
Substitutions vi
Equipment viii
Storage ix

CHAPTER 1:
Old-Timey Plain Pound Cakes 1

CHAPTER 2:
Modern-Day Plain Pound Cakes 19
    Pound Cakes Made with Milk 21
    Pound Cakes Made with Buttermilk 38
    Pound Cakes Made with Half-and-Half 45
    Pound Cakes Made with Evaporated Milk 47
    Pound Cakes Made with Whipping Cream 48
    Pound Cakes Made with Sour Cream 51
    Pound Cakes Made with Eggnog 58
    Pound Cakes Made with Yogurt 60
    Pound Cakes Made with Cream Cheese 66
    Pound Cakes Made with Other Cheeses 70
    Pound Cakes Made with Water 73
    Pound Cakes Made with Carbonated Drinks or Sodas 74

CHAPTER 3:
Chocolate Pound Cakes 77
    Pound Cakes Made with Unsweetened Chocolate 79
    Pound Cakes Made with Sweet Chocolate 84
    Pound Cakes Made with Chocolate Chips 93
    Pound Cakes Made with Chocolate Syrup 97
    Pound Cakes Made with Powdered Cocoa 100
    Pound Cakes Made with White Chocolate 126
    Pound Cakes Made with Chocolate Cookies 128

CHAPTER 4:
Brown Sugar, Butterscotch and Butternut Pound Cakes 131
    Pound Cakes Made with Light Brown Sugar 133
    Pound Cakes Made with Dark Brown Sugar 149
    Pound Cakes Made with Molasses 154
    Pound Cakes Made with Butternut Flavoring 155
    Pound Cakes Made with Butterscotch Morsels 158

CHAPTER 5:
Pound Cakes Made with Fruits, Berries, Nuts and Vegetables 161
    Pound Cakes Made with Almonds 163
    Pound Cakes Made with Apples 166
    Pound Cakes Made with Apricots 179
    Pound Cakes Made with Bananas 182
    Pound Cakes Made with Benne Seeds 188
    Pound Cakes Made with Blackberries 189
    Pound Cakes Made with Blueberries 190
    Pound Cakes Made with Cherries 194
    Pound Cakes Made with Coconut 201
    Pound Cakes Made with Cranberries 206
    Pound Cakes Made with Currants 212
    Pound Cakes Made with Dates 214
    Pound Cakes Made with Figs 215
    Pound Cakes Made with Hazelnuts 216
    Pound Cakes Made with Lemons 217
    Pound Cakes Made with Lime 229
    Pound Cakes Made with Macadamia Nuts 232
    Pound Cakes Made with Mixed Fruit 234
    Pound Cakes Made with Oranges 235
    Pound Cakes Made with Peaches 243
    Pound Cakes Made with Peanuts 245
    Pound Cakes Made with Pecans 248

 Pound Cakes Made with Pineapple 256
 Pound Cakes Made with Pistachio Nuts 263
 Pound Cakes Made with Plums 264
 Pound Cakes Made with Poppy Seeds 265
 Pound Cakes Made with Potatoes 267
 Pound Cakes Made with Prunes 269
 Pound Cakes Made with Pumpkin 271
 Pound Cakes Made with Quince 275
 Pound Cakes Made with Raisins 277
 Pound Cakes Made with Raspberries 280
 Pound Cakes Made with Strawberries 282
 Pound Cakes Made with Sweet Potatoes 285
 Pound Cakes Made with Tangerines 291
 Pound Cakes Made with Walnuts 293

CHAPTER 6:
Pound Cakes Made with Wines, Liqueurs and Other Spirits 297
 Pound Cakes Made with Sherry 299
 Pound Cakes Made with Whiskey 301
 Pound Cakes Made with Rum 306
 Pound Cakes Made with Brandy 323
 Pound Cakes Made with Liqueurs 329

CHAPTER 7:
Spicy Pound Cakes 339

CHAPTER 8:
Cake Mix Pound Cakes 371
 Plain Pound Cakes 373
 Chocolate Pound Cakes 375
 Brown Sugar, Butterscotch and Butternut Pound Cakes 384
 Fruit, Nut and Berry Pound Cakes 386
 Spirit Pound Cakes 400
 Spicy Pound Cakes 403

INTRODUCTION

The classic pound cake, made with one pound each of butter, sugar, flour and eggs, is widely known as a traditional Southern dessert. An early pound cake recipe is found in *The Virginia Housewife or Methodical Cook*, written by Mary Randolph in 1824, and generally regarded as the first "Southern" cookbook. However, the pound cake is most probably of British origin - it was not new when it appeared in *The Art of Cookery Made Plain and Easy*, written by Hannah Glasse and published in England in 1747.

Some of the old pound cake recipes call for weighing the eggs and taking their weight in butter, sugar and flour. The weight of eggs can vary significantly, depending on their size and freshness, and some master cooks won't hear of measuring pound cake ingredients by volume. They point out that the proportions must be of equal weights to assure success.

The original pound cake was leavened only with the air that was beaten into the batter or with separately beaten egg whites. Air bubbles caused by creaming the butter with the sugar cause the cake to rise. When egg whites are beaten stiff and folded in separately, the cake rises even more because of the additional air trapped in the batter. Either way, pound cakes don't need baking powder, although nowadays it often is added as insurance.

Most modern recipes are adaptations that create rich and moist variations on the original recipe, but don't call for the same amounts of ingredients. Liquids can replace some of the butter and eggs. Cream cheese or vegetable shortening can replace some of the butter. Milk or sour cream can replace some of the eggs. Eggs can be used whole as other leavening agents replace whipped egg whites. Small amounts of baking soda or baking powder add volume and lightness. Low fat modifications create a healthier product. Flavorings vary with the cook's imagination.

Although the ingredients vary, the basic procedure hasn't changed. Air bubbles in the batter still cause the cake to rise and produce a satiny appearance. This characteristic texture, with a golden, tender crust, makes the pound cake unique in spite of the many variations on the original theme.

This book is a collection of over 300 pound cake recipes gathered over many years, from many cooks in many states. They range from the basic to the bizarre, but all are delicious, with velvety textures and terrific tastes. Enjoy!

TIPS FOR PERFECT POUND CAKES EVERY TIME

Read the directions. Take time to read the entire recipe before starting. Be sure of equipment and ingredients needed and how much time the recipe will take. Avoid surprises!

Use the correct size pan. Most pound cake recipes are designed for a 10-inch tube pan, which holds 16 cups (more than a standard 12 cup Bundt pans). If the pan is too small, the batter will run over the sides. If the pan is too large, the sides will slow the baking.

Grease and flour the pan to prevent the cake from sticking. Grease the pan with solid shortening. Substitute butter, margarine, or vegetable cooking spray only if the recipe calls for it. Always flour the greased pan, because a slippery surface keeps the cake from adhering to the sides of the pan and rising properly.

Have all ingredients at room temperature for best results. Let them come to room temperature for about one hour. More than an hour of unrefrigerated time may cause the butter to become too soft, and other items, such as eggs, may spoil.

Avoid making substitutions and take care to measure all ingredients accurately. Plain, all-purpose flour doesn't really need to be sifted (unless the recipe calls for sifted flour).

Creaming the butter or shortening with the electric mixer is the single most important step in making a pound cake. Air whipped into a cake is what makes it rise during baking.

Add eggs one at a time, blending just until the yellow disappears. Over-mixing at this stage adds too much air and the cake won't have pound cake's classic velvety texture.

Add flour or flour mixture alternately with liquid, beating at low speed of electric mixer. Begin and end with the flour mixture, mixing only until each addition is blended in.

Spread batter evenly in pan. Place pan in center of oven and bake at the temperature directed in the recipe. Keep the oven door closed during baking, at least until the minimum baking time has elapsed. Even a quick peek may cause the cake to fall.

Test the cake for doneness with a cake tester or wooden toothpick. Insert it into the center of the cake; it should come out with no batter or crumbs clinging to it.

Cool the cake in the pan, right side up, on a wire rack for 10 to 15 minutes. Before re-moving from pan, run a metal spatula around sides, pressing it against sides of the pan.

Invert pan onto a wire rack to remove the cake; invert cake onto another wire rack so that the rounded top is up. Let the cake cool completely, keeping it away from drafts.

POUND CAKE PROBLEM SOLVING

PROBLEM	POSSIBLE CAUSE
Batter overflows	Too much batter for pan Over-mixing
Sticky crust	Too much sugar Under-baking
Damp cake	Cooled too long in pan Under-baking
Tough crust	Over-mixing Not enough sugar, fat, or leavening
Sinking in center	Under-baking Removed from pan too soon Exposed to draft Too much liquid, sugar, or leavening
Heavy texture	Not enough leavening Old baking powder or soda Over-mixing Oven too cold Too much fat, sugar or liquid
Bottom crust too brown	Use of dark baking pan Pan placed too low in oven
Cake falls	Under-baking Oven temperature too low Removed from pan too soon

SUBSTITUTIONS

Serious cooks wouldn't dream of substitutions in their own special recipes for pound cake. The pound cake is regarded almost as an art form - it takes time, thought, and advance planning to have exactly the right ingredients on hand. The recipes in this collection are known to work with the ingredients listed and it's best to follow the recipe exactly. On the other hand, this cookbook contains so many variations on the basic pound cake recipe that you probably can look around until you find one that uses the ingredients available in your kitchen!

That said, good cooks like to experiment and it is true that almost any recipe has some room to make substitutions. The final product may not look or taste the same, but you'll probably still be successful with simple substitutions such as stick margarine for butter, skim or low fat milk for whole milk, or artificial vanilla flavoring for vanilla extract. Even egg substitutes or "instant" buttermilk will work in a pinch. Don't be shy, but don't expect to create the same cake unless you use the same ingredients.

Use the following table as a guide for emergency substitutions.

1 teaspoon baking powder	¼ teaspoon baking soda + ½ teaspoon cream of tartar
1 cup buttermilk	1 cup milk + 1 Tablespoon vinegar or lemon juice
1 ounce semi-sweet chocolate	1 ounce unsweetened chocolate + 1 Tablespoon sugar OR 3 Tablespoon semi-sweet chocolate chips
1 cup semi-sweet chocolate chips	6 ounces semi-sweet chocolate
1 ounce unsweetened chocolate	3 Tablespoon cocoa + 1 Tablespoon shortening
1 cup half & half	7/8 cup milk + 3 Tablespoon butter
1 cup honey	1 ¼ cup sugar + ¼ cup liquid
1 cup milk	½ cup evaporated milk + ½ cup water
1 cup self-rising flour	1 cup plain flour + 1 ½ teaspoon baking powder + ½ teaspoon salt
1 cup sour cream	1 cup plain yogurt

EQUIPMENT

Having the right equipment will make your baking much more enjoyable and successful. You will need these basic items to make pound cakes:

<u>Baking pans</u>: For best results, use shiny aluminum or tin baking pans. Dark surface pans require shorter baking time and cause the cake to brown more quickly. The standard pound cake pan is a 10-inch tube pan, but the batter can be split into two 9 x 5-inch loaf pans with good results. Smaller recipes can be baked in a 12-cup Bundt pan, which makes a more decorative cake.

<u>Bowls</u>: A set of four nesting bowls, made of glass or stainless steel. Plastic bowls may retain odors or colors.

<u>Electric mixer</u>: A free-standing electric mixer is needed for pound cakes to handle the large quantity of batter and the long mixing times.

<u>Grater</u>: A metal or plastic grater with surfaces for fine to coarse shredding.

<u>Measuring cups</u>: Glass measuring cups for measuring liquids and a set ($1/4$, $1/3$, $1/2$, and 1 cup) of metal or plastic measuring cups for dry ingredients.

<u>Spoons</u>: Metal or plastic measuring spoons ($1/8$, $1/4$, $1/2$, and 1 teaspoon and 1 tablespoon) for measuring small amounts of either dry or liquid ingredients; metal, plastic or wooden spoons of varying sizes for mixing ingredients.

<u>Spatulas</u>: Flat metal spatula for leveling off ingredients and for frosting cakes and a rubber scraper for scraping the sides of the bowl during mixing.

<u>Timer</u>: An accurate timekeeper, with a loud tone, for monitoring baking times.

<u>Wire racks</u>: At least metal two racks, for cooling cakes. They must be at least as large as the cake pan.

<u>Cake Tester</u>: Metal or wooden pick to test cake for doneness.

STORAGE

Pound cakes can be stored in an airtight container up to three days. Cakes can be wrapped with plastic wrap and aluminum foil and refrigerated up to one week or frozen up to two months. Frozen cakes should be thawed before unwrapping.

THE POUND CAKE COOK BOOK

CHAPTER 1

OLD-TIMEY PLAIN POUND CAKES

This chapter opens with the original "classic" pound cake recipe - one pound each of butter, sugar, flour and eggs. It also contains another 13 recipes that are variations on that basic theme. The major ingredients vary in proportion to each other, but all are alike in depending on eggs (sometimes lots of eggs) as the only liquid in the recipe.

CLASSIC POUND CAKE

This is it -- the original recipe that calls for a pound of each of the four main ingredients - flour, sugar, butter and eggs. Beaten egg whites are folded in at the end of the mixing for a light texture.

- 1 lb (2 cups) butter (do not substitute)
- 1 lb (4 cups) plain flour
- 1 lb (2 1/3 cups) sugar
- 1 lb (about 10 large) eggs, separated
- 1 teaspoon mace
- 1 teaspoon lemon extract

Beat egg whites until very foamy, add half the sugar and beat until stiff but not dry. In another bowl, cream butter and remaining sugar, beat in egg yolks, and then stir in flour. Stir in flavorings. Fold in egg whites and pour into greased and floured 10-inch tube pan. Bake at 350° for 1 hour or until toothpick comes out clean. Cool in pan 10 minutes; remove from pan to wire rack and cool completely.

MOTHER-IN-LAW'S POUND CAKE

This old-timey recipe makes a BIG cake, even without separating the eggs. There's lemon flavoring in the cake and in the icing.

> 1 lb (2 cups) butter or margarine
> 1 lb sugar (2 ⅓ cups)
> 1 lb eggs (10-12 eggs)
> 1 lb plain flour (4 cups, before sifting)
> ¼ teaspoon salt
> juice of one large lemon

Cream the butter. Add sugar gradually and beat until smooth. Add eggs, one at a time, and beat after each addition. Add flour a little at a time and mix after each addition. Stir in salt and lemon flavoring. Pour into a greased and floured 10-inch pan. Bake at 300° for 1 hour and 30 minutes or until cake tests done. Cool in pan 10 minutes, then remove from pan and cool completely on wire rack.

FROSTING

> 1 Tablespoon shortening or butter
> 1 box powdered sugar
> juice of 2 lemons
> evaporated milk OR whipping cream

Cream ingredients together. Add a few teaspoons of cream or evaporated milk to achieve desired consistency for spreading.

GRANDMOTHER'S POUND CAKE

Lots of butter, lots of eggs! Grandmother's secret was the use of top quality ingredients.

    1 pound salted butter
    4 cups sugar
    12 eggs
    4 cups plain flour
    1-ounce bottle lemon extract

Cream butter and sugar together. Add one egg at a time, mixing well. Add flour gradually. Mix in entire bottle of lemon extract. Pour mixture into large Bundt pan or tube pan, greased with shortening and floured to about 1-2 inches from the top. Place in pre-heated 350° oven and bake for 1 hour or until knife comes out clean. Allow cake to cool completely, then serve.

TEN-FOUR POUND CAKE

Ten eggs and four cups of flour - this is another big cake. Make it fancy by serving with vanilla ice cream and apple cider sauce.

> 2 cups shortening
> 3 ½ cups sugar
> 10 eggs
> 4 cups plain flour, sifted
> ½ teaspoon salt
> 4 teaspoons vanilla extract

Cream shortening and sugar; add eggs. Beat until well blended. Add flour and salt; beat until mixture is smooth and well mixed. Stir in vanilla. Pour into greased and floured 10-inch tube pan. Bake at 250° for 2 hours or until cake tests done. Cool in pan 10 minutes; remove from pan and cool completely on wire rack.

APPLE CIDER SAUCE

> 3 cups apple cider
> 1 cup whipping cream
> ¼ teaspoon vanilla extract
> 2 drops lemon extract
> 2 Tablespoons (¼ stick) unsalted butter, cut into small pieces

Boil apple cider in large skillet until reduced to ½ cup, about 18 minutes. Add cream; boil until slightly thickened, about 2 minutes. Transfer to bowl. Whisk in butter and both extracts. Cool slightly, and then chill until cold, at least 1 hour. Can be made 1 day ahead. Keep chilled. (The rich, creamy sauce is also delicious on crisps, puddings and cobblers.)

BILL BROWN'S POUND CAKE

Bill Brown must have been a chicken farmer -- who else would put so many eggs into one cake! A lot of different flavorings, too.

- 1 lb (2 cups) margarine
- 3 cups sugar
- 1 Tablespoon shortening (rounded)
- 10 large eggs
- 2 teaspoons vanilla extract
- 1 teaspoon almond extract
- 2 teaspoons lemon extract
- ¼ teaspoon mace
- 4 cups plain flour

Cream margarine, sugar and shortening. Add whole eggs, one at a time, beating after each addition. Add flavoring, then flour; mix well. Turn into a greased and floured 10-inch tube pan. Bake at 325° for 1 hour and 30 minutes or until cake tests done. Cool 10 minutes in pan; remove from pan and cool completely on wire rack.

Glaze

- 2 cups powdered sugar
- 1 lemon rind, grated
- 3 Tablespoons lemon juice
- ½ Tablespoon water

Mix ingredients together; add more water if needed, but do not let mixture get too thin.
Spoon on top of cake and let run down sides.

GREGG STREET POUND CAKE

This unusual recipe calls for lining the bottom of the pan with waxed paper, with none of the greasing and flouring that is standard procedure for most pound cake recipes.

　　1¾ sticks margarine
　　¾ cup butter
　　3 cups sugar
　　10 eggs
　　3 cups plain flour, sifted
　　pinch salt
　　1 teaspoon vanilla or almond extract

Cream together margarine and butter and add sugar until well blended. Then mix 2 Tablespoons sifted flour into sugar and butter. Add eggs, one at a time, beating slightly between each addition. Fold in gently the sifted flour and salt on lowest speed of mixer. This cake doesn't have to be beaten vigorously. Pour batter into tube pan with bottom lined with waxed paper. Do not grease sides of tube. Bake at 300° for 1 hour and 50 minutes or until cake tests done. Do not open the door until at least 1 hour and 40 minutes. Cool 10 minutes in pan; remove from pan and cool completely on wire rack.

EIGHT EGG POUND CAKE

Not quite a pound of each of the four main ingredients, but beaten egg whites and baking powder combine to make it a full size cake.

> 1¾ cups butter
> 2¾ cups sugar
> 8 eggs, separated
> 3¾ cups plain flour, sifted
> 1½ teaspoons baking powder
> 1 teaspoon grated lemon rind
> 1 teaspoon nutmeg

Sift together flour and baking powder three times. Add lemon rind and nutmeg to butter and cream until fluffy. Gradually add 1¾ cups of sugar and beat until light. Beat egg yolks very thoroughly until light colored. Add to butter mixture and beat thoroughly. Beat egg whites until they stand in peaks. Add remaining sugar to the egg whites 2 Tablespoon at a time, beating after each addition. Stir in ⅓ of flour, then half of egg whites, and alternate until all are used – beat well after each addition. Turn into greased and floured 10-inch tube pan. Bake at 325° for 1 hour and 20 minutes or until cake tests done. Cool 10 minutes in pan; remove from pan and cool completely on wire rack.

COLUMBIA POUND CAKE

This recipe calls for separating the eggs and for adding baking powder. This cake will rise, so be sure to use a 10-inch tube pan. Make it special by serving with crème anglaise.

- 2 cups butter
- 2 cups sugar
- 9 eggs, separated
- 3 cups plain flour, sifted
- 1 teaspoon baking powder
- 1 teaspoon almond or vanilla extract

Sift flour and baking powder together three times. Cream butter and flavoring; add 1 ¼ cups sugar gradually and cream well. Add egg yolks, one at a time, beating hard after each. Sift flour over creamed mixture and mix in gently but thoroughly. Beat egg whites until they stand in frothy peaks. Then add remaining sugar gradually, beating hard until you have smooth satiny meringue. Mix into creamed batter very gently, but enough to hide all egg white patches. Pour into greased and floured tube pan. Bake at 325° for 1 hour and 10 minutes or until done. Let cool 10 minutes in pan. Remove from pan and cool completely on wire rack.

Crème Anglaise

- 1 cup milk
- 1 cup light cream
- 1 vanilla bean, split
- 6 egg yolks
- ⅓ cup sugar
- 1 teaspoon vanilla extract

Combine egg yolks, sugar and a pinch of salt in a large bowl and beat until thick and pale lemon colored, 1 to 2 minutes. Scald milk with the vanilla bean and set aside, allowing to cool to about 100°. Add the milk and vanilla bean, to the egg mixture. Stir, and then pour the milk/egg mixture back into saucepan. Cook over moderate heat stirring mixture until it thickens, but don't allow mixture to come to a boil. Mixture will be ready when it coats the back of a spoon. Strain custard, and then scrape the seeds from the vanilla bean into mixture. Stir in the vanilla extract. Cool mixture, stirring occasionally, and then chill, covered. Makes 2-½ cups.

OLD DOMINION POUND CAKE

This recipe calls for baking soda, salt and cream of tartar - a mixture sometimes suggested as a substitute for baking powder.

- 1½ cups butter, softened
- 2¼ cups sugar
- 8 large eggs, separated
- 2¼ cups plain flour, sifted
- ¼ teaspoon baking soda
- ⅛ teaspoon salt
- 1½ teaspoons cream of tartar
- 2 Tablespoons lemon juice
- 2¼ teaspoons vanilla extract

Sift together flour, soda, and 1¼ cups sugar. With electric mixer at low speed, just barely blend butter with flour mixture, then with lemon juice and vanilla. Still at low speed, beat in egg yolks, one at a time, just until yolks are blended. In another bowl, with electric mixer at high speed, beat egg whites until frothy; add salt, then gradually add 1 cup sugar with cream of tartar, beating well after each addition. Then beat all until soft peaks form. Gently fold beaten egg whites into cake batter. Turn into well-buttered and floured 10-inch tube pan. Using a rubber spatula, gently cut through the batter 1 or 2 times. Bake at 325° for 1 hour and 30 minutes or until tests done (do not peek during first hour). Turn off oven and let cake remain in oven for 15 minutes. Remove to rack and cool for 15 minutes more before removing from pan to cool completely on wire rack.

PERFECT POUND CAKE

How about a three quarter pound cake? This one has a nice mix of flavorings -- lemon, vanilla and almond.

    1½ cups butter
    2½ cups sugar
    8 eggs
    3 cups plain flour
    1 teaspoon lemon extract
    1 teaspoon vanilla extract
    1 teaspoon almond extract

Cream butter and sugar. Add eggs, one at a time, beating well after each addition. Add flour; stir well. Stir in flavorings. Pour into greased and floured 10-inch tube pan. Bake at 325° for 1 hour and 30 minutes or until cake tests done. Cool 10 minutes in pan; remove to wire rack and cool completely.

SLOW OVEN POUND CAKE

This recipe doesn't take long to mix, but it cooks for a long time in a very slow oven.

> 2 cups margarine
> 2 cups sugar
> 6 eggs
> 2 1/3 cups plain flour
> 2 Tablespoons vanilla extract

Cream margarine and sugar. Add eggs, one at a time, beating well after each addition. Stir in flavoring. Sift flour three times, and then add a little at a time, blending well. Pour batter into a greased and floured 10-inch tube pan. Bake at 275° for 2 hours and 30 minutes or until cake tests done. Cool 10 minutes in pan; remove from pan and cool completely on wire rack.

CONFECTIONERS' POUND CAKE

Confectioners' sugar replaces granulated sugar, and a teaspoonful of baking powder makes it rise. Dust cake with a little additional powdered sugar before serving.

 1¾ cups butter
 1 box (1 lb) confectioners' sugar
 8 eggs
 3 ½ cups plain flour
 1 teaspoon baking powder
 ½ teaspoon salt
 ¼ teaspoon mace
 1 teaspoon vanilla extract
 ½ teaspoon almond extract
 ½ teaspoon lemon extract

Cream butter and add sugar gradually until mixture resembles whipped cream. Add eggs, one at a time beating well after each addition. Sift dry ingredients together 2 times. Add one-half of dry ingredients and mix well. Stir in flavorings. Add remaining dry ingredients and mix well. Pour mixture into greased and floured 10-inch tube pan. Bake at 325° for 1 hour and 5 minutes, or until cake tests done. Remove from pan to cool on rack.

CRUNCHY POUND CAKE

This is a cold-oven pound cake, with a nice topping made from vanilla wafers and pecans.

> 2 cups butter
> 2 cups confectioners' sugar
> 7 eggs
> 3 cups plain flour
> 2 teaspoons vanilla extract

Blend butter and sugar together until light and fluffy. Add the eggs one at a time, beating well after each addition. Slowly stir in the flour. Add the vanilla extract. Pour the batter into a greased and floured 10-inch tube pan. Place pan in cold oven and set temperature to 325°. Bake for 1 hour or until cake tests done. Cool the cake in the pan for 1 hour before inverting onto serving platter.

Topping

> ½ cup crushed vanilla wafers
> (14 wafers)
> 1 Tablespoon melted butter
> ½ cup pecans, finely ground
> 2 Tablespoons sugar

EASY POUND CAKE

Here's a quick and easy recipe. Everything's easy to measure, and it is simple to put together. It will even work without sifting the sugar.

    1 lb (2 cups) butter
    1 lb box powdered sugar, sifted
    6 eggs
    1 lb package plain flour
    1 teaspoon vanilla extract
    ½ teaspoon almond extract

Cream butter and sugar. Add eggs, one at a time, beating after each addition. Add flour and flavorings; mix well. Pour batter into greased and floured tube pan. Bake at 325° for 1 hour and 15 minutes, or until cake tests done. Cool in pan 10 minutes; remove from pan and cool completely on wire rack.

SLOP JOB POUND CAKE

This recipe has ingredients similar to the others in this chapter, but it ignores the traditional rules for mixing. It's a smaller cake, suitable for a Bundt pan. Note also that this is a cold oven cake.

- 1 cup butter, softened.
- 1¾ cups sugar
- 5 eggs
- 2 cups self-rising flour
- 1 teaspoon vanilla extract

Place all ingredients in a bowl. Beat 12 minutes on medium speed. Pour into a greased and floured Bundt pan. Place in cold oven and bake at 325° for 1 hour and 15 minutes. Let cool in pan for 15 minutes, then invert on wire rack and allow to cool completely.

CHAPTER 2

MODERN-DAY PLAIN POUND CAKES

Here are 48 recipes that are "plain" in name only; they use all manner of liquids in place of some of the eggs and/or butter in the old-timey recipes. These include cakes made with every imaginable milk product (even eggnog), as well as recipes that call for other liquids such as ginger ale.

POUND CAKES MADE WITH MILK

MILLION DOLLAR POUND CAKE

This is the "gold standard" for modern-day pound cakes—it's a nice, big cake that turns out perfect every time. No other recipe can beat its taste and texture.

- 2 cups butter, softened
- 3 cups sugar
- 6 eggs
- 4 cups plain flour
- ¾ cup milk
- 1 teaspoon vanilla extract
- 1 teaspoon almond extract

Cream butter and sugar until light and fluffy (beat for about 7 minutes). Add eggs, one at a time, beating 1 minute after each addition. Add flour and milk alternately, beating well after each addition. Stir in flavorings. Pour batter into greased and floured 10-inch tube pan. Bake at 300° for 1 hour and 40 minutes, or until cake tests done. Cool in pan for 10 minutes; remove from pan and cool completely on wire rack.

OLD-FASHIONED POUND CAKE

With a hint of nutmeg flavoring, this recipe makes a handsome cake. Serve it warm, with ice cream on the side.

- 2 cups butter, softened
- 2¾ cups sugar
- 6 large eggs
- 3¾ cups plain flour
- ⅛ teaspoon salt
- ¼ teaspoon ground nutmeg
- ½ cup milk
- 1 teaspoon vanilla extract

Beat butter at medium speed with an electric mixer about 2 minutes or until soft and creamy. Gradually add sugar, beating at medium speed 5 to 7 minutes. Add eggs, one at a time, beating just until yellow disappears. Combine flour, salt, and nutmeg; add to creamed mixture alternately with milk, beginning and ending with flour mixture. Mix at low speed just until blended after each addition. Stir in vanilla. Pour batter into a greased and floured 10-inch tube pan. Bake at 325° for 1 hour and 15 minutes or until a wooden pick inserted in center of cake comes out clean. Cool in pan on a wire rack 10 to 15 minutes; remove from pan, and let cool completely on a wire rack.

NEW FASHIONED POUND CAKE

This smaller cake, which uses mace for flavoring, does nicely in a Bundt pan. Make it fancy with crème anglaise or orange glaze.

- 1 cup butter or margarine
- 1⅓ cups sugar
- 4 large eggs
- 2¼ cups plain flour
- ½ teaspoon baking powder
- ½ teaspoon salt
- ¼ cup milk
- 1 teaspoon vanilla extract
- ¼ teaspoon mace

Sift flour, baking powder and salt together. Cream butter, sugar, vanilla, and mace on high speed of mixer until smooth. Add eggs, one at a time, beating 1 minute after each, on medium speed. Stir in dry ingredients, ½ at a time, alternately with milk. Beat 2 minutes on low speed. Turn into greased and floured Bundt pan or 10-inch tube pan. Bake at 325° for 1 hour and 5 minutes, or until cake tests done. Cool 10 minutes before removing from pan. Cool completely on a wire rack.

Creme Anglaise:

- 2 cups whipping cream
- 6 large egg yolks
- ½ cup sugar
- 2 teaspoons vanilla extract

Heat whipping cream in heavy saucepan until bubbles just form at edge. In bowl, whisk together yolks and sugar. Slowly whisk a little of the whipping cream into egg mixture and return all to saucepan. Continue to heat over low heat, stirring constantly with wooden spoon, until slightly thickened. Stir in vanilla. Makes 2½ to 3 cups. Spoon over cake slices to serve.

Orange Glaze:

1 cup sifted powdered sugar
3 Tablespoons orange-flavored liqueur
½ teaspoon grated orange zest

Stir ingredients together briskly and drizzle over cooled cake. Makes enough to frost 1 cake.

PLAIN OLD POUND CAKE

This recipe has a mix of butter and shortening, and a double dose of vanilla flavoring.

 1 cup butter
 ½ cup vegetable shortening
 3 cups sugar
 5 eggs
 3 cups plain flour
 1 teaspoon baking powder
 1 cup milk
 2 teaspoons vanilla extract

Cream butter, shortening and sugar. Add eggs, one at a time, beating well after each addition. Combine flour and baking powder, and add alternately with milk to creamed mixture, mixing well after each addition. Stir in vanilla. Pour batter into a greased and floured 10-inch tube pan. Bake at 350° for 1 hour and 15 minutes or until cake tests done. Cool 10 minutes before removing from pan; let cool completely on wire rack.

WEDDING POUND CAKE

This recipe is for everyone who ever wondered how to achieve that special taste and texture that is unique to wedding cakes.

½ lb (1 cup) butter
½ cup vegetable shortening
3 cups sugar
6 eggs
3¼ cups plain flour
¼ teaspoon salt
½ teaspoon baking powder
1 cup milk

Combine sugar, butter, and shortening; cream until light and fluffy. Add eggs, one at a time, beating well after each addition. Add flour mixed with salt and baking powder to creamed mixture, alternating with milk and beat well after each addition. Pour batter into well-greased and floured 10-inch tube pan. Bake at 300° for 1 hour and 40 minutes, or until cake tests done. Cool in pan for 10 minutes; remove from pan and cool completely on wire rack.

QUICK FIX POUND CAKE

This one mixes quickly because everything is easy to measure. It even uses self-rising flour, not often seen in pound cake recipes.

 1 cup butter
 2 cups sugar
 4 eggs
 3 cups self-rising flour
 1 cup milk
 2 teaspoons vanilla extract

Cream butter and sugar. Add eggs, one at a time, beating after each addition. Add flour and milk (with vanilla in it) alternately and mix well. Pour batter into greased and floured 10-inch tube pan. Bake at 325° for 1 hour or until cake tests done. Cool 10 minutes before removing from pan. Cool completely on wire rack.

COLD OVEN POUND CAKE

This recipe uses self-rising flour and plain flour. A local legend claims that this recipe was developed by a rural miller who was trying to get his customers to use both of his flour products. This one makes a big cake.

- 1 cup butter
- ½ cup vegetable shortening
- 3 cups sugar
- 6 large eggs
- 3 cups plain flour
- 1 cup self-rising flour
- 1 cup milk
- 2 teaspoons vanilla extract
- 1 teaspoon lemon extract

Start with a cold oven. Do not preheat. Cream butter, shortening and sugar together. Add eggs, one at a time, mixing thoroughly after each addition. Add flour and milk alternately, again mixing well after each addition. Add extracts and mix again. Pour batter into a well-greased and floured 10-inch tube pan. Bake at 325° for 1 hour and 15 minutes or until cake tests done. Cool 10 minutes in pan; remove from pan and cool completely on wire rack.

MORAVIAN POUND CAKE

Nutmeg and lemon provide a unique flavor combination. For variation, 1 teaspoon of almond extract may be substituted for the lemon juice and nutmeg.

> 1 cup butter
> ½ cup shortening
> 3 cups sugar
> 5 eggs
> 3 cups sifted plain flour
> ½ teaspoon salt
> ½ teaspoon baking powder
> 1 cup milk
> 1 teaspoon lemon juice
> ⅛ teaspoon nutmeg

Blend butter and shortening; add sugar gradually. Add eggs, one at a time, mixing well after each addition. Sift flour, salt and baking powder; add to butter mixture alternately with milk; mix well after each addition. Stir in lemon juice and nutmeg. Pour into greased and floured 10-inch tube pan. Bake at 350° for 1 hour and 30 minutes or until cake tests done. Cool in pan 10 minutes; remove from pan and cool completely on wire rack.

DOUBLE VANILLA POUND CAKE WITH RUM-VANILLA GLAZE

Vanilla lovers, this one's for you. It calls for vanilla bean, vanilla extract, and vanilla sugar. Vanilla sugar can be made by adding a vanilla bean cut in 1-inch pieces to 2½ cups of white granulated sugar. Cover and let sit for 2 days before using.

> 1 large vanilla bean, split or cut into pieces
> 1 cup milk
> 4 cups flour, sifted
> 1 Tablespoon pure vanilla extract
> 1 Tablespoon baking powder
> 2 cups butter
> 2½ cups vanilla sugar
> 6 eggs

Pour milk into a saucepan, add the vanilla bean and scald the milk. Let mixture cool to room temperature. Remove vanilla bean, rinse it off, and set aside. Resift the flour with the baking powder and the salt onto a sheet of waxed paper; set aside. In a large bowl, cream the butter with an electric mixer on moderately high speed until light, about 3 minutes. Add the vanilla sugar in two portions, beating thoroughly after each portion is added. Beat in eggs, one at a time, periodically scraping down the sides of the bowl to ensure an even mixture. Blend in vanilla extract. On low speed, add the sifted dry ingredients alternately with the milk, beginning and ending with the dry ingredients. Pour and scrape the batter into a lightly buttered, floured 10-inch tube pan, a large square baking pan or three loaf pans. Bake the cake at 350° for about 1 hour, or until a toothpick inserted into the cake emerges clean and dry. Cool the cake in the pan on a rack for 10 minutes. Prick holes all over the top of the cake with a thin knife or toothpick and slowly spoon glaze over the cake, allowing the syrup to absorb into the cake.

Rum-Vanilla Glaze

1 cup sugar
1 cup water
1 tablespoon pure vanilla extract
¼ cup rum or brandy (optional)

Place sugar and water in a small saucepan, add in the reserved vanilla bean, and bring to a boil. Reduce heat and simmer for 10 minutes, or until syrup begins to thicken. Allow to cool slightly before adding extract and rum. Spoon glaze over cake, as described above.

BUTTER CREAM POUND CAKE

This recipe calls for butter, margarine, shortening and butter flavoring! It is extra moist – the warm cake is wrapped in plastic wrap and then allowed to cool.

- 1 cup butter
- ½ cup margarine
- ½ cup shortening
- 3 cups sugar
- 5 large eggs
- 3 cups plus 2 Tablespoons plain flour
- 1 teaspoon baking powder
- 1 cup milk
- 2 teaspoons butter flavoring
- 2 teaspoons vanilla extract

Cream butter, margarine, shortening, and sugar for 5 minutes or until creamy. Add eggs, one at a time, beating at medium speed after each addition. Sift flour and baking powder; add to mixture alternately with milk and flavorings, beating at low speed after each addition. Pour into greased and floured 10-inch tube pan. Bake at 325° for 1 hour; reduce heat to 300° and bake for 30 minutes. Cool in pan for 3 minutes. Remove from pan and wrap in plastic wrap until completely cool.

Butter Frosting

- 1 cup light brown sugar
- ½ cup margarine
- ½ cup milk
- 3 cups powdered sugar
- 1 teaspoon butter flavoring

Combine brown sugar, margarine, and milk; boil for 4 minutes. Remove from heat and cool. Add powdered sugar and flavoring; beat until smooth. Spread over cake.

BROKEN RULE POUND CAKE

This recipe breaks all the rules - not adding eggs one at a time, not alternating flour with milk, not beating the butter and sugar until fluffy - but it still yields a delectable dessert. Give it a try for a tall, beautiful cake with velvety texture and buttery flavor.

    4 cups plain flour
    3 cups sugar
    2 cups butter
    ¾ cup milk
    6 eggs
    2 teaspoons vanilla

Place flour, sugar, butter, milk, eggs, and vanilla (in that order) in a 4-quart bowl. Beat at low speed with a heavy-duty electric mixer for 1 minute, stopping to scrape down sides of bowl. Beat at medium speed for 2 minutes. Pour into a greased and floured 10-inch tube pan. Bake at 325° for 1 hour and 30 minutes or until cake tests done. Cool in pan on wire rack 10 minutes. Remove from pan; cool completely on wire rack.

CRUSTY POUND CAKE

This is a cold-oven cake; it gets an extra crusty top by raising the oven temperature for the last 15 minutes of cooking. It should be very brown on top.

- ½ cup vegetable shortening
- 1 cup whipped margarine
- 3 cups sugar
- 5 large eggs
- 3 cups plain flour
- 1 cup milk
- 5 drops yellow food coloring
- 2 teaspoons flavoring (vanilla or lemon extract or one of each) (add to milk)

Blend sugar with margarine and shortening, and cream with mixer - about 15 minutes. Add eggs, one at a time, and beat after each for ½ minute. Add food coloring. Add ¼ of flour and beat 2 minutes; add ¼ of milk and beat 1 minute. Continue alternating flour and milk, mixing after each addition. Pour batter into well-greased and floured 10-inch tube pan. Do not preheat oven. Place cake in middle of oven and set temperature at 325°. Bake for 1 hour and 15 minutes, then set temperature to 350° for 15 minutes. Remove cake from pan immediately and cool on rack.

CHOLESTEROL-FREE POUND CAKE

Not only is there no cholesterol, it's a smaller cake so there's not as much to eat! For variation, use 1 teaspoon of lemon extract instead of the butter flavoring.

- 1 cup vegetable oil margarine
- 2 cups sugar
- 1¼ cups egg substitute
- 3 cups plain flour
- 2 teaspoons baking powder
- 1 cup skim milk
- 1 teaspoon vanilla extract
- 1 teaspoon butter flavoring

Sift together flour and baking powder in a small bowl and set aside. In medium-size mixing bowl, cream margarine and sugar, gradually adding egg substitute and flavorings. Alternately blend in flour mixture and skim milk. Pour into greased and floured Bundt pan or 10-inch tube pan. Bake at 350° for 50 minutes or until cake tests done. Cool a few minutes in pan, then invert onto wire rack.

CORNMEAL POUND CAKE

Cornmeal gives this pound cake a slightly gritty texture that is pleasing with the buttery crumb. It is a small recipe, suitable for a loaf pan (or double it for a 10-inch tube pan).

- 1 cup butter
- 1 cup sugar
- 4 eggs
- ½ cup yellow cornmeal
- 1½ cups plain flour
- 1½ teaspoon baking powder
- 1 teaspoon grated nutmeg
- 3 to 6 Tablespoons milk

Cream the butter until it is light and fluffy. Add the sugar a little at a time, beating well after each addition. Add the eggs, one at a time, beating well after each addition. Combine dry ingredients. Add half the cornmeal mixture to the batter, followed by 3 tablespoons of milk, followed by the remaining cornmeal mixture. Add up to 3 additional tablespoons of milk, if necessary (batter should just fall from the spoon). Pour batter into a loaf pan that has been buttered, the bottom lined with waxed paper, the waxed paper buttered, and then all dusted with flour. Bake at 350° for 1 hour and 10 minutes or until cake tests done. Leave in pan on a wire rack for 30 minutes, and then turn out to cool.

CITRUS CORNMEAL POUND CAKE

This is a simple, but delicious cake - it tastes even better the day after it's made. Cornmeal adds a delicate and pleasant crunch.

- 1 cup margarine, softened
- 1 pound (1 box) powdered sugar
- 1½ teaspoons baking powder
- 4 eggs
- 2¼ cups plain flour
- 1 cup milk
- ¾ cup yellow cornmeal
- 1 Tablespoon each freshly grated lemon and orange peel

Beat margarine, sugar and baking powder in large bowl on low speed until blended. Increase speed to high; beat until pale and fluffy. Add eggs, one at a time, beating well after each addition. With mixer on low speed, beat in flour and milk in 3 additions until smooth. Beat in cornmeal and citrus peels until blended. Pour batter into a greased and floured 10-inch tube pan. Bake at 350º for 1 hour or until a toothpick inserted near the center comes out clean. Cool in pan on wire rack 10 minutes, then invert cake on rack.

GLAZE:

- ⅓ cup granulated sugar
- ¼ cup each fresh lemon and orange juice

Mix ingredients; brush over warm cake. Let cool.

POUND CAKES MADE WITH BUTTERMILK

BUTTERMILK POUND CAKE

This is a good basic recipe for buttermilk pound cake. For variation, try 2 teaspoons lemon extract and 1 teaspoon almond extract instead of the orange and vanilla flavorings.

>　1 cup butter or shortening
>　2 cups sugar
>　4 eggs
>　3 cups plain flour
>　½ teaspoon salt
>　½ teaspoon soda
>　½ teaspoon baking powder
>　1 cup buttermilk
>　1 teaspoon vanilla extract
>　1 teaspoon orange extract

Cream butter (or shortening) and sugar until light and fluffy. Add eggs, one at a time, and beat well after each addition. Stir in vanilla and orange flavorings. Sift dry ingredients together three times. Add dry ingredients alternately with buttermilk, mixing after each addition. Spoon mixture into a greased and floured 10-inch tube pan. Bake at 350° for 1 hour or until cake tests done. Cool in pan 10 minutes; remove from pan and cool completely on wire rack.

LEMON BUTTERMILK POUND CAKE

This cake is extra moist because it's allowed to cool in a tight-fitting container. Serve with bourbon whipped cream for a special treat.

- 1 cup margarine
- ½ cup shortening
- 3 cups sugar
- 5 eggs
- 3 cups plain flour
- 2 level teaspoons baking powder
- 1 cup buttermilk
- 2 teaspoons vanilla extract
- 2 teaspoons lemon extract

Cream margarine, shortening, and sugar together. Add eggs and mix well. Combine milk and flavorings. Mix in alternately with flour and baking powder. Mix with electric mixer for 2 to 3 minutes or until batter is smooth. Pour batter into greased and floured 10-inch tube pan. Bake at 350° for 1 hour and 30 minutes or until toothpick comes out clean. Remove from oven and while still hot, run sharp knife around edges of cake. Remove cake from pan immediately. Store at room temperature in tight fitting cake plate with cover. Wipe moisture from cake cover after cake cools.

Bourbon Whipped Cream

- 2 cups chilled whipping cream
- 6 Tablespoons light brown sugar
- 3 Tablespoons bourbon

Combine all ingredients in medium bowl and beat to soft peaks. Can be prepared 4 hours ahead. Cover and refrigerate. Makes about 3½ cups.

LOW FAT BUTTERMILK POUND CAKE

Here's to your health – this recipe cuts the fat without sacrificing the taste.

¼ cup vegetable oil spread
2 cups sugar
¼ cup applesauce
½ cup fat-free sour cream
1 cup egg substitute
1 cup buttermilk
1 teaspoon vanilla extract
1 teaspoon lemon extract
3 cups self-rising flour

In a large mixing bowl, thoroughly blend vegetable oil spread and sugar with an electric mixer. Blend in the applesauce, sour cream, egg substitute, buttermilk, vanilla and lemon extracts until smooth. Add flour and continue to beat for 1 minute or until smooth. Pour batter into a Bundt pan sprayed with vegetable oil cooking spray. Bake at 325° for 45-50 minutes or until tester comes out clean. Cool.

GLAZE

2 Tablespoons buttermilk
¼ cup sugar
1½ teaspoons cornstarch
⅛ teaspoon baking soda
1 Tablespoon low-fat margarine
¾ teaspoon vanilla extract
⅔ cup powdered sugar

In a small saucepan, combine buttermilk, sugar, cornstarch and baking soda. Stirring constantly, bring to a boil over medium heat. Blend in remaining vegetable oil spread, stirring until melted. Remove from heat. Blend in remaining vanilla and powdered sugar. Let glaze cool slightly before drizzling over cake.

VANILLA POLENTA POUND CAKE

Polenta is cornmeal, cooked slowly and usually served alone or with various toppings. Its popularity has spread from simple Italian "home" cooking to become a versatile ingredient in many dishes.

1½ cups buttermilk
1 cup polenta (not instant)
3¼ cups flour
1 Tablespoon baking powder
½ teaspoon baking soda
¾ teaspoon salt
1 Tablespoon vanilla extract
1½ cup unsalted butter, softened
6 eggs

Mix together buttermilk and polenta; let soak for 45 minutes. Sift together flour, baking powder, baking soda and salt. Cream together butter and sugar until light and fluffy. Add eggs one at a time, beating well after each addition. Stir in vanilla extract. Fold soaked polenta and dry ingredients alternately into creamed mixture, in 3 additions. Pour batter into greased and floured 10-inch tube pan. Bake at 350° about 60 minutes, or until a cake tester comes out clean. Let cake cool 10 minutes before turning out on a wire rack to cool. Sift powdered sugar over cake as soon as you remove it from pan. When cake is completely cool, sprinkle powdered sugar over it again. The cake may now be wrapped and stored for at least four days. It can be frozen for as long as a month. If you freeze it, dust with powdered sugar again before serving.

BUTTERMILK CHESS POUND CAKE

This cake takes its name from another Southern tradition, Chess Pie - which often was served at afternoon teas.

- 1 cup butter
- 2½ cups sugar
- 1 teaspoon vanilla
- 5 eggs
- 2 cups plain flour
- 1 cup self-rising corn meal
- 1 cup buttermilk

In large bowl, beat butter, sugar and vanilla until light and fluffy. Add eggs, one at a time, beating well after each addition. In medium bowl, stir together flour and corn meal; add to creamed mixture alternately with buttermilk, beginning and ending with flour. Mix well after each addition. Pour batter into a greased and floured 10-inch tube pan. Bake at 350° for one hour or until toothpick inserted in center comes out clean. Cool upright in pan for 30 minutes; invert onto serving plate.

SOUTHERN CHESS POUND CAKE

This cake will look somewhat fallen and crusty, much like a true chess pie, and its taste will be wonderful.

1 cup butter, softened
½ cup Crisco
3 cups sugar
5 eggs, room temperature
2¼ cups flour
¾ cup yellow cornmeal
1 teaspoon baking powder
¼ teaspoon salt
½ teaspoon baking soda
1 cup buttermilk, room temperature
1 Tablespoon vanilla extract
2 Tablespoons lemon juice

Butter and flour a 10-inch tube pan. Cream the softened butter and Crisco until lightened in color, about 3 minutes. Slowly add the sugar and then beat at high speed for 5 minutes. Add the eggs, one at a time, beating well after each addition. Sift together the flour, cornmeal, baking powder, salt and baking soda. Add ⅓ of the flour to batter, gently blending in, and then add ½ cup buttermilk. Repeat with the remaining flour mixture and buttermilk, ending with the flour. Mix in the vanilla and lemon juice. Bake at 300° for about 1 hour and 15 minutes, or until the cake tests done. Cool in the pan for 15 minutes, and then turn out on a cake rack to cool completely.

POUND CAKES MADE WITH HALF-AND-HALF

GRANNY'S POUND CAKE

This cake relies on carefully folded-in egg whites to give it a light texture.

- 2 cups butter
- 2⅔ cups sugar
- 7 large eggs
- 3½ cups sifted plain flour
- ½ cup half-and-half
- 1 Tablespoon vanilla extract

Separate eggs and beat the whites with 6 Tablespoons of sugar, added gradually; put in refrigerator. Cream butter and remaining sugar well, then add egg yolks and blend on medium speed on electric mixer. Set mixer at lowest speed and add flour and half & half alternately; stir in vanilla, then quickly fold in egg whites. Pour into greased and floured 10-inch tube pan; bake at 325° for approximately 1 hour and 10 minutes or until cake tester comes out clean. Cool in pan 10 minutes; remove from pan and cool completely on wire rack.

SUGAR COOKIE POUND CAKE

This recipe has just a touch of flour along with finely crushed sugar cookies.

- 3 cups sugar cookie crumbs
- 2 cups sliced almonds
- 1 cup unsalted butter, softened
- 2 cups sugar
- 6 eggs
- ½ cup flour
- ½ cup half and half
- 1 Tablespoon vanilla extract
- 2 teaspoons almond extract

Crush sugar cookies to a fine crumb-like texture and grind almonds in a blender or nut grinder. Cream butter and gradually add sugar. Add eggs one at a time until thoroughly incorporated. Stir until mixture has no lumps. In a separate bowl, mix flour and sugar cookie crumbs. At low speed, add cookie crumb mixture and half and half intermittently. Add extracts and continue to mix. Add almonds last, mixing in thoroughly being careful no to over beat. Cut parchment paper to line the bottom of a 9-inch tube pan. Grease pan and parchment paper and flour heavily. This cake does not rise very much. Bake at 300° for 2 hours. Cool in the pan on a wire rack. When completely cool, remove from pan; peel away parchment paper and dust cake heavily with powdered sugar.

POUND CAKES MADE WITH EVAPORATED MILK

BUTTERY POUND CAKE

Butter flavoring gives an extra buttery taste that blends well with caramel frosting.

- 1 cup margarine
- ½ cup butter
- 3 cups sugar
- 6 eggs
- 3 cups plain flour
- 1 teaspoon baking powder
- 1 cup evaporated milk
- 1 teaspoon vanilla extract
- 1 teaspoon butter flavoring

Cream butter, margarine and sugar well; add eggs, one at a time, beating well after each addition. Sift flour and baking powder together. Add flour mixture alternately with milk, beating after each addition. Stir in vanilla and butter flavorings. Bake in large well-greased and floured tube pan at 325° for 1 hour and 30 minutes or until cake tests done. Cool 10 minutes in pan, then let cool completely on wire rack before icing.

CARAMEL FROSTING

- ½ cup margarine
- 1 cup light brown sugar, packed
- ¼ cup milk
- 3 cups confectioners' sugar

Boil margarine and brown sugar for 2 minutes; add milk and mix well. Let cool for 10 minutes. Add powdered sugar and beat until smooth. Spread on cake.

POUND CAKES MADE WITH WHIPPING CREAM

MIKE JARRETT'S OLD FASHIONED POUND CAKE

Mike Jarrett, Commissioner of the SC Department of Health and Environmental Control from 1986 to 1992, was an excellent cook. His mother taught him how to make this crusty cake. Try it warm from the oven and you'll be hooked.

- 1 cup butter
- 3 cups sugar
- 6 eggs, beaten slightly
- 3 cups plain flour, sifted 3 times
- 1 teaspoon baking powder
- 1 cup whipping cream
- 1 teaspoon vanilla extract

Cream butter and sugar until fluffy. Add eggs, one at a time, mixing well after each addition. Sift flour with baking powder. Alternately add flour and whipping cream, beginning and ending with flour. Stir in vanilla. Pour batter into greased and floured 10-inch tube pan. Bake at 325° for 1 hour and 15 minutes or until cake tests done. Let cool 10 minutes in pan; remove cake from pan and cool completely on wire rack

FRENCH VANILLA POUND CAKE

This cake is placed in a cold oven and has a more intense vanilla taste because of the real vanilla bean.

> 1 vanilla bean, cut into thirds
> 1 cup whipping cream, room temperature
> 1¼ cups butter, room temperature
> 2½ cups sugar
> 6 eggs, room temperature
> 3 cups cake flour
> 1 teaspoon baking powder
> 1 Tablespoon vanilla extract
> 1 teaspoon lemon extract

Butter and flour a large (10-¼ inch) decorative Bundt pan. With a small knife, split in half the vanilla bean pieces. Place the vanilla bean and cream in a small saucepan. Warm the mixture just to a simmer, making sure it doesn't come to a boil. Remove from the heat and allow the mixture to steep while preparing the cake. Cream the butter on high speed and then slowly add the sugar; continue beating for about 5 minutes. Add the eggs, one at a time, mixing well after each addition. Sift the cake flour with the baking powder, and set aside. Remove the vanilla bean pieces from the cream; using a small knife, thoroughly scrape the insides of the pieces into the cream. Discard the pieces. Alternately add the flour and cream to the butter, beginning and ending with the flour. Beat in the extracts and then pour the batter into the prepared pan. Place in a COLD oven and bake at 325° for 65 minutes, or until a tester comes out clean. Allow the cake to cool in the pan on a wire rack for about 15 minutes, then turn out and cool completely.

WHIPPING CREAM POUND CAKE

Moist, flavor-changing, light pound cake. You may change flavors by using ⅔ cup whipping cream and ⅓ cup flavored coffee creamer.

- 1 cup butter
- 3 cups white sugar
- 6 eggs
- 3 cups cake flour
- 1 cup heavy whipping cream
- 2 teaspoons vanilla extract
- 1 teaspoon almond extract (optional)

Grease and flour a 10-inch tube pan. In a large bowl, cream butter for 2 minutes. Add sugar and continue beating for 5 minutes. Add eggs one at a time, beating well with each addition. Add flour alternately with whipping cream beginning and ending with flour. Stir in vanilla and almond extract (if desired). Spoon into prepared pan and bake at 325° for 1 hour and 10 minutes. Turn out onto cooling rack covered with a clean, cotton dishtowel. When cooled completely, sprinkle with powdered sugar and serve with fruit or plain.

POUND CAKES MADE WITH SOUR CREAM

SOUR CREAM POUND CAKE

This cake is excellent served warm, with any of these sauce recipes—or try a favorite of your own. For variation, add 1 cup of chopped pecans to the batter.

- 1 cup butter, softened
- 3 cups sugar
- 6 large eggs
- 3 cups plain flour
- ¼ teaspoon baking soda
- 1 cup sour cream
- 1 teaspoon vanilla extract
- 1 teaspoon almond extract (optional)

Beat butter at medium speed with an electric mixer about 2 minutes or until soft and creamy. Gradually add sugar, beating at medium speed 5 to 7 minutes. Add eggs, one at a time, beating just until yellow disappears. Combine flour and baking soda; add to creamed mixture alternately with sour cream, beginning and ending with flour mixture. Mix at lowest speed just until blended after each addition. Stir in flavorings. Pour batter into a greased and floured 10-inch tube pan. Bake at 325° for 1 hour and 20 minutes or until a wooden pick inserted in center comes out clean. Cool in pan on a wire rack 10 to 15 minutes; remove from pan and cool completely on a wire rack.

Lemon-Blueberry Cream

- ¾ cup whipping cream
- ⅓ cup sifted powdered sugar
- 1 cup fresh blueberries
- ½ cup sour cream
- 2 teaspoons freshly grated lemon rind

Beat whipping cream and powdered sugar at medium speed with an electric mixer until soft peaks form. Fold in blueberries, sour cream, and lemon rind. Serve with pound cake. Garnish with lemon zest and fresh blueberries, if desired.

RASPBERRY-ORANGE SAUCE

2 cups fresh or frozen raspberries, thawed
¾ cup sifted powdered sugar
¼ cup Cointreau or other orange-flavored liqueur
1 Tablespoon frozen orange juice concentrate, thawed

Place raspberries in container of an electric blender or food processor; process until smooth. Add powdered sugar and remaining ingredients; process until blended. Pour through a wire-mesh strainer; press mixture with back of a spoon against the sides of the strainer to squeeze out liquid. Discard seeds. Serve with pound cake and additional fruit.

AMARETTO-CHOCOLATE SAUCE

1 cup whipping cream
⅓ cup sugar
2 (4 oz.) bittersweet chocolate bars, chopped
2 Tablespoons butter or margarine
3 to 4 Tablespoons Amaretto

Combine first 4 ingredients in a small saucepan. Cook over low heat, stirring constantly, until thickened and smooth. Remove from heat and stir in liqueur. Serve warm or at room temperature with pound cake, ice cream and strawberries.

ORANGE GLAZE

⅔ cup sugar
¼ cup melted butter
⅓ cup orange juice

While cake is hot, combine ingredients; mix well. Stir until sugar is dissolved. Pour hot glaze over warm cake.

OLD-FASHIONED SOUR CREAM POUND CAKE

This recipe calls for beaten egg whites to be folded into the batter, giving the cake an extra lightness. For variation, add 1 teaspoon lemon extract or almond extract or both.

- 1 cup margarine, softened
- 3 cups sugar
- 6 eggs, separated
- 3 cups plain flour, sifted
- ¼ teaspoon baking soda
- ½ teaspoon salt
- 1 teaspoon vanilla extract
- 1 cup sour cream

Beat egg whites with ¼ teaspoon salt until stiff peaks form. Sift flour and soda together 3 times. Cream margarine and sugar until light and fluffy. Stir in remaining salt (¼ teaspoon) and vanilla. Add egg yolks, one at a time, mixing well after each addition. Add flour mixture alternately with sour cream, beginning and ending with flour mixture; mix well after each addition. Fold in egg whites and pour mixture into a greased and floured 10-inch tube pan. Bake in a 350° oven for one hour or until cake tests done. Cool 10 minutes in pan; remove from pan and cool completely on wire rack.

CREAM CHEESE FROSTING

- 1 (8 oz.) package cream cheese
- evaporated milk
- ½ cup margarine
- 1 teaspoon vanilla extract
- 1 (1 lb) box confectioners' sugar
- 1 cup chopped pecans

Soften the cream cheese and margarine. Place in a mixing bowl and cream well. Mix in the sugar gradually and add enough milk for spreading consistency. Add vanilla and pecans and mix well. Spread on cake.

COFFEE CAKE POUND CAKE

This cake can be served any time of the day, but it is a particular treat at brunch.

1 cup butter, room temperature
2¼ cups sugar
3 eggs, room temperature
1 cup sour cream, room temperature
1¼ teaspoons vanilla extract
2½ cups cake flour
½ teaspoon baking powder
¼ teaspoon baking soda
¼ teaspoon salt

Topping

6 Tablespoons light brown sugar
1½ teaspoons cinnamon
1 cup chopped pecans

Butter and flour a 9-½ inch Bundt pan. Cream the butter well, then slowly add the sugar and continue creaming the mixture at high speed for about 3 minutes. Add the eggs, one at a time, beating well after each addition. Combine the sour cream and vanilla and then add to the batter. Sift the flour with the baking powder, baking soda, and salt. Mix the flour gently but thoroughly into the batter. In a small bowl combine the topping ingredients. Pour ½ the batter into the prepared baking pan, and then sprinkle ⅔ of the topping mixture over the batter. Spread the remaining batter on top and sprinkle with the last ⅓ of the topping. Bake at 350° for approximately 45-50 minutes. Let cake cool in pan on a wire rack about 10-15 minutes, then turn out cake and let it cool completely.

AZTEC POUND CAKE

Corn meal gives this cake a yellow color and a somewhat grainy texture, and the orange rind provides a tangy flavoring. It is a small cake—bake it in a loaf pan.

- 1 cup butter
- 1 Tablespoon grated orange rind
- 2 cups sugar
- 6 large eggs, separated
- 2 cups plain flour
- 1 cup yellow corn meal
- ½ teaspoon baking soda
- ¼ teaspoon salt
- 1 cup sour cream
- 1 teaspoon vanilla extract

Beat butter and orange rind until fluffy; gradually add sugar, beating well. Add egg yolks, one at a time, beating just until yellow disappears. Combine flour, cornmeal, soda and salt; add to butter mixture alternately with sour cream, beginning and ending with flour mixture. Beat at low speed until just blended after each addition. Stir in vanilla. Beat egg whites until stiff peaks form; fold into batter. Pour batter into a greased and floured 9- × 5- × 3-inch loaf pan. Bake at 325° for 2 hours or until a wooden pick inserted into center of cake comes out clean. Cool in pan for 10 minutes; remove from pan and cool completely on wire rack.

POUND CAKES MADE WITH EGGNOG

COCONUT-EGGNOG POUND CAKE

This is a fun way to use the eggnog that hangs around in your refrigerator after the holiday season.

- 1 cup butter or margarine, softened
- ½ cup shortening
- 3 cups sugar
- 6 eggs
- 3 cups plain flour
- 1 cup commercial eggnog
- 1 cup flaked coconut
- 1 teaspoon lemon extract
- 1 teaspoon vanilla extract
- ½ teaspoon coconut extract

Cream butter and shortening; gradually add sugar, beating well at medium speed of an electric mixer. Add eggs, one at a time, beating well after each addition. Add flour to creamed mixture alternately with eggnog, beginning and ending with flour. Mix just until blended after each addition. Stir in coconut and flavorings. Pour batter into a greased and floured 10-inch tube pan. Bake at 325° for 1 hour and 30 minutes or until a wooden pick inserted in center of cake comes out clean. Cool in pan 10 minutes; remove from pan, and cool completely on a wire rack.

EGGNOG-PECAN POUND CAKE

This flavorful use for holiday eggnog is made extra special by the addition of chopped pecans.

- 1 cup butter or margarine, softened
- ½ cup vegetable oil
- 3 cups sugar
- 6 large eggs
- 3 cups plain flour
- 1 Tablespoon ground mace
- 1 teaspoon baking powder
- 1½ cups commercial eggnog
- 1 teaspoon vanilla extract
- 1 teaspoon lemon extract
- 2 cups coarsely chopped pecans

Beat butter and oil at medium speed with an electric mixer for about 2 minutes. Gradually add sugar, beating well. Add eggs, one at a time, beating after each addition. Combine flour, mace, and baking powder; add to butter mixture alternately with eggnog, beginning and ending with flour mixture. Mix at low speed until just blended after each addition. Stir in flavorings; fold in pecans. Pour batter into a greased and floured 10-inch tube pan. Bake at 350° for 1 hour and 15 minutes or until cake tests done. Cover loosely with aluminum foil after 45 minutes to prevent excessive browning. Cool in pan on wire rack for 10 to 15 minutes. Remove from pan and cool on a wire rack.

POUND CAKES MADE WITH YOGURT

YOGURT POUND CAKE

This is about as "healthy" as a pound cake can get—corn oil margarine, egg substitute, and low fat yogurt. It's a small cake, best made in a loaf pan.

> ½ cup corn oil margarine, softened
> ⅔ cup sugar
> ⅓ cup egg substitute
> 2½ cups plain flour, sifted
> ½ teaspoon baking powder
> ¼ teaspoon baking soda
> ¼ teaspoon salt
> 1 (8 oz.) carton low-fat vanilla yogurt
> 1 teaspoon vanilla extract
> ¾ teaspoon almond extract

Beat margarine at medium speed with an electric mixer until fluffy. Gradually add sugar; beat well. Add egg substitute; beat until blended. Combine flour and next 3 ingredients; add to creamed mixture alternately with yogurt, beginning and ending with flour mixture. Mix just until blended after each addition. Stir in flavorings. Spoon batter into 9 × 5 × 3-inch loaf pan that has been coated with cooking spray and dusted with flour. Bake at 350° for 1 hour and 5 minutes or until a wooden pick inserted in center comes out clean. Cool in pan on a wire rack 10 minutes; remove from pan and let cool completely on wire rack.

YUMMY YOGURT POUND CAKE

Not only yogurt, but brown sugar and poppy seeds, too - topped off with a delicious apricot frosting. Love at first bite. Stores best in refrigerator.

> 1 cup butter or margarine, softened
> 3 cups light brown sugar, firmly packed
> 6 eggs
> 2 teaspoons vanilla
> 3 cups plain flour
> ½ teaspoon salt
> ¼ teaspoon soda
> 1 cup (8 oz.) plain yogurt
> 3 Tablespoons poppy seeds

Cream butter and sugar until light and fluffy. Add eggs one at a time, beating well after each addition. Blend in vanilla. Sift together flour, salt and soda; add alternately with yogurt to creamed mixture, beginning and ending with dry ingredients. Stir in poppy seeds. Spoon batter into greased and floured 10-inch tube pan. Bake at 325° for 1 hour and 10 minutes or until toothpick inserted in center comes out clean. Cool in pan 10 minutes; turn out onto wire rack and cool completely.

Apricot Yogurt Frosting

> ¼ cup butter, softened
> ¼ cup apricot preserves
> ¼ cup plain yogurt
> ⅛ teaspoon salt
> 1 pound powdered sugar, sifted

Combine ingredients in order listed. Beat until smooth and creamy.

ALMOND YOGURT POUND CAKE

This is an easy recipe; you can even substitute lemon extract for the almond extract for a lemon yogurt pound cake.

    1 cup unsalted butter, softened
    2 cups packed light brown sugar
    4 eggs
    3 cups all purpose flour
    1 teaspoon baking soda
    ½ teaspoon baking powder
    ½ teaspoon salt
    1 cup plain yogurt
    1 teaspoon almond extract
    Powdered sugar for dusting

Butter and lightly flour the inside of a 10-inch tube pan or Bundt pan. In a large bowl, blend butter and sugar. Add eggs, one at a time, beating well after each addition. Sift together flour, baking soda baking powder and salt in a medium sized bowl. Add flour mixture to butter mixture alternately with yogurt; stir in vanilla and almond extract. Pour batter into the pan and bake at 350° for 1 hour, or until a toothpick inserted in the cake comes out clean. Cool in the pan for 10 minutes; remove and cool completely on a rack. Dust with powdered sugar. Serve plain or with ice cream, chocolate sauce or fresh summer fruits.

STRAWBERRY YOGURT POUND CAKE

The subtle mix of strawberry and almond flavoring makes this cake one to remember. This is a small cake, suitable for a loaf pan.

- 2 cups all-purpose flour
- 2 teaspoons baking powder
- ½ teaspoon salt, optional
- ½ cup butter, softened
- 1 cup sugar
- 4 eggs
- 1 carton (6 oz.) fat strawberry yogurt
- ¼ teaspoon almond extract

In medium bowl, stir together flour, baking powder and salt, if desired. Set aside. In large mixing bowl at medium speed, beat together butter and sugar until light and fluffy. Beat in eggs, yogurt and extract until well blended. Reduce mixer speed to low. Add reserved flour mixture, ½ cup at a time, beating just until blended. Spread evenly in greased and floured 9 × 5 × 3-inch loaf pan. Bake at 325° until cake tester inserted near center comes out clean, about 70 minutes. Cool on wire rack 10 minutes. Remove from pan and cool completely.

ONE-STEP POUND CAKE

Use your favorite yogurt to flavor this cake. Serve it with fresh fruit or frozen yogurt or sorbet.

> 1 cup butter, softened
> 2 cups granulated sugar
> 2¼ cups plain flour
> ½ teaspoon baking soda
> ½ teaspoon salt
> 1 cup (8 oz.) of flavored yogurt
> 4 eggs
> 1 teaspoon grated lemon or orange zest
> 1 teaspoon vanilla extract

Mix together all ingredients in a large bowl until well-blended. Increase speed to medium and beat 3 minutes. Pour batter into greased and floured Bundt pan. Bake at 325° for 50 to 60 minutes or until cake tests done. Transfer pan to a wire rack and cool 15 minutes. Turn cake out onto rack to cool completely.

GLAZE

> ½ cup powdered sugar
> 1 to 2 Tablespoons lemon juice

Whisk together powdered sugar and lemon juice in small bowl until well blended and smooth. Drizzle over cake.

SPICED YOGURT POUND CAKE

This is a rich, moist and delicious spiced pound cake. It needs no frosting but a dusting of confectioners' sugar will dress it up.

- 2 cups butter
- 3 cups sugar
- 4 cups plain flour
- 1 cup plain yogurt
- 6 eggs
- 2 teaspoons vanilla
- 2 teaspoons ground cinnamon
- 2 teaspoons ground allspice
- 1 teaspoon ground nutmeg
- ½ teaspoon ground cloves
- 1 teaspoon salt
- 1 teaspoon baking soda.

In a large bowl, cream the butter with the sugar until light and fluffy. Beat in the flour, yogurt, eggs, vanilla, and remaining ingredients. Mix until combined then beat on high speed for 2 minutes. Pour the batter into a greased and floured 10-inch tube pan. Bake at 350° for 1 hour and 10 minutes or until cake tests done. Cool cake in pan on a wire rack for 15 minutes; remove from pan to cool completely.

POUND CAKES MADE WITH CREAM CHEESE

CREAM CHEESE POUND CAKE

This recipe calls for placing a measuring cup full of water in the oven during baking—the result is a very moist cake with a velvety-smooth texture and delicate cream cheese flavor.

- 1½ cups butter
- 1 (8 oz.) package cream cheese, softened
- 3 cups sugar
- 6 eggs
- 3 cups sifted plain flour
- ⅛ teaspoon salt
- 1½ teaspoon vanilla extract

Beat butter and cream cheese at medium speed with electric mixer for 2 minutes or until creamy. Gradually add sugar, beating 5 to 7 minutes. Add eggs, one at a time, beating just until yellow disappears. Add vanilla, mixing well. Combine flour and salt; gradually add to butter mixture, beating at low speed until just blended after each addition. Spoon mixture into a greased and floured 10-inch tube pan. Place a 2-cup ovenproof measuring cup filled with water in the oven with the tube pan. Bake at 300° for 1 hour and 30 minutes or until cake tests done. Cool in pan on a wire rack for 10 to 15 minutes. Remove from pan and cool completely on wire rack.

CREAM CHEESE GLAZE

- ¼ package (2 ounces) cream cheese, softened
- 1 cup powdered sugar
- 1-2 teaspoons lemon juice or milk

Beat cream cheese, sugar and enough lemon juice (or milk) to make glaze proper consistency. Drizzle over cake and garnish with candied cherries and/or pecans (if desired). Refrigerate cake. Let stand at room temperature 1 to 1½ hours before serving.

BISQUICK POUND CAKE

Using a baking mix certainly reduces the preparation time for this cake but in no way reduces the wonderfully rich flavor and light texture. You may substitute other fruit preserves - try peach or strawberry glaze, instead of the apricot.

> 3 cups Bisquick
> 1½ cups sugar
> ½ cup flour
> ¾ cup butter or margarine, softened
> 6 eggs
> 8 oz. cream cheese, softened
> 1 teaspoon vanilla
> ⅛ teaspoon salt

Grease and flour a 10-inch tube pan. Beat Bisquick, 1½ cups sugar, ½ cup flour, butter, eggs, cream cheese, vanilla and salt in large bowl on low speed, scraping bowl frequently, about 30 seconds. Beat on medium speed for about 4 minutes, scraping bowl occasionally. Pour batter into pan. Bake at 350° until cake tester comes out clean, about 55-60 minutes. Cool 10 minutes; remove from pan.

TOPPING

> ½ cup sugar
> ½ cup water
> ¼ cup orange flavored liqueur

Heat sugar and water to boiling; reduce heat and simmer uncovered, for 2 minutes. Cool to lukewarm. Stir in liqueur. Slowly drizzle over cake.

Glaze

1 cup apricot preserves
¼ cup sugar

Press preserves through sieve. Heat preserves and sugar to boiling, stirring constantly; reduce heat. Simmer uncovered until slightly thickened, about 1 to 2 minutes. Cool slightly; spread over top, allowing some to drizzle down sides.

CREAM CHEESE-STREUSEL POUND CAKE

Streusel: 1 cup light brown sugar
¼ cup baking mix, such as Bisquick
½ teaspoon ground cinnamon
¼ cup unsalted butter, softened

Cake: 3½ cups baking mix (Bisquick)
1½ cups sugar
¾ cup unsalted butter, softened
1 package (8 oz.) cream cheese, softened
6 eggs
1 teaspoon vanilla extract

Grease and flour a 10-inch tube pan, preferably with removable bottom.

For Streusel: In small bowl, stir together light brown sugar, baking mix, cinnamon and butter with a fork until mixture is crumbly. Set aside.

For cake: In large bowl, combine baking mix, sugar, butter, cream cheese, eggs and vanilla. With mixer on low speed, beat 1 minute, scraping down sides of bowl, until blended. On high speed, beat 3 minutes. Spread one-third (about 2 cups) of batter into prepared pan. Sprinkle with one-third (about ⅓ cup) of streusel. Repeat twice with remaining batter and streusel. Bake at 350° for 70 to 80 minutes, or until wooden skewer inserted in center of cake comes out clean. Remove pan to wire rack; let cake cool in pan for 15 minutes. Remove side of pan and let cake cool completely. Remove cake from bottom of pan and tube.

POUND CAKES MADE WITH OTHER CHEESES

CHEDDAR CHEESE POUND CAKE

This sweet blend of cream cheese and sharp Cheddar is extra nice when served with apple butter.

- 1½ cups butter
- 1 (8-ounce) package cream cheese, softened
- 3 cups sugar
- 6 large eggs
- 3 cups plain flour
- 1 dash of salt
- 2 cups (8 ounces) finely shredded sharp Cheddar cheese
- 1 Tablespoon vanilla extract

Beat butter and cream cheese at medium speed with mixer about 2 minutes or until creamy. Gradually add sugar, beating 5 to 7 minutes. Add eggs, one at a time, beating just until yellow disappears. Combine flour and salt; gradually add to butter mixture. Beat at low speed just until blended after each addition. Stir in Cheddar cheese and vanilla. Pour into greased and floured 10-inch tube pan. Bake at 325° for 1 hour and 45 minutes or until a wooden pick inserted in cake comes out clean. Cool in pan 15 minutes; remove from pan and cool completely on wire rack.

SAVORY CHEESE POUND CAKE

This tasty, slightly sweet pound cake is perfect with tea or served at lunch with a bowl of soup or a crisp, green salad. It requires cheddar and Parmesan cheeses.

- ½ cup lightly toasted pine nuts
- 1 cup butter, room temperature
- ¾ cup sugar
- 5 eggs, room temperature
- 2 cups flour
- ½ teaspoon baking powder
- ¼ teaspoon cayenne pepper
- ¼ cup milk, room temperature
- 1 cup grated sharp cheddar cheese
- ½ cup freshly grated Parmesan cheese

Butter and flour a 9-inch Bundt pan. Toast the pine nuts in a dry skillet, stirring constantly and watching closely to make sure they brown only enough to release their oils – about 2 to 3 minutes. Remove the pine nuts from the skillet and place in a small bowl. Set aside to cool. Cream the butter. Gradually add the sugar, beating well. Continue beating another 3 to 4 minutes. Scrape the sides of the bowl and mix well. Add the eggs, one at a time, mixing well after each addition. Whisk together the flour, baking powder, and cayenne pepper. Add half the flour mixture to the butter, mixing well. Add the ¼ cup milk, and follow with the remaining flour. Fold in (with a rubber spatula) the cheeses and cooled pine nuts. Scrape the sides of the bowl and stir. Transfer the batter to the prepared pan. Bake at 350° for 35 to 40 minutes, or until a cake tester comes out clean. Let the cake cool in the pan on a wire rack for 15 minutes. Remove from pan and allow cake to cool completely.

RICOTTA CHEESE POUND CAKE

This recipe shows that there is a pound cake for every taste. This one calls for whole wheat flour, and it is delicious!

- 1 cup unsalted butter, softened
- 2 cups packed light brown sugar
- 6 eggs
- 2 teaspoons vanilla extract
- Finely grated zest of 2 lemons
- 2 cups unbleached flour
- 2 cups whole-wheat flour
- 1 Tablespoon baking powder
- 1 teaspoon salt
- 1 teaspoon nutmeg
- 1¾ cups milk or light cream
- 1 cup Ricotta cheese

Butter and lightly flour a 10-inch tube pan. In a large mixing bowl, cream the butter with an electric mixer, gradually beating in the brown sugar. Add the eggs, one at a time, beating well after each egg. Beat in the vanilla and lemon zest. Sift the flours, baking powder, salt, and nutmeg into another bowl, add any pieces of bran that remain in the sifter; set aside. Puree the milk or cream and ricotta cheese in a blender. Stir the dry ingredients into the creamed mixture alternately with the milk/ricotta; do this is several stages, beginning and ending with the dry ingredients. Do not beat the batter. Distribute the batter evenly in the prepared pan, then bake at 350° for 1 hour and 15 minutes or until a tester inserted near center comes out clean. Cool the pan on a rack for 10 minutes, then invert it onto the rack and cool the cake for at least one hour before cutting. Transfer cake to a serving plate.

POUND CAKES MADE WITH WATER

4X POUND CAKE

This recipe calls for water as added liquid. Powdered sugar gives this cake a fine texture.

> 1½ cups butter
> 1 box (1 lb) powdered sugar
> 6 large eggs
> 3⅓ cups plain flour
> ⅛ teaspoon salt
> ½ cup water
> 1 teaspoon vanilla extract
> 1 teaspoon almond extract

Cream butter. Sift sugar, and add gradually to butter, creaming until fluffy. Add eggs, one at a time, beating well after each addition. Stir salt into flour. Add flour mixture, alternating with water, to creamed mixture; mix well after each addition. Fold in flavorings and pour into a greased and floured 10-inch tube pan. Bake at 325° for 1 hour and 25 minutes or until cake tests done. Cool in pan 10 minutes; remove from pan and cool completely on wire rack.

POUND CAKES MADE WITH CARBONATED DRINKS OR SODAS

GINGER ALE POUND CAKE

Ginger ale provides the liquid for this recipe and adds a bit of flavoring as well. Adventuresome cooks may want to try their own favorite soda!

- ½ cup shortening
- 1 cup margarine
- 2½ cups sugar
- 5 eggs
- 3 cups plain flour
- 6 oz. bottle ginger ale
- 2 teaspoons lemon extract

Cream sugar, margarine, and shortening. Add eggs, one at a time, and beat after each addition. Stir in lemon extract. Add flour alternately with ginger ale; mix well after each addition. Turn batter into a greased and floured 10-inch tube pan. Bake for 1 hour at 325° or until done. Cool 10 minutes in pan; remove from pan and cool completely on wire rack.

7-UP POUND CAKE

Any lemon-lime soda will give the cake a nice lemony flavor.

    1 cup butter, softened (no substitutions)
    ½ cup vegetable shortening
    3 cups sugar
    5 large eggs
    3 cups plain flour, sifted
    ¼ teaspoon salt
    1½ teaspoons vanilla extract
    ½ teaspoon lemon extract
    1 cup 7-Up or other lemon-lime soda

Combine flour and salt in bowl. Combine remaining ingredients except soda in large mixer bowl; beat at medium speed for about 5 minutes or until light and fluffy, scraping sides occasionally. Reduce speed to low; add dry ingredients and soda, beginning and ending with dry ingredients; mix well after each addition. Pour batter into greased and floured 10-inch tube pan. Bake at 325° for 1 hour and 30 minutes or until cake tests done. Cool in pan 15 minutes. Invert onto wire rack, remove from pan and cool completely.

ORANGE CRUSH POUND CAKE

This recipe's distinctive orange flavor is further enhanced by the glaze made with orange juice and powdered sugar.

> 2¾ cups sugar
> 1 cup shortening
> ¼ cup margarine
> 1 cup Orange Crush
> 5 eggs
> ½ teaspoon salt
> 3 cups plain flour, sifted
> 1 teaspoon vanilla extract
> 1 teaspoon orange extract

Cream sugar, shortening and margarine. Add eggs, one at a time, mixing well after each addition. Cream until fluffy. Sift salt and flour together and add to sugar mixture alternately with Orange Crush; mix well after each addition. Stir in flavorings. Pour batter into greased and floured 10-inch tube pan. Bake at 325° for 1 hour and 10 minutes, or until cake tests done. Cool 10 minutes in pan; remove from pan and cool on wire rack.

GLAZE

> 1¼ cups sifted powdered sugar
> ¼ cup orange juice
> 1 teaspoon orange extract

Mix all ingredients until smooth. Add more powdered sugar if too thin. Spread on warm cake.

CHAPTER 3

CHOCOLATE POUND CAKES

Since the Aztecs first introduced it to Cortez, chocolate has become the most widely eaten confection in the world. The 40 recipes in this chapter take advantage of many forms of chocolate—unsweetened, sweet, chocolate chips, chocolate syrup, cocoa, German chocolate, white chocolate, even chocolate cookies.

POUND CAKES MADE WITH UNSWEETENED CHOCOLATE

CHOCOLATE ALMOND POUND CAKE

This recipe goes together quickly and has a little crunch, thanks to the almonds and corn meal.

- ½ cup finely chopped almonds
- 1½ cups sugar
- 4 oz butter, melted
- 4 eggs
- 4 oz. unsweetened chocolate, melted
- 1½ teaspoons almond extract
- 2 cups flour
- 1 cup corn meal
- 1 teaspoon salt (optional)
- ½ teaspoon baking powder
- 1 cup milk

Generously grease a 12-cup Bundt pan. Coat sides with almonds. In a large bowl, beat sugar and butter until light and fluffy. Add eggs, one at a time, mixing well after each egg. Stir in chocolate and almond extract. Combine flour, corn meal, salt and baking powder. Add alternately with milk to chocolate mixture, mixing at low speed until well blended. Spoon batter into pan. Bake at 350° for 50-60 minutes. Cool 10 minutes, remove from pan and cool on rack.

MOCHA POUND CAKE

Mocha! The luxurious taste of coffee and chocolate.

> 1½ cups shortening
> 2½ cups sugar
> 6 eggs
> 4 cups sifted plain flour
> 1 teaspoon salt
> ½ teaspoon baking soda
> 1 teaspoon cream of tartar
> 4 (1 oz.) squares unsweetened chocolate, melted
> 4 to 5 teaspoons instant coffee granules
> 1 cup water
> 2 teaspoons vanilla extract

Cream shortening; gradually add sugar, beating until light and fluffy. Add eggs, one at a time, beating well after each addition. Add melted chocolate, mixing well. Dissolve coffee granules in water; stir well and set aside. Combine flour, salt, cream of tartar, and soda; gradually add to chocolate mixture alternately with coffee mixture, beginning and ending with flour mixture. Mix well after each addition. Stir in vanilla. Pour batter into greased and floured 10-inch tube pan. Bake at 325° for 1 hour and 30 minutes or until a wooden pick inserted in center comes out clean. Cool in pan 10 minutes; remove from pan onto wire rack and cool completely.

CHOCOLATE PECAN POUND CAKE

This cake gets its buttery, nutty flavor from butternut flavoring. This is a mixture of vanilla, butter and nut flavorings; southern cooks will find it in any supermarket—in other parts of the country, it may take a little more effort.

> 1 cup butter, softened
> ½ cup butter flavored Crisco
> 3 cups sugar
> 5 large eggs
> 1 (1 oz.) square unsweetened chocolate, melted
> 3 cups plain flour
> ½ teaspoon baking powder
> ½ teaspoon salt
> ⅓ cup cocoa
> 1 cup milk
> ½ cup chopped pecans
> 1 teaspoon butternut flavoring
> 1 teaspoon vanilla extract

Beat butter and shortening at medium speed with an electric mixer about 2 minutes or until creamy. Gradually add sugar, beating at medium speed 5 to 7 minutes. Add eggs, one at a time, beating after each addition just until yellow disappears. Stir in melted chocolate. Combine flour and next 3 ingredients; add to butter mixture alternately with milk, beginning and ending with flour mixture. Mix at low speed just until blended after each addition. Stir in pecans and flavorings. Spoon batter into a greased and floured 10-inch tube pan. Bake at 325° for 1 hour and 35 minutes or until a wooden pick inserted in center of cake comes out clean. Shield cake with aluminum foil for the last 10 minutes. Cool in pan on a wire rack 10 to 15 minutes; remove from pan and let cool completely on wire rack.

SOUR CREAM CHOCOLATE POUND CAKE

Butter and sour cream combine for a rich taste. This recipe is unusual in calling for boiling water to be added to the cake batter.

- 1 cup butter
- 2 cups sugar
- 2 eggs
- 2 (2 oz) squares unsweetened chocolate, melted
- 2½ cups plain flour
- 1 teaspoon soda
- ¼ teaspoon salt
- 1 (8 oz.) carton sour cream
- 1 cup boiling water

Cream butter and sugar. Add eggs one at a time and mix well after each addition. Add melted chocolate and mix well. Sift dry ingredients together and add to butter mixture alternately with sour cream, mixing well after each addition. Add boiling water last and mix well. Pour into greased and floured 10-inch tube pan. Bake at 325° for 1 hour or until cake tests done. Cool 10 minutes in pan; remove from pan and cool completely on wire rack.

Glaze

- 2 Tablespoons cocoa
- 1 Tablespoon water
- 1 Tablespoon light corn syrup
- 2 Tablespoons butter or margarine
- ¼ teaspoon vanilla
- ½ cup powdered sugar

In a small saucepan, combine cocoa, water, corn syrup and butter. Cook over low heat until mixture thickens, stirring constantly. Remove from heat. Stir in vanilla and powdered sugar; beat until smooth. Spread glaze over top of cooled cake, allowing some to run down sides.

CHOCOLATE ALMOND MARBLE POUND CAKE

The almond flavoring in this cake blends well with the chocolate and vanilla. The light and dark swirls of color give it a striking appearance.

1 Tablespoon shortening
1 (1 oz.) square unsweetened chocolate
½ cup butter or margarine, softened
½ cup shortening
2 cups sugar
4 eggs
3 cups plain flour
½ teaspoon baking soda
⅛ teaspoon salt
1 cup buttermilk
2 teaspoons vanilla extract
1 teaspoon almond extract

Melt 1 Tablespoon shortening and 1 square chocolate in a small saucepan, stirring until smooth. Set aside. Cream butter and shortening; gradually add sugar, beating well at medium speed of an electric mixer. Add eggs, one at a time, beating after each addition. Dissolve soda in buttermilk. Combine flour and salt; add to creamed mixture alternately with buttermilk, beginning and ending with flour mixture. Mix until just blended after each addition. Stir in flavorings. Remove 2 cups of batter and add chocolate mixture, stirring until blended. Spoon ⅓ of remaining plain batter into a greased and floured 10-inch tube pan; top with half of the chocolate batter. Repeat layers, ending with plain batter. Gently swirl batter with a knife to create marble effect. Bake at 350° for 1 hour and 10 minutes or until cake tests done. Cool in pan 10 minutes; remove from pan and cool completely on wire rack.

POUND CAKES MADE WITH SWEET CHOCOLATE

BUTTERY CHOCOLATE POUND CAKE

This cake has a mild chocolate and buttery flavor.

- 1 cup shortening
- 2 cups sugar
- 4 eggs
- ½ teaspoon baking soda
- 3 cups plain flour
- ½ teaspoon salt
- 1 (4 oz.) package sweet baking chocolate, melted
- 1 cup buttermilk
- 2 teaspoons vanilla extract
- 2 teaspoons butter flavoring

Cream shortening; gradually add sugar, beating well. Add eggs, one at a time, beating well after each addition. Dissolve baking soda in buttermilk. Combine flour and salt; add to creamed mixture alternately with buttermilk mixture, beginning and ending with flour mixture. Mix well after each addition. Add chocolate, beating well. Stir in flavorings. Pour batter into a well-greased 10-inch tube pan. Bake at 325° for 1 hour and 25 minutes or until cake tests done. Cool in pan 15 minutes; remove cake from pan and let cool completely on wire rack.

MILK CHOCOLATE POUND CAKE

With milk chocolate bars and chocolate syrup, this cake is delicious plain, or with powdered sugar sifted over the top, or topped with caramel icing.

> 1 cup butter, softened
> 2 cups sugar
> 4 eggs
> 6 (1.55 oz.) milk chocolate candy bars, melted
> 2½ cups plain flour
> ¼ teaspoon baking soda
> pinch of salt
> 1 cup buttermilk
> 1 cup chopped pecans (optional)
> 1 cup chocolate syrup
> 2 teaspoons vanilla extract

Cream butter; gradually add sugar, beating well at medium speed of an electric mixer. Add eggs, one at a time, beating after each addition. Add melted candy bars. Combine flour, soda, and salt; add to chocolate mixture alternately with buttermilk, beginning and ending with flour mixture. Mix just until blended after each addition. Add pecans, chocolate syrup, and vanilla, blending well. Pour batter into a greased and floured 10-inch tube pan. Bake at 325° for 1 hour and 15 minutes or until a wooden pick inserted in center of cake comes out clean. Cool in pan 15 minutes; remove from pan, and cool completely on wire rack.

Caramel Icing

> ½ cup light brown sugar
> ½ cup dark brown sugar
> ½ cup butter
> ¼ cup evaporated milk
> 2 cups powdered sugar

Melt sugars in double boiler with butter; bring to boil. Add evaporated milk (room temperature) and bring back to boil. Mix with powdered sugar; beat well. Spread on cake.

SWEET CHOCOLATE POUND CAKE

This recipe makes nice use of cinnamon. It is unusual in calling for the cake pan to be lined with waxed paper, in addition to the standard greasing and flouring (no way this one will stick!)

- 1 cup butter or margarine
- 1¾ cups sugar
- 3 eggs
- 1 egg yolk
- 2¾ cups plain flour, sifted
- 1 teaspoons salt
- ½ teaspoons soda
- ¼ teaspoons cinnamon
- 1 (4 oz.) bar sweet cooking chocolate
- ¾ cup milk
- ¾ teaspoon cream of tartar
- 1 teaspoon vanilla extract

Melt chocolate over hot water; cool. Sift dry ingredients. Cream butter; add dry ingredients, milk and vanilla. Mix to dampen; beat for 2 minutes at medium speed. Add eggs, yolk, and chocolate. Beat for 1 minute longer. Pour batter into greased and floured 10-inch tube pan with bottom also lined with waxed paper. Bake at 350° for 1 hour and 5 minutes, or until cake tests done. Cool in pan for 15 minutes. Remove from pan and finish cooling on wire rack.

SUNDAE POUND CAKE

Chocolate lovers will love this one. It's delicious plain or with fresh strawberries and ice cream. For a real feast, make it fancy with a dark chocolate glaze and two kinds of chocolate drizzle. Note that this is a small cake, suitable for a Bundt pan or a loaf pan.

> ½ cup butter
> 3 eggs
> ⅔ cup sour cream
> ½ of a 4-ounce bar sweet baking chocolate, cut up
> 2 Tablespoons milk
> 1 Tablespoon water
> 1-⅓ cups all-purpose flour
> ¼ teaspoon baking powder
> ⅛ teaspoon baking soda
> 1¼ cups sugar
> 1 teaspoon vanilla
> 1 teaspoon finely shredded lemon peel

Grease and flour a 6-cup fluted tube pan or 9×5×3-inch loaf pan; set aside. In a small heavy saucepan melt the sweet baking chocolate with milk and water over low heat, stirring until smooth. Remove from heat; cool slightly. In a small mixing bowl combine flour, baking powder, and baking soda; set aside. In a large mixing bowl beat butter with an electric mixer on medium to high speed until softened. Gradually add sugar, beating until very light and fluffy. Add vanilla. Add eggs, 1 at a time, beating on low to medium speed for 1 minute after each addition. Alternately add flour mixture and sour cream, beating on low speed just until combined. Stir in lemon peel. Spread batter in prepared pan. Bake at 325° for

50 to 60 minutes or until a wooden toothpick inserted into the center of the cake comes out clean. Cool cake in pan on a wire rack for 10 minutes. Remove cake from pan and cool completely. Spoon Dark Chocolate Glaze over cake. If desired, using a pastry bag with a small tip, pipe Milk Chocolate Drizzle and/or White Chocolate Drizzle over glaze.

Dark Chocolate Glaze

1 ounce unsweetened chocolate
2 Tablespoons butter
2 Tablespoons milk
1 cup sifted powdered sugar
½ teaspoon vanilla extract

In a small saucepan combine chocolate, butter, and milk, stirring over low heat until chocolate is melted. Remove from heat. Stir in powdered sugar and vanilla. Beat until smooth.

Milk Chocolate Drizzle

½ ounce milk chocolate
1 Tablespoon butter
1 Tablespoon milk
½ cup sifted powdered sugar
¼ teaspoon vanilla extract

In a small saucepan combine milk chocolate, butter, and milk, stirring over low heat until melted. Remove from heat. Stir in powdered sugar and vanilla. Beat until smooth.

White Chocolate Drizzle

½ ounce white baking bar
1 Tablespoon butter
1 Tablespoon milk
½ cup sifted powdered sugar
¼ teaspoon vanilla extract

In a small saucepan combine white baking bar, butter, milk, stirring over heat until melted. Remove from heat. Stir in powdered sugar and vanilla. Beat until smooth.

GERMAN CHOCOLATE POUND CAKE

German sweet chocolate is a blend of unsweetened chocolate, sugar and cocoa butter; it has a light, mild flavor. It's scrumptious with chocolate glaze, or embellished with coconut pecan frosting.

>   4 oz. German sweet chocolate
>   2¾ cups sifted plain flour
>   1¾ cups sugar
>   1 teaspoon salt
>   ¾ teaspoon cream of tartar
>   ½ teaspoon baking soda
>   ¼ teaspoon cinnamon
>   1 cup butter, softened
>   ¾ cup milk
>   1 teaspoon vanilla extract
>   3 eggs
>   1 egg yolk

Melt chocolate in double boiler and set aside to cool. Sift dry ingredients together. Cream softened butter. Add dry ingredients, milk and vanilla extract, mixing only to combine. Beat 2 minutes at medium speed with electric mixer. Add eggs, egg yolk and chocolate. Beat 1 minute longer. Pour batter into a greased and floured 10-inch tube pan that has been lined with wax paper. Bake at 350° for 1 hour and 5 minutes, or until cake tests done. Cool in pan for 15 minutes. Turn out of pan, remove waxed paper and cool completely on wire rack.

Chocolate Glaze

>   4 oz. German sweet chocolate
>   1 Tablespoon butter
>   ¼ cup water
>   1 cup confectioners' sugar, sifted
>   ⅛ teaspoon salt
>   ½ teaspoon vanilla extract

Melt chocolate, butter and water in a double boiler over low heat. Combine confectioners' sugar and salt. Gradually stir in chocolate mixture and vanilla extract, blending well. Pour over cooled cake.

Coconut Pecan Frosting

1 cup sugar
1 cup evaporated milk
½ cup butter or margarine
3 eggs, beaten
1⅓ cups flaked coconut
1 cup chopped pecans
1 teaspoon vanilla extract

In medium saucepan, combine sugar, milk, butter and eggs. Cook over medium heat, stirring constantly, until mixture starts to bubble. Stir in coconut, pecans and vanilla. Cool to room temperature. Spread frosting on cake.

POUND CAKES MADE WITH CHOCOLATE CHIPS

CHOCOLATE CHIP COOKIE POUND CAKE

This cake has all the ingredients of a true chocolate chip cookie and will become just as loved, especially with household with children (no matter what their ages).

- 1½ cups chocolate chips
- 1 cup butter, room temperature
- 1 cup sugar
- 1½ cups light brown sugar
- 5 eggs, room temperature
- 3 cups flour
- 1 cup sour cream
- 1 Tablespoon vanilla extract
- 1 teaspoon baking powder
- ½ teaspoon baking soda
- ½ teaspoon salt
- 1 cup chopped pecans

Butter and flour a 10-inch tube pan. Place chocolate chips in a food processor, pulsing just until the chips are chopped finely but not so long that they become powdery. Set aside. Beat the butter until light. Add the sugars, a little at a time and cream very well – until the mixture is light and fluffy. Beat in the eggs, one at a time, beating slightly after each addition. Mix in ½ of the flour. Mix together the sour cream and vanilla and add to the butter, mixing well. Combine the baking powder, soda and salt with remaining flour and add to the butter. Mix well. Add the chopped chocolate chips and the cup of pecans, incorporating well with the rest of the butter but being careful not to overbeat at this point. Bake at 325° for 55 to 60 minutes or until cake tests done. Let the cake cool in the pan for 15 to 20 minutes before turning out on a cake rack. Cool completely before slicing.

PECAN CHOCOLATE CHIP POUND CAKE

A layer of chopped pecans on the bottom of the pan produces a delightful crunchy topping, and chocolate chip mini-morsels are small enough to remain suspended in the batter (the larger ones tend to sink toward the bottom).

2¾ cups sugar
1¼ cups butter, softened
5 eggs
1 teaspoon almond extract
3 cups plain flour
1 teaspoon baking powder
¼ teaspoon salt
1 cup milk
1 cup semi-sweet mini-morsel chocolate chips
1 cup chopped pecans

In a large mixing bowl, beat sugar, butter, eggs and almond extract on low speed, until just mixed. Beat on high for 5 minutes, scraping sides of bowl occasionally. In a separate bowl, combine flour, baking powder and salt. On low speed, add flour mixture alternately with milk, mixing until just blended. Fold in chocolate chips. Sprinkle pecans in bottom of a greased and floured 10-inch tube pan. Carefully pour batter over pecans. Bake at 325° for 1 hour and 40 minutes or until cake tests done. Cool 20 minutes in pan before removing to wire rack to cool completely.

MINI-MORSEL POUND CAKE

This cake will remind you of a giant chocolate chip cookie. Dress it up with a sprinkling of confectioners' sugar.

- 1 cup butter, softened
- 2 cups sugar
- 4 eggs
- 3 cups plain flour
- 1 teaspoon baking powder
- ½ teaspoon salt
- ¾ cup milk
- 3 teaspoons vanilla extract
- 1 package (12 oz.) semi-sweet chocolate mini-morsels

In small bowl, combine flour, baking powder and salt; set aside. In large mixer bowl, beat sugar, butter and vanilla extract until creamy. Beat in eggs, one at a time, beating well after each addition. Gradually beat in flour mixture alternately with milk, mixing after each addition. Stir in semi-sweet chocolate mini-morsels. Pour into greased and floured 10-inch tube pan. Bake at 325° for 1 hour and 15 minutes or until cake tests done. Cool in pan 15 minutes. Remove from pan and cool completely on wire rack.

LUXURY POUND CAKE

Chocolate chips and walnuts, with the zesty taste of orange—it deserves its name. Be sure to chill the chocolate chips so they can be ground in a food chopper.

    2 cups soft shortening
    2 cups sugar
    8 eggs, unbeaten
    4 cups sifted plain flour
    ½ teaspoon salt
    1 teaspoon baking powder
    1 (12 oz.) package chilled semi-sweet chocolate chips
    2 teaspoons vanilla extract
    grated rind of 2 oranges
    ½ cup orange juice
    1 cup chopped walnuts

Cream together shortening and sugar; add eggs, one at a time, beating well after each addition. Sift together flour, salt, and baking powder. Finely grind chocolate chips in a food chopper. Mix orange rind and orange juice and add alternately with flour mixture, mixing after each addition. Add vanilla, walnuts, and chocolate and beat until just smooth. Turn into greased and floured 10-inch tube pan. Bake at 300° for 1 hour and 40 minutes or until done. Cool 10 minutes in pan; turn onto wire rack to completely cool.

POUND CAKES MADE WITH CHOCOLATE SYRUP

CHOCOLATE MARBLE POUND CAKE

With beaten egg whites and self rising flour, this cake will rise nicely. It makes a good-sized cake, which is very pretty when dusted with confectioners' sugar.

- 1½ cups butter
- 2¼ cups sugar
- 6 eggs, separated
- 3 cups self-rising flour
- ¾ cup milk
- 1 small can (5½ oz.) chocolate syrup
- 1½ teaspoons vanilla extract

Cream butter and sugar until light and fluffy. Add egg yolks and vanilla and beat until well blended. Alternately add flour and milk to batter a little at a time until blended. Beat the egg whites until stiff and gently fold them into the batter. Remove ⅓ of the batter to another bowl and stir in the chocolate syrup. Layer batter in a greased and floured 10-inch tube pan as follows: Pour half of white batter into a greased cake pan. Pour in chocolate batter and top with the remaining half of white batter. Gently swirl batter with a knife to create marble effect. Bake at 300° for 1 hour and 50 minutes or until cake springs back when lightly touched with the fingertips. When cake has cooled for 15 minutes in pan, turn out of pan and cool completely on wire rack.

MALTED MILK BLACK AND WHITE POUND CAKE

During baking of this recipe, the chocolate layer is 'swallowed' by the light batter and is only revealed when you cut into the cake. Look for malted milk powder in the supermarket, where dry milk is sold. This cake is best when baked several hours ahead or the day before serving.

- ½ cup fine dry bread crumbs
- 1½ cups unsalted butter
- 1 Tablespoon vanilla extract
- ½ teaspoon salt
- 2½ cups sugar
- 7 eggs
- ½ cup milk
- 3½ cups all-purpose flour, sifted
- ½ cup malted milk powder
- ¾ cup chocolate syrup
- ¼ teaspoon baking soda
- ½ teaspoon almond extract

Coat a 10-inch tube pan with nonstick cooking spray. Dust inside of pan with dry breadcrumbs, tapping out any excess crumbs. Beat butter, vanilla and salt in a large bowl with mixer on medium speed 1 to 2 minutes until smooth and creamy. Add sugar, about ¼ cup at a time, beating well between additions. Scrape bowl; beat 6 to 7 minutes until fluffy and pale. Beat in eggs 1 at a time, beating well after each. Increase speed to high; beat 1 to 2 minutes until well blended. On low speed, beat in milk, then flour and malted milk powder, beating just until well combined. Scrape 5 cups batter into prepared pan; smooth top with a spatula. Beat chocolate syrup, baking soda and almond extract into remaining batter just until well blended. Pour chocolate batter over light batter and smooth top. Bake at 350° for 70 – 80 minutes, until cake springs back when lightly pressed and a wooden pick inserted in thickest part comes out clean. Cool in pan on a wire rack 20 minutes. Run a narrow thin-bladed knife around cake and tube. Invert cake on rack and cool completely.

CHOCOLATE-SWIRL POUND CAKE

This delicious cake can be made fancy with chocolate sauce that can be made ahead. Simply reheat before serving, adding additional water if needed.

> 2 cups butter
> 3 cups sugar
> 6 large eggs
> 4 cups plain flour
> ¾ cup milk
> 1 teaspoon vanilla extract
> ½ cup chocolate syrup

Beat butter at medium speed with electric mixer until creamy (about 2 minutes). Gradually add sugar, beating 5 to 7 minutes. Add eggs, one at a time, beating just until yellow disappears. Add flour to butter mixture alternately with milk, beginning and ending with flour. Mix at low speed just until blended after each addition. Stir in vanilla. Combine 1 cup batter and chocolate syrup, stirring until blended. Divide remaining batter in half; pour one portion into a greased and floured 10-inch tube pan. Spoon half of chocolate batter on top; repeat layers. Gently swirl batter with a knife. Bake at 300° for 1 hour and 40 minutes or until a wooden pick inserted in center comes out clean. Cool in pan on wire rack for 10 minutes; remove from pan and cool completely on a wire rack.

CHOCOLATE SAUCE

> 6 (1-ounce) squares semi-sweet chocolate
> ¼ cup butter
> ⅔ cup sifted confectioners' sugar
> 2 Tablespoons water
> 1 teaspoon vanilla extract

Melt chocolate and butter in a medium saucepan over low heat, stirring occasionally. Remove from heat; stir in confectioners' sugar, water and vanilla. Serve over pound cake.

POUND CAKES MADE WITH POWDERED COCOA

CHOCOLATE POUND CAKE WITH FROSTING

This basic recipe for chocolate pound cake calls for the addition of baking powder to ensure that it rises. For extra moist cake, try one of the smooth, mouth-watering toppings.

>   1 cup butter, softened
>   ½ cup margarine, softened
>   3 cups sugar
>   5 eggs
>   3 cups plain flour
>   ½ teaspoon baking powder
>   ½ teaspoon salt
>   ½ cup cocoa
>   1 cup milk
>   1 teaspoon vanilla extract

Cream butter and margarine until smooth; add sugar and beat until light and fluffy. Add eggs, one at a time, beating well after each addition. Combine dry ingredients, and add to creamed mixture alternately with milk and vanilla; mix well after each addition. Spoon batter into a well-greased and floured 10-inch tube pan. Bake at 325° for 35 minutes; reduce heat to 200° and bake an additional 35 to 40 minutes. If cake is to be frosted, let it cool 10 minutes in pan, then turn onto wire rack to cool completely. If cake is to be glazed, turn warm cake onto serving dish and add the topping while the cake is still warm.

Chocolate Frosting

>   1 cup sugar
>   ¼ cup butter or margarine
>   ⅓ cup evaporated milk
>   ½ cup semi-sweet chocolate morsels
>   ½ teaspoon vanilla extract

Combine first 3 ingredients in a small saucepan; bring to a boil, and boil 1 minute, stirring occasionally. Stir in chocolate morsels and vanilla. Beat with a wooden spoon about 3 minutes or until desired spreading consistency. Spread on cake.

Fudge Frosting

2 cups sugar
¼ cup cocoa
¼ teaspoon salt
⅔ cup milk
½ cup shortening
1 teaspoon vanilla extract

Combine all ingredients, except vanilla, in a heavy saucepan. Bring to a boil, stirring constantly; boil 2 minutes, stirring constantly. Remove from heat; pour into a small mixing bowl and add vanilla. Beat at high speed with an electric mixer for 5 minutes. Spread on cake.

Creamy Chocolate Glaze

2¼ cups sifted powdered sugar
3 Tablespoons cocoa
¼ cup butter, softened
3 to 4 Tablespoons milk
2 Tablespoons chopped pecans

Combine sugar and cocoa, mixing well. Add remaining ingredients and beat until smooth. Spoon mixture over warm cake. Sprinkle with chopped pecans.

CRUNCHY CHOCOATE POUND CAKE

This cake has a nice crunchy top. Sprinkle it with powdered sugar and serve with mixed berries and whipped cream.

- 1 cup of butter
- 1 cup shortening
- 3 cups sugar
- 6 large eggs
- 3 cups all purpose flour
- ¼ cup cocoa
- ½ teaspoon baking powder
- 1 cup whipping cream
- 1 teaspoon vanilla

Beat butter and shortening until creamy. Gradually add sugar, beating well. Add eggs, one at a time, beating just until yellow disappears. Combine flour and next three ingredients. Add to batter mixture alternating with cream, beginning and ending with flour mixture. Mix until blended after each addition. Stir in vanilla. Pour into greased Bundt pan or 10-inch tube pan. Bake at 325° for 1 hour and 30 minutes. Test for doneness with a toothpick. Remove from oven, cool for 30 minutes. Invert to a serving plate.

BUTTERMILK CHOCOLATE POUND CAKE

This is one those pound cakes that really does taste better on the second or third day. Remember that chocolate cakes tend to bake more quickly than other cakes, so be careful not to overcook.

- Sifted cocoa, for dusting the pan
- 2 cups butter, room temperature
- 3 cups sugar
- 6 eggs, room temperature
- 3¼ cups flour
- ¼ teaspoon salt
- ½ teaspoon baking soda
- ¾ cup cocoa
- ¾ cup buttermilk, room temperature
- 1½ teaspoons vanilla

Butter a 10-inch tube pan and dust with sifted cocoa (instead of flour). Cream the butter with an electric mixer. Add the sugar gradually and continue to beat for 5 minutes. Add the eggs, one at a time, mixing well after each egg. In a separate bowl, using a wire whisk or fork, mix together the flour, salt, baking soda, and cocoa. Alternately add the dry ingredients and the buttermilk and vanilla to the batter, ending with the flour. Pour into the prepared tube pan and bake at 350° for approximately 1 hour and 10 to 15 minutes, being extra careful not to overcook. Let the finished cake cool in the pan for 10 minutes. Then, turn the cake out on a wire rack and let it cool completely.

CHOCOLATE HAZELNUT CAKE

Rich dark cocoa and ground toasted hazelnuts turn this cake into a chocolate lover's dream. All you need on top is a shake of powdered sugar and maybe a spoonful of freshly whipped cream.

- 1 cup hazelnuts, toasted
- 2½ cups sugar
- 2¼ cups all-purpose flour
- 1 cup unsweetened cocoa
- ¾ teaspoon salt
- ½ teaspoon baking powder
- ½ teaspoon baking soda
- 1 cup butter or margarine, softened
- 4 eggs
- 1 Tablespoon vanilla extract
- 1¼ cups buttermilk
- Confectioners' sugar (optional)
- whipped cream (optional)
- mint leaves and fresh fruit for garnish

Grease 10-inch tube pan; dust with cocoa. In food processor, pulse hazelnuts with ½ cup sugar until nuts are very finely ground, occasionally stopping processor and scraping side with rubber spatula. Transfer nut mixture to medium bowl; stir in flour, cocoa, salt, baking powder, and baking soda; set aside. In large bowl, with mixer at low speed, beat butter with remaining 2 cups sugar until blended, scraping bowl often with rubber spatula. Increase speed to medium high; beat until creamy, about 3 minutes, occasionally scraping bowl. Reduce speed to low, add eggs, one at a time, beating well after each addition. Beat in vanilla. Alternately add flour mixture and buttermilk, beginning and ending with flour mixture; beat just until smooth. Spoon batter into pan and spread evenly. Bake at 325° for 1 hour and 15 minutes or until cake tests done. Cool cake in pan on wire rack for

15 minutes. For tube pan, with small metal spatula, loosen cake from side and center tube of pan. Invert cake onto cake plate, immediately invert again (so top side is up) onto wire rack to cool completely. For fluted pan, loosen cake from pan. Invert cake directly onto wire rack to cool completely.

CHOCOLATE NUT POUND CAKE

This simple recipe for chocolate pound cake can be made with or without the nuts, or it can be made with nuts other than pecans.

    1 cup butter or margarine, softened
    ½ cup shortening
    2½ cups sugar
    5 eggs
    3 cups plain flour
    ½ cup cocoa
    1 cup milk
    1 cup chopped pecans

Combine butter and shortening, mixing well; gradually add sugar, beating until light and fluffy. Add eggs, one at a time, beating well after each addition. Combine flour and cocoa; add to creamed mixture alternately with milk, beginning and ending with flour mixture. Mix well after each addition. Pour batter into a greased and floured 10-inch tube pan. Sprinkle pecans evenly over batter. Bake at 325° for 1 hour and 30 minutes or until cake tests done. Cool in pan 15 minutes; remove from pan and let cake cool completely on wire rack.

CHOCOLATE WALNUT POUND CAKE

This recipe has a double dose of chocolate and stays fresh and moist for several days. You can double the recipe for a larger cake to be made in a tube pan.

 1 cup butter, softened
 1⅓ cups sugar
 3 eggs, room temperature
 1⅔ cups flour
 ⅓ cup cocoa
 ½ teaspoon baking soda
 ¼ teaspoon salt
 1 cup vanilla yogurt, room temperature
 1 teaspoon vanilla extract
 ⅔ cup coarsely chopped walnuts
 2 3-oz. bittersweet chocolate bars, chopped

Butter a 9 × 5 × 3 inch loaf pan. Dust with sifted cocoa (instead of flour). Cream the butter with an electric mixer. Add the sugar gradually and continue to beat for 5 minutes. Add the eggs, one at a time, mixing well after each egg. In a separate bowl, sift together the flour, cocoa, soda, and salt. Alternately add the dry ingredients and the vanilla yogurt to the batter, ending with the flour. Mix in the vanilla extract, nuts, and chopped chocolate. Pour into the prepared pan and bake at 325° for approximately 1 hour and 10 to 15 minutes, being extra careful not to overcook. Let the finished cake cool in the pan for 10 minutes. Then turn the cake out on a wire rack and let it cool completely.

CHOCOLATE PEPPERMINT POUND CAKE

This would make a great seasonal gift, maybe garnished with peppermint pieces.

- 3 cups plus 2 Tablespoons flour
- 3 teaspoons baking powder
- 1 teaspoon salt
- 2/3 cup unsweetened cocoa powder
- 1 cup unsalted butter, room temperature
- 3 cups granulated sugar
- 4 eggs, room temperature
- 1 Tablespoon vanilla flavoring
- 1 teaspoon butter flavoring
- 1 Tablespoon chocolate extract
- 2 teaspoons peppermint extract
- 1½ cups milk, room temperature
- ¼ cup sour cream, room temperature

Lightly grease and flour a 10-inch tube pan. Line the bottom with a circle of waxed paper cut to fit pan. Grease the waxed paper. Sift together flour, baking powder, salt, and cocoa. Set aside. Cream butter at high speed for 3 minutes. Add sugar to margarine or butter 1 cup at a time, beating well after each addition. Beat in eggs, one at a time. Continue beating for at least 3 minutes after adding the last egg. Add vanilla flavoring, butter flavoring, chocolate extract and peppermint extract. Reduce speed to low. Alternately add the sifted dry ingredients (one third at a time) with the milk (one half at a time). Add sour cream. Beat for 4 minutes at low speed. Carefully pour and scrape batter into tube pan. Gently shake and tap pan to level batter. Bake at 325° on the lower third level rack of the oven for 75 to 90 minutes, or until tester comes out clean. Allow cake to cool in pan for 5 minutes. Carefully invert on rack to remove from pan. Remove waxed paper. Allow cake to cool completely.

CHOCOLATE SNICKERS POUND CAKE

Can't get enough chocolate? Try this cake! If you don't like peanuts, substitute Milky Way bars for the Snickers bars.

> 3 cups flour
> ½ cup sifted Dutch-processed cocoa powder
> 1 teaspoon baking powder
> ½ teaspoon salt
> 1½ cups unsalted butter, softened
> 1⅔ cups sugar
> 5 eggs
> 1¼ cups milk
> 1 Tablespoon chocolate extract
> 25 miniature or 10 fun-size Snickers bars, diced, 7 oz total

Grease and flour 10-inch tube pan. In bowl, whisk flour, cocoa, baking powder and salt. In large bowl, beat butter and sugar on medium speed 5 minutes, until fluffy. Beat in eggs, one at a time. Mix chocolate extract with milk. On low speed, alternately beat in flour mixture with milk mixture, until blended and smooth. Fold in diced candy bars. Scrape into prepared baking pan. Bake at 325° 1 hour and 15 minutes, until wooden pick inserted near center comes out clean. Cool in pan on rack for 45 minutes; invert cake onto wire rack. Cool cake completely.

GLAZE

> ½ cup heavy cream
> 1 Tablespoon each unsalted butter
> 1 Tablespoon sugar
> 18 Dove Promises (dark chocolate miniatures)

In medium saucepan, over medium-high heat, stir together heavy cream, butter and sugar until sugar dissolves. Bring to a boil. Add chocolate; remove from heat. Let stand 3 minutes; whisk until smooth. Let cool 5 minutes, until glaze is slightly thickened but still pourable. Set wire rack with cake on large jellyroll pan. Pour glaze over cake; with spatula, gently spread to cake edges; push excess glaze over edges. Spread glaze over sides of cake to cover, refrigerate 1 hour to set glaze. Transfer cake to serving plate. Garnish with peanut butter M&M's.

CHOCOLATE SOUR CREAM POUND CAKE

This rich cake calls for sour cream and brown sugar. It makes a pretty cake when sprinkled with powdered sugar.

 1 cup butter or margarine, softened
 2 cups sugar
 1 cup firmly packed brown sugar
 6 large eggs
 2½ cups plain flour
 ¼ teaspoon baking soda
 ½ cup cocoa
 1 (8 oz.) carton sour cream
 2 teaspoons vanilla extract

Beat butter at medium speed with an electric mixer about 2 minutes or until soft and creamy. Gradually add sugars, beating at medium speed 5 to 7 minutes. Add eggs, one at a time, beating after each addition just until yellow disappears. Combine flour, baking soda, and cocoa; add to creamed mixture alternately with sour cream, beginning and ending with flour mixture. Mix at lowest speed just until blended after each addition. Stir in vanilla. Spoon batter into a greased and floured 10-inch tube pan. Bake at 325° for 1 hour and 20 minutes or until a wooden pick inserted in center comes out clean. Cool in pan on a wire rack 15 minutes; remove from pan, and cool completely on a wire rack.

CHOCOLATE TRUFFLE POUND CAKE

This is the ultimate chocolate pound cake, one rich and elegant enough to please all chocolate lovers and to serve at the most special occasions.

   1 cup butter, room temperature
   3 cups light brown sugar
   6 eggs, room temperature
   2½ cups flour
   1 teaspoon baking soda
   ½ teaspoon salt
   ½ cup cocoa
   1 cup buttermilk, room temperature
   6 ounces bittersweet chocolate, melted
   1 Tablespoon vanilla extract

Butter and flour a 10-inch tube pan. Cream the butter until lightened in color. Add the brown sugar gradually until well combined. Continue to beat for about 5 minutes. Add the eggs, one at a time, mixing well after each addition. In a bowl, whisk together the flour, soda, salt and cocoa. Add one third of the flour mixture to the batter, mix well, and then add ½ cup of the buttermilk. Add the next one third of the flour mixture, the remaining buttermilk, and finally the lat one third of the flour mixture. Beat about 1 minute to mix well. Gently fold in the melted chocolate and vanilla. Pour the batter into prepared pan and smooth the top. Bake at 325° for 1 hour and 15 to 20 minutes or until a cake tester comes out clean. (Be careful not to overbake, checking the cake after 70 minutes.) Let the cake rest in the pan for 15 to 20 minutes; turn out, then let cool completely before icing.

Chocolate Truffle Icing

¾ cup butter, softened
1 box confectioners' sugar
½ cup plus 1 Tablespoon cocoa
5-6 Tablespoons buttermilk cocoa, for dusting
½ cup chopped toasted almonds

Combine all ingredients until light and fluffy, adding additional buttermilk if necessary to make spreadable. Ice the cooled cake. Dust the top with cocoa (shaking through a strained or sifter), and sprinkle chopped almonds on top.

MOCHA MARBLE POUND CAKE

This flavorful cake uses ingredients that are lower in fat and calories. It's a small cake, made in a loaf pan, but the recipe can be doubled for a full-size cake.

¼ cup margarine, softened
1 cup sugar
1 teaspoon vanilla extract
½ cup egg substitute
1 (8 oz.) container coffee-flavored low-fat yogurt, divided
2 cups plain flour
2 teaspoons baking powder
1 teaspoon baking soda
½ teaspoon salt
⅓ cup cocoa, divided
vegetable oil cooking spray
½ cup sifted powdered sugar
½ to 1 teaspoon fat-free milk

Beat margarine at medium speed until creamy; gradually add sugar, beating 5-7 minutes. Add vanilla and egg substitute; beat just until blended. Reserve 1½ Tablespoons yogurt in a small bowl. Combine flour and next three ingredients and add mixture to margarine mixture alternately with remaining yogurt, beginning and ending with flour mixture. Beat just until blended after each addition. Divide batter in half; stir ¼ cup cocoa into one portion. Alternately spoon batters into a 9 × 5-inch loaf pan coated with cooking spray. Swirl gently with a knife to create marbled effect. Bake at 350° for 1 hour or until a toothpick inserted in center comes out clean. Cool in pan for 10 minutes, remove from pan and cool completely on a wire rack. Whisk remaining cocoa and powdered sugar into reserved yogurt; add milk, as needed, for desired consistency. Pour over cooled cake.

MOCHA POUND CAKE WITH COFFEE CRÈME ANGLAISE

The coffee and cocoa compliment one another nicely in this recipe and make a moist, delicious pound cake that is liked by all, especially when served the Coffee Crème Anglaise.

> 1 cup butter, room temperature
> ½ cup Crisco
> 3¼ cups sugar
> 5 eggs, room temperature
> 3 cups flour
> 4 Tablespoons cocoa
> ½ teaspoon baking powder
> ½ teaspoon baking soda
> 1 cup coffee yogurt, room temperature
> ½ cup strong coffee
> 1 Tablespoon vanilla extract

Butter and flour a 10-inch tube pan. Cream together the butter and Crisco, beating well. Add the sugar and beat until fluffy. Add the eggs one at a time. Whisk together the flour, cocoa, baking powder, and baking soda. Alternately add the dry ingredients and the coffee yogurt to the batter, ending with the flour mixture. Combine the coffee and vanilla extract and carefully fold into the batter. Bake at 325° for one hour and 15 to 20 minutes of until a cake tester comes out clean. Cool in the pan on a rack for 15 minutes, then turn out onto a rack and cool completely. Serve with Coffee Crème Anglaise.

Coffee Crème Anglaise

> 2 cups milk
> 1 Tablespoon instant coffee
> 5 egg yolks
> 2 teaspoons cornstarch
> ½ cup sugar
> 1½ teaspoons vanilla extract
> 2 Tablespoon strong coffee

Warm the milk and coffee until hot, but don't let the mixture simmer. In a medium saucepan, combine the egg yolks, cornstarch and sugar. Whisk over low heat until mixture thickens. Slowly add the warm milk and instant coffee, stirring until the mixture coats the back of a spoon. Stir in the vanilla extract and strong coffee. All the custard to cool. Place a piece of plastic wrap directly on the custard and then refrigerate. This recipe can be made 2 to 3 days ahead of time.

MOCHACCINO POUND CAKE

Look for "Special Dark – Dutch Processed" cocoa powder at the grocery store. It makes any pound cake super dark with maximum chocolate impact.

1 cup butter
8 oz. cream cheese
3 cups sugar
6 eggs
2¼ cups flour
¾ cups cocoa
⅓ instant coffee granules or ¼ cup instant espresso powder
1 Tablespoon vanilla extract

Butter and flour a 10-inch tube pan. Cream together butter, cream cheese and sugar for about 5 minutes. Add eggs, one at a time, blending well after each addition. Combine flour and cocoa and sift together 3 times. Add in three additions to batter, scraping sides and bottom of bowl after each addition. Do not beat batter, just blend until flour is mixed well. Stir in coffee or espresso, along with vanilla extract. Pour batter into pan. Bake at 325° for 1 hour and 30 minutes, or until cake tester comes out clean when inserted into center of cake. Remove from oven and let cool in pan for 10 minutes. Remove cake from pan and place on cooling rack; let cool thoroughly.

DUTCH CHOCOLATE POUND CAKE

This cake has a deep chocolate flavor and a dense texture. It's too rich for frosting, but a big scoop of ice cream is a nice touch. Note that this is a COLD oven recipe.

- 3 cups plain flour
- ½ teaspoon baking powder
- ½ cup cocoa
- ¼ teaspoon salt
- 1½ cup butter
- 3 cups sugar
- 5 large eggs
- 1¼ cups milk
- 1 teaspoon vanilla extract

Beat butter and sugar together until fluffy, about 8 or 9 minutes. Beat in the eggs one at a time, mixing well after each addition. Mix in the combined dry ingredients alternately with the milk. Beat in the vanilla. Pour the batter into a greased and floured 10-inch tube pan. Place the pan in a cold oven and set the temperature to 325°. Bake for 1 hour and 20 minutes, or until cake tests done. Allow cake to cool in the pan on wire rack for 30 minutes before removing to wire rack to cool completely.

LOW CAL CHOCOLATE POUND CAKE

This recipe cuts calories by using margarine, corn oil and skim milk. Egg substitute can be used to reduce the cholesterol as well.

1 cup margarine
½ cup corn oil
3 cups sugar
5 eggs
3 cups plain flour
½ teaspoon salt
½ teaspoon baking powder
½ cup cocoa
¾ cup skim milk
1 Tablespoon vanilla extract
1 Tablespoon lemon extract

Cream margarine, oil and sugar together. Add eggs, one at a time, beating after each addition. Stir in flavorings. Sift together dry ingredients and add alternately with milk, beating after each addition. Turn into greased and floured 10-inch tube pan. Bake at 325° for 1 hour and 30 minutes or until cake tests done. Cool in pan 10 minutes; remove from pan and cool on wire rack.

CHOCOLATE RIPPLE POUND CAKE

This is a big, rich cake. It's similar to many old fashioned recipes, with a pound of this and a pound of that, but the chocolate makes it memorable.

    3 Tablespoons shortening
    ½ cup plus 1 Tablespoon cocoa
    2 cups butter or margarine
    3 cups sugar
    10 large eggs
    4 cups flour, sifted
    2 teaspoons vanilla extract

Melt shortening in a small pan; add cocoa, stirring until smooth. Set aside. Beat butter at medium speed with an electric mixer until creamy; gradually add sugar, beating well. Add eggs, one at a time, beating after each addition. Add flour and vanilla, mixing well. Remove 2 cups of batter and add chocolate mixture, stirring until blended. Spoon ⅓ remaining batter into a greased and flour 10-inch tube pan; top with half of the chocolate batter. Repeat layers, ending with plain batter. Draw a knife through batter to make a swirl design. Bake at 325° for 1½ hours or until wooden pick inserted in the center comes out clean. Cook cake in pan on a wire rack for 10 minutes; remove from pan and cool completely on a wire rack.

NO-FAT CHOCOLATE POUND CAKE

Can there be such a thing as a fat-free cake? Prune butter is the magic ingredient in this recipe, but be warned — there are still plenty of calories! Substitute 6 egg whites or equivalent egg substitute to reduce cholesterol.

> 3 cups plain flour
> 1 cup powdered cocoa
> 1 Tablespoon baking powder
> ¼ teaspoon salt
> ½ cup prune butter (see below)
> 3 cups sugar
> 1½ teaspoons vanilla
> 3 eggs
> 1¼ cups skim milk

Stir together the flour, cocoa powder, baking powder and salt; set aside. In a large bowl, place prune butter, sugar and vanilla; beat with electric mixer until well blended. Add eggs, one at a time, beating after each addition. Add flour mixture and milk alternately, in 3 additions, beating well after each addition. Spread into well-greased and floured 10-inch tube pan. Bake at 350° for about 1 hour, or until cake tester inserted in center comes out clean. Invert onto wire rack; cool.

PRUNE BUTTER

> ¼ cup corn syrup
> 2 Tablespoons granulated sugar
> 1 12-oz. package whole pitted prunes
> ⅔ cup water

Place first three ingredients in a food processor or blender and process for 30 seconds. Continue running the processor or blender and slowly add water until very smooth. Note: Can be stored in refrigerator for several months.

RED VELVET POUND CAKE

This cake is deep red (with the cocoa added) or bright red (without the cocoa) in color, with creamy white icing, and it is just perfect to dress up for special occasions. Add some holly or other greenery for a festive Christmas cake; garnish with blueberries for the fourth of July; add candy hearts for Valentine's Day. Use your imagination! (Note: This makes a very tall cake; for a smaller version, reduce or omit the baking powder.)

- 1 cup butter or margarine, softened
- ½ cup shortening
- 3 cups sugar
- 7 eggs
- 3 cups plain flour
- ½ cup cocoa
- 1 teaspoon baking powder
- ¼ teaspoon salt
- 1 cup milk
- 1 Tablespoon vanilla extract
- 1 (1 oz.) bottle red food coloring

Combine butter or margarine, shortening and sugar; cream until light and fluffy. Add eggs, one at a time, beating well after each addition. Stir in vanilla and food coloring. Combine flour, cocoa, baking powder and salt; add to creamed mixture alternately with milk, beating well after each addition. Pour batter into a greased and floured 10-inch tube pan. Bake at 325° for 1 hour and 20 minutes or until cake tests done. Cool cake in pan for 10 minutes; remove from pan and cool completely on wire rack.

Cream Cheese Frosting

½ cup butter, softened
8 oz. package cream cheese, softened
1 teaspoon vanilla extract
1 box powdered sugar, sifted
1 to 2 Tablespoons milk

Combine butter and cream cheese, blend until smooth. Stir in vanilla, mixing well. Stir in powdered sugar. Beat frosting until creamy; add enough milk to make spreading consistency.

DOUBLE CHOCOLATE POUND CAKE

This recipe is for chocolate lovers – cocoa and unsweetened chocolate combine for a rich velvety cake. Delicious with vanilla ice cream or Brown Sugar Sour Cream.

3 cups flour
¾ cup cocoa
½ teaspoon baking powder
½ teaspoon salt
1½ cups butter, softened
3 cups sugar
5 eggs
1¼ cups milk
4 oz. unsweetened chocolate, grated
1 Tablespoon vanilla
Powdered sugar for dusting

Grease and flour a 10-inch tube pan. In sifter, mix flour, cocoa, baking powder and salt. Sift into large bowl; set aside. In large bowl, with mixer at high speed, beat butter until fluffy. Gradually beat in sugar, beating until light and fluffy. Beat in eggs, one at a time, beating well after each addition. Alternately beat in flour mixture (in fourths) and milk (in thirds), beginning with flour. Beat in grated chocolate and vanilla. Pour into prepared pan, spreading top evenly; bake at 350° for 1 hour and 15 minutes or until cake tester inserted in cake comes out clean. Cool cake in pan 10 minutes; invert onto rack. Cool completely. Before serving, dust with powdered sugar or serve with Brown Sugar Sour Cream.

Brown Sugar Sour Cream

1½ cups sour cream
3 Tablespoons dark brown sugar
¾ teaspoon vanilla

In a small bowl, stir together all ingredients until smooth. Mixture will keep, covered and chilled for 1 week.

POUND CAKES MADE WITH WHITE CHOCOLATE

WHITE CHOCOLATE POUND CAKE

This elegant cake features white on white, with white chocolate in the cake and the icing.

> 1 cup shortening
> 2½ cups sugar
> 6 eggs
> ¼ pound white chocolate
> 3 cups flour
> ½ teaspoon baking powder
> ½ teaspoon salt
> ¾ cup milk
> 1 teaspoon vanilla

Cream shortening and sugar together. Add eggs, one at a time, beating well after each addition. Melt white chocolate in top of double boiler. Cool and add to sugar mixture. Sift flour with baking powder and salt. Add dry ingredients alternately with milk, beginning and ending with dry ingredients. Stir in vanilla. Pour batter into a greased and floured 10-inch tube pan. Bake at 300° for 1 hour and 15 minutes, or until cake tests done. Cool in pan for 15 minutes, then invert onto wire rack to finish cooling completely.

WHITE CHOCOLATE ICING

> ¼ cup margarine
> ½ cup evaporated milk
> 2 cups sugar
> ¼ pound white chocolate
> 1 teaspoon vanilla

Combine margarine, milk, sugar and white chocolate in a heavy saucepan. Cook over low heat, stirring constantly, until mixture comes to a boil. Boil 1 minute; remove from heat. Add vanilla and beat until thick. Pour over cooled cake.

WHITE CHOCOLATE-WALNUT POUND CAKE

The rich combination of butter, cream cheese, white chocolate and walnuts makes this cake out of this world! A sprinkle of confectioners' sugar is optional.

> 1 cup unsalted butter
> 1 (8 oz.) package cream cheese
> 2 cups sugar
> 4 large eggs
> 2 cups plain flour, sifted
> 2 teaspoons baking powder
> 1 teaspoon coffee extract
> 2 teaspoons vanilla extract
> 6 oz. white chocolate, chopped into chip-sized pieces
> ½ cup finely chopped walnuts
> Confectioners' sugar

Cream butter, cream cheese, and sugar until fluffy, then stir in the extracts. Add eggs, one at a time, beating well after each addition. Sift together baking powder and flour. Add to batter and beat at medium to high speed until flour is completely incorporated. Stir in flavorings and chocolate bits. Butter a 10-inch tube pan and coat it with the chopped nuts. Do sides of pan first then coat bottom of pan with the remaining nuts. Spoon batter into pan and bake at 325° for 1 hour and 20 minutes, or until a toothpick inserted in the center comes out clean. Cool in pan for 10 minutes; remove from pan and cool completely on wire rack.

POUND CAKES MADE WITH CHOCOLATE COOKIES

OREO POUND CAKE

The name alone makes this cake a real hit with children, but it's also loved by grown-ups as well.

- 2 cups crushed Oreo cookies (about 18-20 cookies)
- 1½ cups butter, softened
- 2 cups sugar
- 5 eggs, room temperature
- 2 cups flour
- 1 teaspoon baking powder
- 1 cup cream, room temperature
- 1 Tablespoon vanilla extract

Butter and flour a 10-inch tube pan. Crush between two pieces of waxed paper enough Oreo cookies (approximately 18 to 20) to measure 2 cups after crushing. Put aside. Cream together the butter and sugar until light and smooth. Add eggs, one at a time, beating after each addition. Combine the flour and baking powder. Add half of the flour mixture to the batter and beat well. Add the cream and vanilla to batter and mix. Add the remaining half of flour and mix well. Add the crushed Oreos and mix just until incorporated well, being careful not to over mix. Pour the batter into prepared tube pan. Bake at 325° for 1 hour and 10-15 minutes or until the cake pulls away from the sides of the pan and a tester inserted near center of the cake comes out clean. Let the cake cool in the pan on a wire rack for 10-15 minutes. Turn the cake out on a rack to cool completely.

OREO COOKIE POUND CAKE II

Here's another cake with Oreo cookies, but this time they're in chunks in the batter. This cake freezes well and is good cold from the refrigerator.

- 25 Oreo cookies
- 3 cups all-purpose flour
- 1½ cups granulated sugar
- 1¼ cups milk
- 1 cup butter-flavor shortening
- 1½ teaspoons salt
- 1 teaspoon vanilla extract
- 4 large eggs

Preheat oven to 350°. Grease and flour a 9-inch fluted tube pan (Bundt pan). Cut each cookie into quarters. In large bowl, with mixer at low speed, beat flour and remaining ingredients, except cookies. Increase speed to high; beat 2 minutes, scraping bowl. Spoon about ¾ cup batter into pan. Gently stir cut-up cookies into remaining batter and spoon into same pan. Bake at 350° for 50 minutes or until cake springs back when lightly touched with finger (wooden pick test will not work). Cool cake in pan on wire rack for 10 minutes; remove from pan; cool completely on rack.

CHOCOLATE GLAZE:

- 6 ounces semisweet chocolate chips
- 3 Tablespoons butter-flavored shortening
- 1 Tablespoon milk
- 1 Tablespoon corn syrup

In 1-quart saucepan over low heat, heat chocolate chips, shortening, milk and corn syrup, stirring constantly until melted and smooth. Place rack with cake over large plate to catch drips, then pour warm glaze over top and side of cake. Slide it on a plate for serving.

CHAPTER 4

BROWN SUGAR AND BUTTERNUT POUND CAKES

This chapter contains only 21 recipes, but they are very special ones that fit no other category. First, there are brown sugar pound cakes that use light or dark brown sugar or molasses for a different taste and texture—often including pecans or other nuts. Then there are butternut pound cakes, with a distinctive taste and color that comes from vanilla, butter and nut flavoring - a Southern favorite known simply as butternut flavoring.

POUND CAKES MADE WITH LIGHT BROWN SUGAR

BROWN SUGAR POUND CAKE WITH WALNUT GLAZE

This warm and rich cake is loaded with nuts, in the cake and in the glaze.

> 1 cup butter, softened
> ½ cup vegetable shortening
> 1 pound light brown sugar
> 1 cup granulated sugar
> 5 eggs
> 3 cups all purpose flour, sifted
> 1 teaspoon baking powder
> ½ teaspoon salt
> 1 cup milk
> 1 teaspoon vanilla extract
> 1 cup finely minced walnuts (black walnuts are especially good)

Cream the butter and shortening together until very fluffy; add the brown sugar gradually; creaming all the while until light, then add the granulated sugar the same way. Beat the eggs into the mixture, one at a time. Sift the flour with the baking powder and salt. Combine the milk and vanilla. Add the sifted dry ingredients to the mixture alternately with the milk, beginning and ending with the dry ingredients and mixing only enough to blend. Fold in the walnuts. Pour batter into a well greased and floured 10 inch tube pan and bake at 350° for about 1 hour and 15 minutes or until cake pulls from sides of pan and when it is pressed lightly with a finger, the imprint vanished slowly. Remove the cake from oven and cool upright in pan on a wire rack for 15 minutes. Loosen cake from sides of pan and around central tube with a thin-bladed spatula, then invert pan onto a large round plate and turn cake out.

Walnut Glaze

1 cup confectioners' sugar
2 Tablespoons butter, softened
6 Tablespoons light cream, room temperature
½ teaspoon vanilla extract
½ cup very finely minced walnuts

Stir together all ingredients; then spoon over the still warm cake. Scoop up any glaze that "puddles" on the cake plate, and reapply it to the sides of the cake for a thicker glaze. Let glaze harden before cutting cake.

PECAN BROWN SUGAR POUND CAKE

Brown sugar and nuts go together! This cake is excellent just plain, or it can be made quite elegant with frosting.

- 1½ cups butter
- 1 box (1 lb) light brown sugar
- 1 cup white sugar
- 5 large eggs
- 3 cups plain flour
- 1 teaspoon baking powder
- 1 cup milk
- 1 teaspoon vanilla extract
- 1 cup chopped pecans

Cream butter until light and fluffy. Add sugars and blend well. Add eggs, one at a time, mixing well after each addition. Mix flour and baking powder together in a separate bowl. Add flour mixture to sugar and egg mixture alternately with milk, starting and ending with flour. Mix well after each addition. Stir in vanilla and pecans. Bake in a greased and floured 10-inch tube pan at 325° for 1 hour and 15 minutes or until cake tests done. Cool in pan for 15 minutes, then invert onto wire rack until completely cooled.

Caramel Frosting

- 2 cups light brown sugar, packed
- 5 Tablespoons cream or evaporated milk
- ½ cup butter
- ½ teaspoon baking powder
- ½ teaspoon vanilla extract

Mix all ingredients together in saucepan. Boil over medium heat for 2 minutes, stirring constantly. Remove from heat and add baking powder and vanilla. Beat until smooth and creamy. Spread on completely cooled cake.

Cream Cheese Frosting

½ cup butter or margarine, softened
1 (8 oz.) package cream cheese, softened
2 teaspoons vanilla extract
1 (16 oz.) package powdered sugar

Combine all ingredients, mixing until smooth. Spread on cooled cake.

CARAMEL NUT POUND CAKE

Black walnut flavoring gives an extra nutty taste to this cake that is made with both buttermilk and sweet milk. Pecan lovers may omit the walnut flavoring and use chopped pecans instead of walnuts.

1 cup butter
½ cup shortening
1 lb (1 box) light brown sugar
6 large eggs
3 cups plain flour
¼ teaspoon salt
½ cup buttermilk
½ cup milk
½ teaspoon vanilla extract
½ teaspoon black walnut flavoring
1 cup chopped walnuts

Cream butter, shortening and sugar until light and fluffy. Add eggs, one at a time, beating well after each addition. Beat 3 minutes after addition of last egg. Sift dry ingredients together, and add alternately with mixture of milk and buttermilk, beginning and ending with flour; mix well after each addition. Stir in flavoring and nuts. Pour batter into greased and floured 10-inch tube pan. Bake at 325° for 1 hour and 15 minutes or until cake tests done. Do not open door during first hour of cooking. Cool in pan for 10 minutes; remove from pan and cool on wire rack.

HUNGARIAN POUND CAKE

Layers of brown sugar, nuts and cinnamon make this cake rich and delicious.

> 1½ cups brown sugar
> 1½ cups ground nuts
> 2 teaspoons cinnamon
> 1 cup butter, softened
> 1¾ cups sugar
> 6 eggs, slightly beaten
> 1¾ cup sour cream
> 1 teaspoon vanilla extract
> 3 cups flour
> 1 teaspoon baking soda
> 1 teaspoon lemon rind, grated

Mix brown sugar, ground nuts and cinnamon; set aside. Cream butter and sugar together; add beaten eggs, one at a time. Add sour cream and beat until thick. Add dry ingredients and mix well. Mix in vanilla and lemon rind. Pour half of batter into thoroughly greased and floured 10-inch tube pan. Sprinkle half of sugar & nut mixture over batter, covering well. Add rest of batter; put remaining sugar & nut mixture over top. Press topping in lightly with fork. Bake at 350° for 1 hour or until cake tests done. Cool pan on wire rack for 15-20 minutes; loosen and turn cake upside down onto wire rack to cool completely.

PRALINE POUND CAKE

Brown sugar and pecans give this cream cheese pound cake a different taste and texture. For a flavor of New Orleans, try topping it with the nut glaze.

    1½ cups butter or margarine, softened
    8 oz. cream cheese, softened
    3 cups brown sugar
    6 eggs, at room temperature
    3¼ cups plain flour
    2 teaspoons vanilla extract
    1½ cups chopped pecans, divided

Grease and flour a 10-inch tube pan and sprinkle ½ cup chopped pecans in pan; set aside. Cream butter and cream cheese. Add brown sugar and cream until light and fluffy (about 5 minutes). Add eggs, one at a time, mixing well after each addition. Fold in flour until just combined. Do not over mix. Stir in vanilla and remaining pecans. Spoon batter into prepared pan and bake at 325° for 1½ hours and or until cake tests done. Cool in pan 10 minutes; remove from pan and place on serving dish for glazing.

Nut Icing

    ½ cup butter
    ¼ cup milk
    1 teaspoon vanilla extract
    1 box (1 lb) confectioners' sugar
    ½ cup chopped pecans

Soften butter; add milk, vanilla, and sugar. Cream together until smooth, and add nuts. Pour over warm cake.

BUTTER PECAN POUND CAKE

This distinctive cake has toasted pecans added to the cake batter and uses ground pecans to "flour" the pan. The buttery glaze sets it off.

2 Tablespoons ground pecans
1½ cups butter, softened
1 (3 oz.) package cream cheese, softened
2 cups firmly packed light brown sugar
1 cup sugar
5 eggs
3 cups plain flour
½ teaspoon baking powder
¼ teaspoon salt
1 teaspoon vanilla extract
1 teaspoon maple extract
¾ cup milk
1 cup chopped pecans, toasted

Toasted pecans: Heat oven to 350°. Spread nuts in a single layer on a cookie sheet. Bake for 5 to 10 minutes or until light golden brown, stirring occasionally. Watch them closely to avoid over-browning.

Grease 10-inch tube pan; sprinkle with ground pecans, coating the bottom and sides of pan. Beat butter, cream cheese, brown sugar and sugar until light and fluffy. Add eggs 1 at a time, beating well after each addition. In small bowl, combine flour, baking powder and salt; mix well. Add vanilla and maple extract to milk. Add flour mixture to butter mixture alternately with milk mixture, beginning and ending with flour; mix well after each addition. Fold in toasted pecans. Pour batter into greased and pecan-coated pan. Bake at 350° for 1 hour and 10 minutes, or until toothpick inserted in center comes out clean. Do not open oven door for first hour of baking. Cool upright in pan 10 minutes; invert onto wire rack and cool completely.

Glaze

2 Tablespoons butter
2 Tablespoons light brown sugar
½ cup powdered sugar
1 teaspoon vanilla extract
1 to 2 Tablespoons hot water

In small saucepan, melt butter with brown sugar. Bring to a boil; boil until thickened, stirring constantly. Remove from heat; stir in remaining ingredients, adding enough water for desired glaze consistency. Spoon over cooled cake.

LIGHT BROWN SUGAR POUND CAKE

This cake has a touch of maple flavor, with egg whites used for a lighter textured cake.

- ½ cup butter or margarine
- 1 cup vegetable shortening
- ⅓ cup white sugar
- 1 box (1 lb) light brown sugar
- 5 egg whites beaten stiff
- 5 egg yolks
- 3 cups plain flour
- ½ teaspoon salt
- ½ teaspoon baking powder
- 1 cup milk
- 1 teaspoon maple extract
- 1 teaspoon vanilla extract
- 1 cup chopped nuts

Cream shortening and butter; add sugars and beat until creamy. Add egg yolks, one at a time, beating well after each addition. Add flour alternately with milk and flavorings, and mix well after each addition. Add nuts and fold in egg whites. Pour into greased and floured 10-inch tube pan and bake at 325° for 1 hour or until cake tests done. Turn out onto wire rack and cool completely.

TOPPING

- 3 oz. cream cheese, softened
- ¼ cup butter (or margarine)
- 2 cups 10X confectioners' sugar
- 1 teaspoon vanilla extract
- ¾ cup finely chopped nuts

Mix all ingredients together thoroughly and spread on cake.

MAHOGANY POUND CAKE

This cake is a delicious blend of caramel and chocolate. Dust it with powdered sugar before cutting, or drizzle with a caramel glaze.

- 1½ cups butter or margarine, softened
- 2½ cups sugar
- 1 cup firmly packed light brown sugar
- 6 large eggs
- 2 ½ cups plain flour
- ½ cup cocoa
- ¼ teaspoon baking soda
- 1 (8-ounce) container sour cream
- 1 teaspoon vanilla extract

Beat butter at medium speed with an electric mixer about two minutes or until creamy. Gradually add sugars, beating 5 to 7 minutes. Add eggs, one at a time, beating just until yellow disappears. Combine flour, cocoa and soda; add to butter mixture alternately with sour cream, beginning and ending with flour mixture. Beat at low speed just until blended after each addition. Stir in vanilla. Pour batter into a greased and floured 10-inch tube pan. Bake at 325° for 1 hour and 40 minutes or until a wooden pick inserted in center comes out clean. Cool in pan on a wire rack 10 to15 minutes; remove from pan and cool on a wire rack.

Caramel Glaze

- ¼ cup butter, softened
- ¼ cup light brown sugar
- ¼ cup sugar
- ¼ cup whipping cream
- 1 teaspoon vanilla extract

Bring first four ingredients to a boil in a heavy saucepan over high heat, stirring often. Boil, without stirring, for 1 minute. Remove from heat; stir in vanilla. Cool until slightly thickened. Drizzle over cake.

MAPLE SUGAR POUND CAKE

Maple glaze adds to the maple flavoring in this cake. This is as close to New England as a Southern pound cake can get.

½ cup butter or margarine, softened
1 cup shortening
1 (1 lb) box light brown sugar
5 eggs
3 cups plain flour
½ teaspoon salt
½ teaspoon baking powder
1 cup evaporated milk
1-2 teaspoons maple extract

Combine butter and shortening in a large mixing bowl; mix well. Gradually add sugar, beating until light and fluffy. Add eggs, one at a time, beating well after each addition. Combine flour, salt and baking powder; add to creamed mixture alternately with milk, beginning and ending with flour mixture. Mix well after each addition. Stir in flavoring. Pour batter into a greased and floured 10-inch tube pan. Bake at 325° for 1 hour and 20 minutes or until cake tests done. Cool in pan 10 to 15 minutes; remove from pan and cool completely on wire rack.

Maple Glaze:

½ cup maple syrup
2 Tablespoons butter
1 Tablespoon milk
1 cup sifted powdered sugar

Bring first three ingredients to a boil in a small saucepan over medium high heat. Boil, stirring constantly, for about 2 minutes. Remove from heat and stir in powdered sugar. Makes about ⅔ cup to drizzle over cake.

MAPLE SYRUP POUND CAKE

This recipe is deliciously different. The light brushing of maple syrup makes it very mellow and moist.

> 1½ cups butter, room temperature
> 1 cup sugar
> 5 eggs, room temperature
> 3 cups flour, sifted
> ½ teaspoon baking powder
> 1 cup maple syrup, plus extra syrup for glaze
> 2 teaspoons vanilla extract
> ⅓ cup cream, room temperature

Butter and flour a 9-inch Bundt pan. Cream together the butter and sugar. Add eggs, one at a time, beating slightly after each addition. Sift together flour and baking powder. Combine the maple syrup, vanilla, and cream. Alternate the wet ingredients with the flour, beginning and ending with the flour. Pour the batter into prepared pan and bake at 350° for approximately 50 minutes, or until the cake tests done. Let the cake sit in the pan for 10 to 15 minutes. Turn the cake out onto a rack. Brush the top of the still warm cake with the extra maple syrup, using only enough to make the cake glisten but not so much as to make it soggy.

MAPLE WALNUT POUND CAKE

Here's another variation of a maple pound cake. This large cake has a crunchy streusel filling that is delicious at brunch, lunch, or dinner, or as we say in the South, suppertime. The maple flavor comes from maple-flavored syrup.

<u>Walnut Streusel:</u>
- 1¼ cups packed brown sugar
- 2 teaspoons ground cinnamon
- ½ cup cold, unsalted butter, cut into pieces
- ¾ cup flour
- 1 cup walnuts – coarsely chopped

In a medium bowl, stir brown sugar, flour, butter and cinnamon with a fork, or rub mixture with fingertips until crumbly. Stir in walnuts.

<u>Maple Pound Cake</u>
- 1½ cups butter, softened
- 1½ cups maple flavored syrup
- ½ cup packed brown sugar
- 1 Tablespoon vanilla
- 2 teaspoons baking powder
- ½ teaspoon baking soda
- ½ teaspoon salt
- 7 eggs
- 4¼ cups flour

With mixer on high speed, beat butter, pancake syrup, brown sugar, vanilla, baking powder, baking soda and salt in a large bowl until blended (mixture will look curdled). Add eggs, one at a time beating well after each addition. With mixer on low speed gradually add flour, beating just until blended and smooth. Spoon half of the batter into lightly greased 10-inch tube pan. Sprinkle with half the streusel. Pour in remaining batter and spread evenly. Sprinkle with remaining streusel. Bake at 325° for 1 hour and 20 minutes or until a cake tester comes out with moist crumbs clinging to it. Cool in pan on a wire rack for 15 minutes. If necessary, run a thin sharp knife around edge of pan to loosen cake. Place cookie sheet over pan and carefully invert both. Remove pan. Place rack over cake and turn cake streusel side up. Cool completely. Store, wrapped airtight, up to 3 days at room temperature or freeze up to 3 months.

WILLARD SCOTT'S POUND CAKE

This simple recipe is good in any weather.

 1 cup butter, softened
 ½ cup shortening
 5 eggs, room temperature
 3¼ cups light brown sugar
 3½ cups flour
 ½ teaspoon baking powder
 1 cup milk

Cream together butter and shortening; add eggs, one at a time, creaming after each egg. Add sugar and mix well. Sift flour and baking powder together and add alternately with milk to batter. Bake in a greased and floured 10-inch Bundt pan for 1¼ to 1½ hours at 325° or until cake tests done.

Frosting

 1 cup pecans, chopped
 ½ cup butter, softened
 1 lb powdered sugar
 3-4 Tablespoons milk

Toast pecans in butter in broiler pan until well browned. Cool slightly and add sugar and enough milk to thin to spreading consistency. Spread on top of cake. Some should drip down sides and center, but spread only on top.

POUND CAKES MADE WITH DARK BROWN SUGAR

DARK BROWN SUGAR POUND CAKE

Dark brown sugar produces a warm, textured cake that can be enjoyed plain or with a caramel frosting.

- 1 cup margarine
- ½ cup shortening
- 1 box (1 lb) dark brown sugar
- 5 eggs
- 3 cups plain flour
- 1 teaspoon baking powder
- 1 cup milk
- 1 teaspoon vanilla extract

Cream margarine, shortening and sugar. Add eggs, one at a time, beating after each addition. Sift baking powder with flour; mix milk and vanilla. Add alternately the milk and flour mixtures, mixing well after each addition. Bake in a greased and floured 10-inch tube pan at 350° for 1 hour and 15 minutes, or until cake tests done. Cool in pan for 10 minutes; remove from pan and cool completely on wire rack.

FROSTING

- 1 box (1 lb) light brown sugar
- 1 small (5 oz.) can evaporated milk
- ½ cup margarine

Bring to a boil and boil 2 minutes. Beat to a creamy consistency and spread on cake. If frosting gets too hard, add a little more milk. If too thin, add some powdered sugar.

BROWN SUGAR POUND CAKE WITH CREAMY RUM GLAZE

This recipe calls for dark brown sugar, which gives it a warm and cozy taste. Make it really special with the rum-flavored glaze.

1 cup butter
1 cup dark brown sugar, firmly packed
1 cup sugar
5 eggs
3 cups all-purpose flour
½ teaspoon baking powder
½ teaspoon baking soda
½ teaspoon salt
1 cup milk
2 teaspoons vanilla extract

Beat butter at medium speed with an electric mixer until creamy; gradually add dark brown and white sugars, beating well. Add eggs, one at a time, beating until blended after each addition. Combine flour and next 3 ingredients; add to butter mixture alternately with milk, beginning and ending with flour mixture. Beat at low speed until blended after each addition. Stir in vanilla. Pour into a greased and floured 10-inch tube pan. Bake at 325° for 1 hour and 30 minutes or until a wooden pick inserted in center comes out clean. Cool in pan on a wire rack for 10 minutes. Remove from pan; cool completely on a wire rack. Serve with creamy rum glaze.

Creamy Rum Glaze

½ cup sugar
½ cup dark brown sugar, firmly packed
½ cup whipping cream
½ cup butter
1 to 2 Tablespoon dark rum or ¼ teaspoon rum extract

Cook sugars, whipping cream and butter in heavy saucepan over medium heat, stirring constantly, until butter melts and sugars dissolve. Increase heat, and bring to a boil; cook, stirring constantly, about 3 minutes or until slightly thickened. Stir in rum. Cool slightly and pour over cake.

CARAMEL POUND CAKE

Light brown sugar has a flavor like honey, while dark brown sugar has the taste of molasses. In combination with the white granulated sugar, this outstanding cake has a mild butterscotch flavor. For a nice variation, add a cup of chopped pecans to the batter.

- 1 cup firmly packed dark brown sugar
- 1 cup firmly packed light brown sugar
- 1 cup granulated sugar
- 1 cup butter or margarine, softened
- ½ cup vegetable oil
- 5 large eggs
- 3 cups plain flour
- ½ teaspoon baking powder
- ½ teaspoon salt
- 1 cup milk
- ½ teaspoon vanilla extract

Beat sugars and butter at medium speed with an electric mixer until blended. Add oil, and beat until blended. Add eggs, one at a time, beating just until yellow disappears. Combine flour, baking powder, and salt; add to butter mixture alternately with milk, beginning and ending with flour mixture. Beat at low speed just until blended after each addition. Stir in vanilla extract. Pour batter into a greased and floured 10-inch tube pan. Bake at 325° for 1 hour and 20 minutes or until a wooden pick inserted in center comes out clean. Cool in pan on wire rack 10 minutes; remove from pan and cool on wire rack. Drizzle with Caramel Glaze, below.

Caramel Glaze

1 (16-ounce) package light brown sugar
½ cup butter or margarine
1 (5-ounce) can evaporated milk
Dash of salt
½ teaspoon baking powder
½ teaspoon vanilla

Bring first four ingredients to a boil in a medium saucepan, stirring often. Boil, stirring constantly, 3 minutes. Remove from heat; add baking powder and vanilla. Beat at medium speed with an electric mixer 5 to 7 minutes or until thickened. Drizzle quickly over cake.

POUND CAKES MADE WITH MOLASSES

MOLASSES POUND CAKE

A big cake—in size and in taste. The combination of brown sugar, molasses, cinnamon, nutmeg and ginger is something to write home about! This recipe calls for light molasses, but dark molasses can be used for even more flavor.

    2 cups butter or margarine
    1¼ cups light brown sugar
    6 eggs
    5 cups plain flour, sifted
    1 Tablespoon ground cinnamon
    2 Tablespoons ground ginger
    1 teaspoon ground nutmeg
    ½ teaspoon salt
    1½ teaspoon soda
    ½ cup milk
    2 cups light molasses

Cream butter and sugar until light and fluffy. Add eggs, one at a time, beating well after each addition. Combine flour, spices, and salt. Dissolve soda in molasses and mix with milk. Add dry ingredients to butter, sugar and egg mixture, alternating with molasses and milk. Mix well after each addition. Spoon mixture into greased and floured 10-inch tube pan. Bake at 325° for 1 hour and 10 minutes or until cake tests done. Cool in pan for 5 minutes; then turn onto wire rack to cool completely.

POUND CAKES MADE WITH BUTTERNUT FLAVORING

BUTTERNUT POUND CAKE

Butternut is the common name for vanilla, butter and nut flavoring. It is bright yellow to orange colored and produces a distinctive flavor for cake and frosting.

- 1 cup butter
- 1 cup shortening
- 2½ cups sugar
- 8 large eggs
- 3½ cups plain flour
- ¼ teaspoon cream of tartar
- 3 teaspoons butternut flavoring

Cream butter, shortening, and sugar at medium speed for 10 minutes. Add one egg at a time, beating well after each addition. Blend in flour, cream of tartar and flavoring. Spoon batter into a greased and floured 10-inch tube pan. Bake at 325° for 1 hour and 15 minutes, or until cake tests done. Cool in pan 10 minutes; remove from pan and cool completely on wire rack.

Frosting

- ½ cup butter
- 1 box (1 lb) confectioners' sugar
- evaporated milk
- 1 Tablespoon butternut flavoring

Blend butter and sugar with enough milk to obtain desired consistency; add flavoring and mix well. Frost cooled cake.

BUTTERNUT CREAM POUND CAKE

This cake uses both self-rising and plain flour. For variation, add 1½ teaspoon of lemon extract to the cake batter and use the lemon glaze for topping.

>   1 cup shortening
>   2 cups sugar
>   4 eggs
>   1 cup self-rising flour
>   2 cups plain flour
>   ⅛ teaspoon salt (optional)
>   1 cup milk
>   1-2 Tablespoons butternut flavoring

Cream shortening with sugar until light. Add eggs, one at a time, beating after each addition. Add salt and self-rising flour; mix well. Add milk alternately with plain flour; mixing well after each addition. Stir in flavoring. Mix well, but lightly. Pour into greased and floured 10-inch tube pan. Bake at 325° for 1 hour or until cake tests done. Cool 10 minutes in pan; remove from pan and cool completely on wire rack.

Butternut Frosting

>   1 (8 oz.) package cream cheese, softened
>   ½ cup margarine, softened
>   1 box (1 lb) confectioners' sugar
>   1 teaspoon butternut flavoring
>   1 cup pecans, chopped

Mix all ingredients thoroughly and spread on cooled cake.

Lemon Glaze

>   1 cup sugar
>   1 cup lemon juice

Bring sugar and juice to a boil and pour over hot cake.

BUTTERNUT POUND CAKE WITH CARAMEL SAUCE

This rich and moist cake becomes a mouth-watering delight with warm caramel sauce.

    1 cup butter, softened
    ½ cup shortening
    5 eggs
    3 cups sugar
    1 (5 oz.) can evaporated milk
    3¼ cups flour
    ¼ teaspoon salt
    1 teaspoon baking powder
    2 Tablespoons butternut flavoring

Beat butter and shortening until creamy. Gradually add sugar and beat 5-7 minutes. Add eggs, one at a time, beating until yellow disappears. Add enough water to milk to measure 1 cup. Combine dry ingredients. Add to butter mixture alternately with milk mixture, beginning and ending with flour mixture. Stir in flavoring. Pour into greased and floured 10-inch tube or Bundt pan. Bake at 325° for 1 hour and 25 minutes. Cool in pan for 10 minutes. Remove and cool completely. Serve with caramel sauce.

CARAMEL SAUCE

    1 cup brown sugar, firmly packed
    1 cup half and half OR liquid whipping cream
    3 Tablespoons butter
    1 teaspoon caramel extract

Combine ingredients in a heavy saucepan, cook over low heat. Stir occasionally for 4-5 minutes or until thickened. Add extract. Serve warm over cake.

POUND CAKES MADE WITH BUTTERSCOTCH MORSELS

GATHER ROUND POUND CAKE

This buttermilk pound cake has an unusual mix of coffee and butterscotch flavors. Delightfully different!

- 1 cup butter
- 1½ cups sugar
- 4 eggs
- 3 cups plain flour
- ½ teaspoon soda
- ¼ teaspoon salt
- 2 Tablespoons instant coffee
- ¾ cup buttermilk
- 1 (6 oz.) package butterscotch morsels
- ¼ cup water

In double boiler, melt together butterscotch morsels, instant coffee, and water. Cream butter and sugar. Blend in butterscotch mixture. Combine flour, soda, and salt. Add to creamed mixture alternately with buttermilk; mixing well after each addition. Add eggs, one at a time, beating after each addition. Pour into a greased and floured 10-inch tube pan. Bake at 350° for 55-60 minutes, or until cake tests done. Cool 10 minutes before removing from pan. Cool on wire rack.

BUTTERSCOTCH-PECAN POUND CAKE

This butternut and cream cheese pound cake contains toasted pecans and butterscotch morsels; it's a rich, savory combination.

- 1 cup butter or margarine, softened
- 1 (8 oz.) package cream cheese, softened
- 2¼ cups sugar
- 6 large eggs
- 2⅔ cups plain flour
- 1 teaspoon vanilla extract
- 1 teaspoon butternut flavoring
- 1 cup chopped pecans, toasted
- ½ cup butterscotch morsels

Beat butter and cream cheese at medium speed for about 2 minutes or until soft and creamy. Gradually add sugar, beating at medium speed 5 to 7 minutes. Add eggs, one at a time, beating after each addition just until yellow disappears. Gradually add flour, mixing at lowest speed just until blended after each addition. Stir in flavorings, pecans, and morsels. Spoon batter into a greased and floured 10-inch tube pan. Bake at 325° for 1 hour and 20 minutes or until a wooden pick inserted in center comes out clean. Cool in pan on a wire rack 10 minutes; remove from pan, and let cool completely on a wire rack.

CHAPTER 5

POUND CAKES WITH FRUITS, NUTS, BERRIES AND VEGETABLES

This chapter contains 103 recipes that prove that just about anything can be added to a pound cake. Fruit varieties range from apples to oranges to bananas; nuts from almonds to peanuts to walnuts; berries from blueberries to strawberries. Vegetables are represented by the potato and sweet potato. With this variety of recipes, there is something here for every taste.

POUND CAKES MADE WITH ALMONDS

ALMOND POUND CAKE

Almonds were mentioned in the Old Testament; they were among the earliest of cultivated foods. This thoroughly modern recipe is full of flavor with the "crunch" of toasted almonds on top.

> 3½ cups plain flour
> 1 teaspoon baking powder
> ⅛ teaspoon salt
> 1 cup unsalted butter, softened
> 2 cups sugar
> 7 eggs
> 1 teaspoon vanilla
> 1 teaspoon almond extract

Mix flour, baking powder and salt; set aside. Beat together butter and sugar in a bowl on medium speed until light and fluffy, about 3 minutes. Beat in eggs, one at a time, beating well after each addition. Beat in vanilla and almond extract. On low speed, beat in flour mixture. Increase speed to medium and beat for 3 minutes. Pour batter into greased and floured 10-inch tube pan. Bake at 350º for 1 hour or until toothpick inserted into center comes out clean. Cool cake in pan on wire rack for 10 minutes. Turn cake out onto wire rack to cool completely.

TOPPING:

> ¼ cup water
> ¼ cup sugar
> ¼ cup sliced almonds, toasted

Bring water to boiling in a small saucepan. Stir in sugar until dissolved. Remove from heat. Generously brush top of cake with syrup. Press almonds into the top of the cake.

TOFFEE POUND CAKE

Almond brickle in the cake batter gives a great taste and a little crunch. Brickle baking chips can be found in the baking section of the supermarket.

> ½ cup butter, softened
> ¼ cup shortening
> 1½ cups sugar
> 5 eggs
> 1½ teaspoons vanilla extract
> 2½ cups plain flour
> 1 teaspoon baking soda
> ½ teaspoon salt
> 1 cup buttermilk
> 1 (6 oz.) package almond brickle baking chips

Beat butter and shortening together until smooth and creamy. Gradually add sugar and beat until fluffy. Add eggs one at a time, mixing well after each addition. Stir in vanilla. In a small bowl, mix together dry ingredients. Alternately add flour mixture and buttermilk, beginning and ending with flour; beat well after each addition. Stir in brickle chips. Pour batter into greased and floured 10-inch tube pan. Bake at 350° for 1 hour or until toothpick inserted in center of cake comes out clean. Cool in pan for 10 minutes; invert onto wire rack and cool completely.

GLAZE

> ⅓ cup butter or margarine
> 2 cups powdered sugar
> 1 teaspoon vanilla extract
> 2 to 3 Tablespoons water

In medium saucepan, heat margarine until golden brown; remove from heat. Blend in powdered sugar and vanilla. Add water until glaze is smooth and of drizzling consistency. Immediately spoon over top of cooled cake, allowing some to run down the sides.

POUND CAKES MADE WITH APPLES

APPLE POUND CAKE

Like apple pie? You'll love this apple pound cake, which gets an extra kick from rum-flavored sauce spooned over the cake while warm.

- 1 cup vegetable oil
- 2 cups sugar
- 3 eggs
- 3 cups plain flour
- 1 teaspoon cinnamon
- 1 teaspoon nutmeg
- 1 teaspoon baking soda
- ½ teaspoon salt
- 1 teaspoon vanilla extract
- 3 cups chopped apples
- 1 cup chopped pecans
- melted margarine

In a large bowl, combine and beat eggs, sugar and vegetable oil. Sift together the dry ingredients and stir into the egg mixture until batter is smooth. Stir in vanilla and fold in chopped apples and nuts. Spoon into a greased and floured Bundt pan. Bake at 325° for 1 hour and 20 minutes. Allow to cool in pan about 10 minutes. Remove from pan and brush outside of cake lightly with melted margarine. Keep covered until served.

RUM-FLAVORED SAUCE

- ½ cup margarine
- ½ cup light brown sugar, packed
- 2 Tablespoons milk
- 1 Tablespoon rum extract

Combine margarine, sugar and milk in small saucepan. Bring to low boil and simmer gently about 2 minutes, until clear and syrupy. Add rum extract. While hot, spoon over warm cake. Keep cake covered until served.

APPLE-PECAN POUND CAKE

This yummy cake will make you think of fall. It's delicious plain, but you can dress it up with a caramel glaze.

- 2½ cups chopped green apples
- 1 cup butter, softened
- 1½ cups sugar
- 1½ teaspoons vanilla
- 5 eggs
- 2 cups flour
- 1 Tablespoon baking powder
- 1 Tablespoon ground cinnamon
- ¾ cup pecans, chopped

In skillet, lightly sauté apple chunks in 2 tablespoons butter. Set aside. In bowl, cream remaining butter with sugar until light and fluffy. Beat in vanilla. Beat in eggs 1 at a time. In a bowl, sift together flour, baking powder and cinnamon. Stir into butter mixture until blended. Fold in apples and pecans. Spoon into greased and floured Bundt pan. Bake at 325° for 1 hour, or until wood pick inserted near center comes out clean. Glaze with Caramel Sauce.

Caramel Sauce

- ½ cup brown sugar—packed
- ½ cup granulated sugar
- ½ cup whipping cream
- 1 Tablespoon butter

Combine brown sugar, sugar and whipping cream in medium saucepan. Bring to boil. Cook and stir, about 2 minutes. Remove from heat. Stir in butter until melted. Cool. Then drizzle over cake.

APPLE CIDER POUND CAKE

This recipe uses a variety of spices, but it gets its distinctive taste from old-fashioned apple cider. Get it from a road-side stand if you're lucky enough to live near the mountains; otherwise, most supermarkets carry it (at least in the fall of the year).

- 1 cup butter or margarine, softened
- ½ cup shortening
- 3 cups sugar
- 6 eggs
- 3 cups plain flour
- ½ teaspoon baking powder
- ½ teaspoon salt
- ¾ teaspoon ground cinnamon
- ½ teaspoon ground allspice
- ½ teaspoon nutmeg
- ¼ teaspoon ground cloves
- 1 cup apple cider
- 1 teaspoon vanilla extract

<u>NOTE</u>: 1½ teaspoons apple pie spice may be substituted for cinnamon, allspice, nutmeg and cloves

Combine butter and shortening, mixing well; gradually add sugar, beating well. Add eggs, one at a time, beating well after each addition. Combine dry ingredients; add to creamed mixture alternately with apple cider, beginning and ending with flour mixture. Mix well after each addition. Stir in vanilla. Pour batter into a greased and floured 10-inch tube pan. Bake at 325° for 1 hour and 50 minutes or until cake tests done. Cool in pan 10 to 15 minutes; remove cake from pan onto wire rack and let cool completely.

Apple Cider Sauce

3 cups apple cider
1 cup whipping cream
2 Tablespoons unsalted butter, cut into small pieces
¼ teaspoon vanilla extract
2 drops lemon extract

Boil apple cider in large skillet until reduced to ½ cup, about 18 minutes. Add cream; boil until slightly thickened, about 2 minutes. Transfer to bowl. Whisk in butter and both extracts. Cool slightly, and then chill until cold, at least 1 hour. (Can be made 1 day ahead. Keep chilled.) Top cake slices with ice cream, sauce and toasted nuts.

APPLE STREUSEL POUND CAKE

With walnut streusel within, a delicious glaze garnished with more walnuts outside, this cake is delicious from start to finish!

- 1 cup walnut pieces, divided
- 1½ cups butter or margarine, divided
- 4 cups cake flour, divided
- ½ cup packed light brown sugar
- ¾ teaspoon ground cinnamon, divided
- 2 cups Granny Smith apples, about 12 oz, peeled, cored and diced, divided
- 5 eggs
- 1 cup plus 2 Tablespoons sour cream, divided
- 1½ cups granulated sugar
- 1½ teaspoons baking powder
- ¼ teaspoon salt

Spread nuts in a single layer over jellyroll pan, bake until fragrant, 3-5- minutes. Cool 3 minutes; coarsely chop. Butter and flour 12-cup Bundt pan.

For streusel, melt ¼ cup butter. In bowl, combine 1 cup flour, brown sugar, ½ teaspoon cinnamon and ½ of walnuts; stir in melted butter until clumps form. Stir in half of the apples; set aside.

For cake, whisk together eggs and 1 cup sour cream; set aside. In another bowl, at low speed, combine granulated sugar, baking powder, salt and remaining flour. With mixer running, gradually beat in remaining butter. Beat in egg mixture, ⅓ at a time. Increase speed to medium; beat until smooth and fluffy, 1-2 minutes. Stir in remaining walnuts and apples. Pour half of batter into pan; top with streusel, then remaining batter. Bake at 350° for 50 minutes or until cake tester comes out clean. Cool in pan on rack for 20 minutes. Remove from pan;

cool completely on rack. Glaze and garnish with walnuts, if desired. If making ahead, wrap cooled *unglazed* cake in plastic and foil; freeze up to one month. Thaw unwrapped at room temperature. Glaze and garnish with walnut halves before serving.

Glaze

2 cups confectioners' sugar
2 teaspoons lemon juice

In bowl, whisk confectioners' sugar with lemon juice and remaining sour cream and cinnamon until smooth; drizzle over cake.

LIGHT LOW-CAL APPLE POUND CAKE

For those in search of a healthier pound cake recipe, here's one that's lower in fat and calories. One slice even counts for ½ fruit exchange!

- 2½ cups all-purpose flour
- ½ cup Splenda artificial sweetener
- 1 Tablespoon baking powder
- ¼ teaspoon baking soda
- 1 teaspoon cinnamon
- ½ teaspoon nutmeg
- ½ teaspoon salt
- 2 eggs
- 4 egg whites
- 2 teaspoons vanilla extract
- ¼ cup sugar
- ⅓ cup butter
- ⅓ cup buttermilk, low-fat
- 3 apples, peeled, cored and diced
- ⅓ cup walnuts, finely chopped

Lightly coat a 10-inch tube pan with cooking spray. Dust with flour. Combine flour, Splenda, baking powder, baking soda, cinnamon, nutmeg and salt. In a separate bowl, whisk together the eggs, egg whites and vanilla. With an electric mixer, beat the sugar, butter and buttermilk until creamy. With the electric mixer still running, add the dry ingredients alternately with the eggs. Beat until fluffy. Fold in the apples and walnuts. Spread batter into prepared pan. Bake at 350° for 1 hour, or until toothpick inserted in center comes out clean. Cool on a wire rack for 10 minutes. Remove from pan and cool.

APPLE GINGER POUND CAKE

This is a delicious apple pound cake, made with Granny Smith apples, especially when paired with the ginger-flavored custard sauce. This is a small recipe, for a loaf pan.

- 1 cup butter, room temperature
- 1¾ cups sugar
- 5 eggs, room temperature
- 2 cups flour
- ¼ teaspoon salt
- 1 teaspoon dried ginger
- ¼ teaspoon cinnamon
- ¼ teaspoon freshly grated nutmeg
- ¼ cup cream, room temperature
- 1 teaspoon finely grated lemon zest
- 1 cup peeled and finely chopped Granny Smith apples, tossed in 2 teaspoons of fresh lemon juice

Butter and flour a 9×5×3 inch loaf pan. Cream the butter for 3 minutes, until lightened in color. Add the sugar and beat on high speed for 5 minutes. Add the eggs, one at a time, beating well after each addition. Sift the flour with the salt, ginger, cinnamon, and nutmeg. Gradually add the flour to the batter, blending well. Add the ¼ cup cream and blend well. Mix in the lemon zest. Fold in the apples and lemon juice. Spoon batter into the loaf pan and bake at 350° for about 1 hour, or until cake tests done.

Custard Sauce

- 1¾ cups half and half
- 5 egg yolks
- ½ cup sugar
- 1 teaspoon vanilla extract
- ½ teaspoon dried ginger
- 1 teaspoon fresh lemon juice

Bring the half and half to a simmer and remove from heat. Beat the egg yolks and sugar in a medium saucepan until they reach a nice pale yellow. Slowly add the warm half and half to the egg yolks, whisking constantly over low heat until the sauce coats a spoon, being especially careful not to curdle the yolks. Transfer the ingredients to a glass bowl. Whisk in the vanilla extract and dried ginger and lemon juice. Allow to cool before refrigerating. The Custard Sauce makes a nice addition this pound cake when spooned on top of each slice or to the side of the dessert plate. The sauce can be refrigerated for 2 days.

APPLESAUCE POUND CAKE

This is a good, old-fashioned applesauce pound cake that will fill your house with the spicy fragrance of fall.

½ cup butter
2 cups brown sugar
2 eggs
3½ cups plain flour
½ teaspoon salt
2 teaspoons ground cinnamon
1 teaspoon ground cloves
3 teaspoons baking soda
3 cups unsweetened applesauce
½ cup raisins
½ cup finely chopped dates
1 cup chopped nuts

Cream together butter and brown sugar, beating until light and fluffy. Mix in eggs, one at a time, and beat thoroughly. Mix together flour, salt, cinnamon, cloves and soda. Add flour mixture into creamed mixture alternately with the applesauce, beginning and ending with the flour mixture. Stir in the raisins, dates and pecans. Pour into a greased and floured tube pan. Bake at 300° for 1 hour and 30 minutes, or until cake tests done. Cool in pan on wire rack 15 minutes; invert onto rack to cool completely.

Brown Sugar Frosting

½ cup butter
1 cup brown sugar
¼ cup milk
1 teaspoon vanilla
2 cups sifted confectioners' sugar

Melt butter in a small saucepan over low heat and stir in brown sugar. Boil for 2 minutes. Stir in milk and continue to stir until the mixture returns to a boil. Remove from heat and cool for 5 minutes. Beat in vanilla and confectioners' sugar. Frost cooled cake.

APPLESAUCE RUM RAISIN POUND CAKE

This is a winning variation with dark Jamaican rum giving it a spicy, rich flavor and the raisins an extra moistness. Set aside some applesauce to serve with each slice.

- 2½ cups all-purpose flour
- 1½ teaspoons ground cinnamon
- 1 teaspoon baking soda
- ½ teaspoon salt
- ¼ teaspoon allspice
- ¾ cup packed brown sugar
- ½ cup granulated sugar
- ½ cup butter or margarine, softened
- 2 eggs
- ⅓ cup dark Jamaican rum
- 2 teaspoons vanilla extract
- 1¼ cups sweetened applesauce
- 1 cup dark raisins

Grease 10-cup tube pan or Bundt pan; dust with flour. On waxed paper, combine flour, cinnamon, baking soda, salt and allspice; set aside. In a large bowl, with mixer at low speed, beat sugars with butter until blended, scraping bowl often with rubber spatula. Increase speed to medium-high; beat until creamy, about 3 minutes, occasionally scraping bowl. Reduce speed to low; add eggs, one at a time, beating well after each addition. Beat in rum and vanilla. Alternately add flour mixture and applesauce, beginning and ending with flour mixture. Stir in raisins. Spoon batter prepared pan and spread evenly. Bake at 350° for 50 to 55 minutes, or until cake tests done. Cool cake in pan on wire rack for 15 minutes. For fluted pan, loosen cake from pan. Invert cake directly onto rack to cool completely. For tube pan, with small metal spatula, loosen cake from side and center tube of pan. Invert cake onto plate; immediately invert again (so top side is up) onto wire rack to cool completely.

Brown Sugar-Rum Glaze

¼ cup packed light brown sugar
3 Tablespoons butter
¼ cup milk
1 Tablespoon dark Jamaican rum
⅓ cup confectioners' sugar

In 1-quart glass measure, heat brown sugar and butter in microwave on High for 1- 2 minutes until bubbly, stirring twice during cooking. With wire whisk, beat in rum, then confectioners' sugar until mixture is smooth. Immediately pour glaze over top of cooled cake, allowing it to run down sides. Let cake stand at least 20 minutes to allow glaze to set before serving.

POUND CAKES MADE WITH APRICOTS

APRICOT BRANDY POUND CAKE

This sour cream pound cake is pretty impressive just plain. The topping made with apricots, apricot brandy, and a little rum really dresses it up.

- 1 cup unsalted butter, softened
- 3 cups sugar
- 6 large eggs
- 3 cups sifted plain flour
- ½ teaspoon salt
- ¼ teaspoon baking soda
- 1 cup sour cream
- ⅔ cup apricot brandy
- 1 teaspoon vanilla extract
- 1 teaspoon orange extract
- 1½ teaspoons rum

Cream the butter, adding sugar a little at a time. Beat until light and fluffy. Add eggs while beating, one at a time. Add sour cream, brandy, vanilla, orange extract, and rum; mix well. Sift together flour, salt, and baking soda in a separate bowl. Add dry ingredients to butter mixture and stir. Transfer batter to greased and floured 10-inch tube pan. Bake at 325° for one hour or until cake tests done. Let cool in pan on wire rack for one hour.

Topping

- 1½ dozen dried apricots
- ½ cup unsalted butter
- ½ cup light brown sugar
- 2 teaspoons milk
- 1 Tablespoon cornstarch
- ½ cup apricot brandy
- ¼ cup rum

Mince 9 apricots in food processor with metal blade. Soak these apricots in the brandy and rum for at least 4 hours. After marinating, combine all ingredients in a small saucepan over low heat and stir constantly until thickened. Spoon slightly cooled mixture over cake and decorate with remaining 9 apricots.

APRICOT WALNUT POUND CAKE

It's hard to go wrong with fresh fruit, cream cheese and nuts, especially when the fruit is as distinctive as apricots. The resulting cake is full of flavor and texture that is a perfect accompaniment to coffee or tea.

- 1 cup butter, softened
- 3 oz cream cheese, softened
- 2 cups sugar
- 5 eggs, room temperature
- 2½ cups flour
- 1 teaspoon baking powder
- ½ teaspoon baking soda
- 1½ teaspoons finely grated orange zest
- ¾ teaspoon orange extract
- 1 teaspoon freshly grated nutmeg
- 1 cup chopped walnuts
- 1½ cups diced fresh apricots (approximately 4-5 medium apricots, unpeeled)

Butter and flour a 10-inch tube pan. Cream together butter and cream cheese for about 5 minutes. Slowly add the sugar to the creamed mixture, beating lighter in texture. Add the eggs to the batter, one at a time, beating well after each. In a bowl, whisk together the flour, baking powder, and soda. Gently but thoroughly blend the dry ingredients into the batter. Beat for 1 minute to incorporate the flour. Add the orange zest, orange extract and nutmeg. Fold in the walnuts and diced apricots. Evenly spread the batter into the prepared pan and bake at 325° for about 1 hour and 10-15 minutes, or until a tester comes out clean. Cool in the pan on a wire rack for about 10 minutes. Turn the cake out onto a wire rack and allow it to cool completely before slicing.

POUND CAKES MADE WITH BANANAS

BANANA SOUR CREAM POUND CAKE

This recipe will remind you of banana bread, but it's much lighter in color and in texture. For variation, add 1 cup of finely chopped pecans.

    1 cup butter, softened and cut in pieces
    1 Tablespoon solid vegetable shortening
    3 cups sugar
    6 eggs
    3 cups sifted plain flour
    ¼ teaspoon baking soda
    1 cup sour cream
    ¼ teaspoon vanilla extract
    ¼ teaspoon lemon extract
    ¼ teaspoon almond extract
    1 cup ripe bananas, mashed

Mix flour, sugar and baking soda. Beat in butter until mixture is crumbly. Beat in shortening, eggs and sour cream. Continue beating 5 minutes. Add flavorings and bananas and beat 2 minutes longer. Pour batter into greased and floured 10-inch tube pan. Bake at 325° for 1 hour and 30 minutes or until a sharp knife inserted deep into the cake comes out clean. Let cool for 5 minutes, then remove from pan and cool completely on wire rack.

GLAZED BANANA POUND CAKE

Don't be misled into thinking this cake is similar to banana nut bread. Instead, it is a spicy pound cake with a light, appealing texture.

- 1 cup butter, softened
- 2¾ cups sugar
- 6 eggs, separated, room temperature
- 1 cup sour cream
- 2 large, very ripe bananas, mashed to make 1 full cup
- 1½ teaspoons vanilla extract
- 3 cups cake flour
- ½ teaspoon baking soda
- ¼ teaspoon salt
- ½ teaspoon freshly grated nutmeg
- ½ teaspoon allspice
- ¼ teaspoon cloves
- ½ teaspoon ginger
- ¼ cup sugar

Butter and flour a 10½-inch decorative tube or Bundt pan. Cream butter well, slowly add the 2¾ cups sugar. Beat the mixture for about 5 minutes. Add egg yolks and beat well. Mix together sour cream, bananas, and vanilla extract. Add sour cream mixture to the batter. In a bowl, whisk together the flour, baking soda, salt and spices. Gently fold the flour into the cake batter. With clean, dry beaters, beat the egg whites until they hold soft peaks. Add ¼ cup sugar to the egg whites and continue beating until firm. Fold egg whites into the batter, being careful not to overmix. Pour the batter into the prepared pan and bake at 325° for 1 hour and 15 minutes, or until cake tests done. Let the cake cool in the pan on a wire rack for 15 minutes. Unmold on a rack and cool completely.

Glaze

2 cups confectioners' sugar
2-3 Tablespoons water

Combine the confectioners' sugar and water, mixing well. Place the cooled cake on a wire rack over a sheet of waxed paper. Slowly drizzle the glaze over the cake, covering it completely.

BANANA BLUEBERRY POUNDCAKE

Another summertime favorite, with lots of fruit and nuts.

    1½ cups canola oil
    2½ cups sugar
    3 eggs
    3 cups flour
    1 teaspoon soda
    ¾ teaspoon salt
    ½ cup buttermilk
    2 bananas, mashed
    1½ teaspoons vanilla
    1 cup pecans, chopped
    ¾ cup fresh or thawed blueberries

Mix oil, sugar and eggs. Add flour, soda, salt and mix together. Toss in pecans, and blueberries. Add buttermilk, bananas, and vanilla. Bake in greased and floured 10-inch tube pan at 325° for approximately 1 hour and 25 minutes or until cake tests done. Place upside down on a cake rack; when cool, invert and turn out onto rack.

BANANA BROWN SUGAR POUND CAKE

This cake is just plain sinful, it's so good. The warmth of brown sugar with bananas and nuts – it's a combination that's hard to beat.

- 1 lb light brown sugar
- 1 cup white sugar
- 1 lb butter
- 5 eggs
- 2 large bananas, mashed
- 3 cups flour
- ½ teaspoon baking powder
- ½ teaspoon salt
- 1 cup milk
- 1 teaspoon vanilla
- 1 cup pecans

Cream sugars together with butter until very light and fluffy. Add eggs, one at a time, beating well after each addition. Stir in bananas. Sift flour with baking powder and salt. Mix milk and vanilla together. Add each to first mixture alternately. Stir in the pecans. Pour into a 10-inch well-greased tube pan. Bake at 350° for 1½ hours, or until firm. Place upside down on a cake rack; when cool, invert and turn out onto rack.

BANANA BREAD POUND CAKE

Banana bread lovers of all ages will appreciate this dense, rich pound cake of the same persuasion. It's equally at home for breakfast or dessert.

1½ cups shortening
2 cups sugar
4 eggs
2 cups mashed ripe bananas
¼ cup plus 2 Tablespoons buttermilk
1 teaspoon vanilla extract
3 cups all-purpose flour
1¼ teaspoons baking soda
¼ teaspoon salt
½ cup chopped pecans

Beat shortening at medium speed 2 minutes or until creamy. Gradually add sugar, beating 5 to 7 minutes. Add eggs, one at a time, beating just until yellow disappears. Combine banana, buttermilk and vanilla. Combine flour, soda and salt; add to shortening mixture alternately with banana mixture, beginning and ending with flour mixture. Mix a low speed after each addition just until blended. Stir in pecans. Spoon batter into a greased and floured 10-inch tube pan. Bake at 325° for 1 hour and 30 minutes or until a wooden pick inserted in center comes out clean. Cool in pan on a wire rack for 15 minutes; remove cake from pan and cool completely on wire rack.

POUND CAKES MADE WITH BENNE SEEDS

BENNE SEED POUND CAKE

According to legend among descendants of slaves along the coast of South Carolina, benne is a good luck plant for those who eat the seeds or plant them in their garden. Benne seed wafers are a favorite type of cookie, made today with sesame seeds. This is a small cake, suitable for a loaf pan. Serve with fruit if desired.

1 cup butter, softened
1 cup granulated sugar
4 eggs
½ cup milk
1 teaspoon vanilla extract
1 teaspoon grated lemon peel
⅓ cup sesame seeds, toasted and divided
2 cups all-purpose flour
1 teaspoon baking powder
½ teaspoon salt

In a mixing bowl, cream butter and sugar. Beat in eggs, one at a time. Combine milk, vanilla extract and lemon peel; set aside. Reserving 1 Tablespoon sesame seeds, combine remaining sesame seeds with flour, baking powder and alt. Add dry ingredients to creamed mixture alternately with milk mixture; mix well. Pour into a greased and floured 9x5-inch loaf pan. Sprinkle with reserved sesame seeds. Bake at 325° for 65 minutes or until a wooden pick inserted near the center comes out clean. Cool in pan for 10 minutes; remove to a wire rack to cool completely.

POUND CAKES MADE WITH BLACKBERRIES

BLACKBERRY POUND CAKE

1 cup butter, softened
2 cups sugar
6 eggs
3½ cups flour
1 (12-ounce) jar blackberry jam
1½ teaspoons lemon flavoring

Oil and flour a 9-inch Bundt pan. In a large mixing bowl, combine butter and sugar and beat until fluffy. Add eggs and beat until creamy. Fold in flour a little bit at a time and then stir in blackberry jam and lemon flavoring. Beat the final mixture until smooth. Turn batter out into pan and bake at 350° for 1 hour. Cool in pan 10 minutes; remove cake from pan and let cool completely on wire rack.

POUND CAKES MADE WITH BLUEBERRIES

BLUEBERRY POUND CAKE

This recipe works best with small Maine blueberries. Large Southern blueberries are sweet and juicy, but they tend to sink to the bottom of the pan. Note that this recipe calls for coating the pan with butter and sugar instead of shortening and flour.

> 1 cup butter or margarine
> 2¼ cups sugar, divided
> 4 eggs
> 3 cups plain flour, divided
> 1 teaspoon baking powder
> ½ teaspoon salt
> 1 teaspoon vanilla extract
> 2 cups fresh blueberries or canned blueberries, well drained and dredged in ¼ cup of flour

Grease a 10-inch tube pan with butter. Sprinkle pan with ¼ cup sugar; set aside. Cream remaining butter; gradually add remaining sugar, beating well. Add eggs, one at a time, beating well after each addition. Add vanilla; mix well. Combine 2¾ cups flour, baking powder, and salt; gradually add to creamed mixture, beating until well blended. Dredge blueberries with remaining ¼ cup flour; stir to coat well. Fold blueberries into batter. Pour batter into prepared pan. Bake at 325° for 1 hour and 10 minutes or until cake tests done. Cool in pan 10 minutes; remove from pan and let cool completely on wire rack.

LOW-FAT BLUEBERRY POUND CAKE

This is a lighter, low-fat version of a blueberry pound cake. It uses low-fat yogurt and low-fat cream cheese.

- 2 cups sugar
- ½ cup light butter
- ½ (8 ounce) block low-fat cream cheese, softened
- 3 large eggs
- 1 large egg white
- 3 cups flour, divided
- 2 cups fresh or frozen blueberries
- 1 teaspoon baking powder
- ½ teaspoon baking soda
- ½ teaspoon salt
- 8 ounce container low-fat lemon yogurt
- 2 teaspoons vanilla extract
- Cooking spray

Beat first 3 ingredients at medium speed of a mixer until well blended (about 5 minutes). Add eggs and egg white, 1 at a time, beating well after each addition. Combine 2 tablespoons flour and blueberries in a small bowl, and toss well to coat. Combine remaining flour, baking powder, baking soda, and salt. Add flour mixture to sugar mixture alternately with yogurt, beginning and ending with flour mixture. Fold in blueberry mixture and vanilla; pour cake batter into a 10-inch tube pan coated with cooking spray. Bake at 350° for 1 hour and 10 minutes or until a wooden pick inserted in center comes out clean. Cool cake in pan 10 minutes; remove from pan.

Lemon Glaze

- ½ cup powdered sugar
- 4 teaspoons lemon juice

Combine powdered sugar and lemon juice in a small bowl; drizzle over warm cake.

BLUEBERRY ORANGE POUND CAKE

This flavorful cake combines the sweetness of blueberry with the zesty taste of orange. This is a small cake, good for a Bundt pan.

- 1 cup blueberries
- 2 cups plain flour
- 2 teaspoons baking powder
- 1 cup unsalted butter
- 1 Tablespoon finely grated orange rind
- 1½ cups powdered sugar
- 4 eggs
- 2 teaspoons vanilla extract
- 2 Tablespoons fresh orange juice

Grease and flour a 10-inch Bundt pan. Combine flour and baking powder and set aside. Cut butter into 1-inch pieces and place in mixing bowl. Add orange rind and soften on low speed. Increase speed to medium-high and cream until smooth and light in color, about 1½ to 2 minutes. Add powdered sugar, a little at a time, scraping bowl often. Beat until well blended, about 3 minutes. Add eggs, one at a time, beating well after each addition. Reduce speed to low and add vanilla and orange juice. The batter will appear curdled. Add flour mixture all at once, scraping sides of bowl again. Increase speed to medium-low and beat 30 seconds more. Spread a third of the batter in the prepared pan. Add half the blueberries. Layer another third of the batter and then add the remaining blueberries. Top with remaining batter. Smooth the surface with the bottom of a spoon. Bake at 350° for 45 to 50 minutes or until cake is golden brown on top and begins to come away from the sides of the pan. Let cake cool in pan on rack for 15 minutes, then invert cake onto serving plate and dust with 2 Tablespoons powdered sugar.

BLUEBERRY PEACH POUND CAKE

Nothing says summertime like peaches and blueberries. This recipe is superb with fresh fruit.

    ½ cup butter, softened
    1¼ cups sugar
    3 eggs
    ¼ cup milk
    2½ cups flour, sifted
    2 teaspoons baking powder
    ¼ teaspoon salt
    2¼ cups fresh peaches, peeled and chopped
    2 cups blueberries, fresh or frozen

Cream butter and sugar together. Beat in eggs, one at a time. Beat in milk. Combine flour, baking powder and salt; add to creamed mixture. Stir in peaches and blueberries. Pour into a greased and floured 10-inch tube pan. Bake at 350° for 60-70 minutes or until cake tester comes out clean. Cool in pan for 15 minutes; remove to a wire rack to cool completely. Dust with confectioners' sugar if desired.

POUND CAKES MADE WITH CHERRIES

CHERRY POUND CAKE

Here's a recipe for George Washington's Birthday—it's colorful and tasty with or without frosting. This recipe has many variations. For example, try adding 1 teaspoon of butternut flavoring and 1 cup chopped nuts. Or, add a few drops of red food coloring to the cake and/or icing. Or, after cooking, prick the top of the cake and pour the leftover cherry juice over the cake before icing it. Note that this is a "cold oven" pound cake—don't preheat the oven!

½ cup margarine
1 cup vegetable shortening
3 cups sugar
6 eggs
½ teaspoon vanilla extract
3¾ cups plain flour
¾ cup milk
½ (10 oz.) jar red maraschino cherries, chopped and drained
½ teaspoon almond extract
½ teaspoon vanilla extract
pinch salt

Cream margarine, shortening and sugar. Add eggs, beating well after each addition. Add flavorings and mix. Combine flour and salt; add to the sugar/egg mixture alternately with milk, beginning and ending with flour. Beat well. Stir in cherries. Pour batter into a greased and floured 10-inch (or larger) tube pan. Place pan in cold oven, then bake at 300° for 2 hours, or until the cake tests done. Cool in pan 10 minutes; remove from pan and cool completely on wire rack.

FROSTING

8 oz. cream cheese
¼ cup margarine
2 cups powdered sugar
½ cup flaked coconut
½ cup chopped pecans
½ (10 oz.) jar chopped red maraschino cherries
½ teaspoon butternut flavoring
OR ½ teaspoon each butter and almond extract
OR ½ teaspoon each lemon and vanilla extract

Combine cream cheese and butter, beating until smooth. Add sugar and beat until light and fluffy. Fold in coconut, nuts, cherries and flavorings. Spread over top and sides of cake.

FRESH CHERRY POUND CAKE

This recipe takes advantage of seasonal fresh cherries; when combined with the richness of ground almonds and the hint of nutmeg, they create a unique and delicious cake.

- 1 cup butter, room temperature
- 1⅓ cups sugar
- 4 eggs, room temperature
- 2 cups cake flour
- pinch of salt
- ¾ cup slivered almonds, toasted and ground
- 1½ teaspoon vanilla extract
- ⅛ teaspoon freshly grated nutmeg
- 2 cups unpitted, fresh sweet cherries (measure, then pit and halve)

Butter and flour a 9-inch Bundt pan. Cream butter at medium speed. Slowly add sugar and continue to beat until light, about 4 to 5 minutes. Add eggs, one at a time, beating well after each addition. With a large rubber spatula, gently fold in the flour. Fold in the almonds, vanilla and nutmeg. Add ⅓ of the batter to the pan, evenly smoothing it. Arrange a single layer of cherry halves on top of the batter being careful not to touch the sides of the pan. Repeat with ⅓ more batter, another layer of cherries, and ending with the remaining batter, evenly smoothing the top. Bake at 325° for 55-60 minutes, or until a tester comes out clean. Cool on a rack for 15 minutes, then turn out of the pan and cool completely.

CHERRY CREAM CHEESE POUND CAKE

This luscious pound cake has a nutty top crust and is moist and flavorful.

> 1 (8 oz.) package cream cheese
> 1 cup butter
> 1½ cups sugar
> 1½ teaspoons vanilla
> 4 eggs
> 2½ cups plain flour, divided
> 1½ teaspoons baking powder
> ⅛ teaspoon salt
> 1 cup candied or maraschino cherries, halved
> ½ cup chopped nuts

Cream the cream cheese, butter, sugar and vanilla together until smooth. Beat in eggs one at a time. Sift together 2¼ cups flour, baking powder and salt; fold into cream cheese mixture. Dredge cherries in ¼ cup flour and fold into batter. Sprinkle nuts over the bottom of a greased 10-inch tube pan; bottom should be completely covered (add a few more nuts if needed). Spoon batter into pan on top of nuts. Bake at 325° for 1 hour and 15 minutes or until cake tests done. Allow cake to cool in pan; run knife around outside edge and center tube. Ease cake out of pan onto serving plate.

CHERRY BUTTERNUT POUND CAKE

This cake is a delicious blend of butternut, cherries and chopped nuts. It's guaranteed not to last too long! NOTE: This is a cold oven recipe.

- ½ cup vegetable shortening
- 1 cup butter
- 2 cups sugar
- ¼ teaspoon salt
- 5 eggs
- 3 cups flour
- 1 small can evaporated milk, with water added to make 1 cup
- 2 Tablespoons butternut flavoring
- 1 cup chopped nuts
- 1 cup chopped Maraschino cherries, drained

Cream shortening and butter until fluffy. Add sugar and salt. Beat in eggs, one at a time. Add flour and milk, alternately, ending with flour. Add flavoring. Fold nuts and cherries into cake mixture. Bake in a greased and floured tube pan for 1 hour and 45 minutes. Start in a cold oven, then set to 300° and do not open door while cooking. Remove from pan immediately after baking. After cooling completely, wrap in Saran wrap to store.

CHOCOLATE CHERRY POUND CAKE

The dates and nuts in this recipe will make you think of fruit cake, but with a different twist.

3 cups flour
2 teaspoons baking powder
½ teaspoon baking soda
1 cup chopped red and green maraschino cherries
1 cup semi sweet chocolate pieces
1 cup chopped dates
1 cup chopped walnuts
1 cup sugar
½ cup butter or margarine
3 eggs
1¼ cups milk
¼ cup cherry-flavored brandy
½ cup confectioners' sugar
2-3 teaspoons water or milk

Grease 10-inch Bundt pan. In medium bowl, stir together flour, baking powder and baking soda. Add cherries, chocolate pieces, dates and walnuts; toss to coat. In large bowl with mixer at medium speed, beat sugar and butter about 2 minutes or until light and fluffy. Add eggs, one at a time, beating until smooth and scraping bowl occasionally. Add milk and brandy; beat until mixed. Add flour mixture; stir until mixed. Pour batter into prepared pan. Bake at 350° for 55 minutes or until wooden toothpick inserted in center comes out clean. Let stand on wire rack 10 minutes. Remove from pan; cool completely. For glaze, in small bowl, stir together confectioners' sugar and 2 teaspoons of the water. If necessary, add more water. Drizzle glaze over cake. Garnish with cherries, if desired.

GOLDEN CROWN HONEY POUND CAKE

This festive cake is excellent for gift giving. Make it in a 10-inch tube pan or 3 loaf pans.

- 1 cup butter or margarine
- 3 eggs
- ½ cup honey
- ½ cup sugar
- 1 Tablespoon vanilla
- 1 Tablespoon grated fresh lemon peel
- 2 cups flour
- 1 teaspoon baking powder
- ¼ teaspoon salt
- ¼ teaspoon baking soda
- 1 cup Maraschino cherries, whole, drained
- ½ cup broken pecans

Bring butter and eggs to room temperature. In large mixer bowl, beat butter on medium speed of electric mixer about 1 minute. Gradually add honey, then sugar; beat 5 to 7 minutes after all the honey and sugar have been added. Add vanilla and lemon peel; mix well. Add eggs one at a time; beating well after each addition. Scrape bowl frequently. Combine flour, baking powder, salt and baking soda; mix well. Add flour mixture to egg mixture, beat on low speed only until ingredients are blended; gently stir in cherries and pecans. Pour batter into three greased and floured loaf pans or one tube pan. Bake at 325° for 40 to 50 minutes or until wooden pick inserted near center comes clean. Cool for 15 minutes in pan. Remove from pan and cool completely on wire rack.

POUND CAKES MADE WITH COCONUT

COCONUT POUND CAKE

With 2 cups of flaked coconut added to the batter, it's best to let this cake cool completely before removing it from pan.

- 1½ cups butter, softened
- 3 cups sugar
- 5 eggs
- 3 cups plain flour
- ½ teaspoon baking powder
- 1 cup milk
- 1½ teaspoons vanilla extract
- 1½ teaspoons almond extract
- 2 cups flaked coconut

Sift together flour and baking powder. Cream butter; add sugar and beat until light and fluffy. Add eggs, one at a time, and beat thoroughly after each addition. Mix flavorings into milk. Alternately beat flour and milk into creamed mixture, starting and ending with flour. Fold in coconut. Pour cake batter into a greased and floured 10-inch tube pan. Bake at 325° for 1 hour and 25 minutes, or until cake tests done. Cool 1 hour. Remove from pan.

COCONUT BUTTERMILK POUND CAKE

This buttermilk pound cake has flaked coconut in the batter and in the topping. It gets an additional flavor boost from coconut extract.

> 1 cup shortening
> 2 cups sugar
> 4 eggs
> 3 cups plain flour
> ½ teaspoon soda
> ½ teaspoon baking powder
> ½ teaspoon salt
> 1 cup buttermilk
> ½ cup flaked coconut
> 3 teaspoons coconut extract

Cream shortening and sugar. Add eggs, one at a time, beating after each addition. Add buttermilk (to which soda has been added) alternately with sifted dry ingredients; mix well after each addition. Add coconut and flavoring, and mix well. Pour batter into a greased and floured 10-inch tube pan. Bake at 350° for 1 hour. Turn off heat and leave in oven for 10 minutes. Remove from oven and let cake cool an additional 10 minutes in pan. Then remove from pan and cool completely on wire rack.

Coconut Topping

> 1 cup sugar
> 1 cup water
> ¼ cup margarine
> ½ cup flaked coconut
> 3 Tablespoons light corn syrup

Combine all ingredients in pan and boil for 5 minutes. Punch holes in top of cake. Spoon hot topping over cooled cake.

COCONUT CREAM POUND CAKE

This recipe calls for cream of coconut, a sweet thick liquid made from fresh coconut. It is sold where you buy ingredients for mixed drinks, such as pina colada.

    1 cup butter or margarine, softened
    ½ cup shortening
    2½ cups sugar
    5 eggs
    3 cups flour
    ½ teaspoon baking powder
    1 cup cream of coconut
    1 teaspoon grated lemon peel
    1 teaspoon vanilla extract

Cream butter or margarine with shortening; gradually add sugar, beating until light and fluffy. Add eggs, one at a time, beating well after each addition. Combine flour and baking power; add to creamed mixture alternately with cream of coconut, beginning and ending with flour mixture. Mix just until blended after each addition. Stir in the lemon peel and vanilla. Pour batter into a greased and floured 10-inch tube pan; bake at 350° for 1 hour and 15 minutes or until a wooden pick inserted near center comes out clean. Cool in pan 10 to 15 minutes; remove from pan and cool completely on a rack.

COCONUT CREAM CHEESE POUND CAKE

This cream cheese pound cake uses frozen coconut, with coconut extract for extra flavor.

- ½ cup butter, softened
- ½ cup shortening
- 1 (8 oz.) package cream cheese, softened
- 3 cups sugar
- 6 eggs
- 3 cups plain flour
- ¼ teaspoon baking soda
- ¼ teaspoon salt
- 1 package (8-oz.) frozen coconut, thawed
- 1 teaspoon vanilla extract
- 1 teaspoon coconut extract

Cream butter, shortening, and cream cheese; gradually add sugar, beating well at medium speed of an electric mixer. Add eggs, one at a time, beating after each addition. Combine flour, soda, and salt; add to creamed mixture, stirring just until blended. Stir in remaining ingredients. Pour batter into a greased and floured 10-inch tube pan. Bake at 325° for 1 hour and 30 minutes or until a wooden pick inserted in center of cake comes out clean. Cool in pan 10 to 15 minutes; remove from pan and let cool completely on a wire rack.

VANILLA WAFER POUND CAKE

This is something different—a cake with no flour. Instead, the recipe uses a pound of finely crushed vanilla wafers! The nuts can be omitted if you wish.

- 1 cup butter
- 2 cups sugar
- 6 eggs
- ½ cup milk
- 1 cup chopped pecans
- 1 cup flaked coconut
- 1 teaspoon vanilla extract
- 1 pound vanilla wafers, crushed

Cream butter and sugar. Add eggs, one at a time. Crush vanilla wafers very fine and add ½ of wafers and ½ of milk and mix well. Then add rest of the wafers and milk. Mix well. Add nuts (chopped fine) and coconut and vanilla. Pour batter into a greased and floured 10-inch tube pan. Bake at 350° for 1 hour and 30 minutes, or until cake tests done. Cool 10 minutes in pan; remove from pan and let cool completely on wire rack.

POUND CAKES MADE WITH CRANBERRIES

CRANBERRY POUND CAKE

New England meets the Deep South.

> 1 cup unsalted butter, softened
> 2 cups sugar
> 4 eggs, room temperature
> 2½ cups flour
> 1 teaspoon baking powder
> ½ teaspoon baking soda
> ½ teaspoon salt
> 2 Tablespoons ground ginger
> ½ cup buttermilk
> 2½ cups cranberries (picked over)

Butter and flour a 3-quart Bundt pan. In a large bowl, cream butter; add sugar, a little at a time, until light and fluffy; add eggs, one at a time, beating well after each addition. Sift flour, baking powder, baking soda, salt and ginger; add to creamed mixture alternately with buttermilk, beginning and ending with flour; fold in cranberries. Spoon into prepared Bundt pan; smooth the top. Bake at 350° for 1¼ hours or until tester comes out clean. Cool on rack for 10 minutes; turn out and cool completely.

GLAZE:

> 1½ cups sugar
> 1½ cups water
> 1½ cups cranberries (picked over)

In a heavy saucepan, cook sugar and water over moderate heat; stir and wash down sides of pan with brush dipped in water; add cranberries; bring to a boil. Boil, undisturbed, until temperature reaches 250°; strain through a fine sieve, pressing hard on solids; let cool slightly. Brush on cake.

CRANBERRY ORANGE POUND CAKE

This rich and flavorful cake makes a colorful addition to a holiday meal. It's small enough to make in a Bundt pan, which makes it all the more decorative. Butter rum sauce or vanilla butter sauce are both delicious with this cake. Or, with orange glaze, the cake can be made ahead, wrapped well and stored up to 2 days.

    1½ cups butter, softened
    2¾ cups sugar
    1 teaspoon vanilla extract
    1 teaspoon grated orange peel
    6 eggs
    3 cups plain flour
    1 teaspoon baking powder
    ½ teaspoon salt
    1 (8 oz.) container sour cream
    1½ cups chopped fresh or frozen cranberries (do not thaw)

Beat butter and sugar until light and fluffy. Add vanilla and orange peel; mix well. Add eggs one at a time, beating well after each addition. In medium bowl, combine flour, baking powder and salt; add alternately with sour cream, beating well after each addition. Gently stir in cranberries. Pour batter into a greased and floured 10-inch tube pan (or Bundt pan). Bake at 350° for 1 hour and 10 minutes or until cake tests done. Cool 15 minutes; remove from pan and cool completely on wire rack.

Butter Rum Sauce

    1 cup sugar
    1 Tablespoon plain flour
    ½ cup half-and-half
    ½ cup butter
    4 teaspoons light rum or ¼ teaspoon rum extract

In small saucepan, combine sugar and flour. Stir in half-and-half and butter. Cook over medium heat until thickened and bubbly, stirring constantly. Remove from heat; stir in rum. Serve warm sauce over cake.

Vanilla Butter Sauce

1 cup sugar
1 Tablespoon all purpose flour
½ cup half and half cream
½ cup butter (no substitutes), softened
½ teaspoon vanilla extract

In a small saucepan, combine sugar and flour. Stir in cream and butter; bring to a boil over medium heat, stirring constantly. Boil for 2 minutes. Remove from heat and stir in vanilla. Serve warm sauce over cake.

Orange Glaze

⅓ cup sugar
⅓ cup fresh orange juice

In small saucepan, combine sugar and orange juice and bring to simmer, stirring until sugar dissolves. Brush warm glaze all over warm cake. Cool completely.

CRANBERRY-ORANGE ZEST POUND CAKE

Garnish this festive cake with powdered sugar and serve with fruit compote for an elegant dessert.

>1¼ cups unsalted butter, softened
>8 ounces cream cheese, softened
>2 cups sugar
>6 eggs
>½ teaspoon vanilla
>2 oranges, grated zest only
>4 cups all-purpose flour
>2 teaspoons baking powder
>Pinch of ground cloves
>Pinch of salt
>2¼ cups fresh cranberries, chopped
>Powdered sugar for garnish

Cream together butter, cream cheese and sugar until light and fluffy. Mix in eggs, one at a time, and vanilla extract and orange zest, scraping the side of the bowl between each addition. Stir together flour, baking powder, cloves and salt. Add to batter and mix on low speed until smooth. Do not overbeat. Fold in cranberries. Pour into non-stick or prepared (greased and floured) 8- or 9-inch Bundt pan. Bake at 350° for 50 to 55 minutes or until an inserted knife comes out clean. Cool thoroughly at room temperature and remove from pan. Dust top with powdered sugar. Spoon compote into center and serve.

Fruit Compote

1 orange, rind sliced off, and juiced (¼ cup juice)
2½ cups sugar, divided
2 cups fresh cranberries, divided
1 cup dried cranberries
1 cinnamon stick
1 teaspoon vanilla

In a sauté pan, combine 1 cup fresh cranberries, dried cranberries, cinnamon, vanilla, 1½ cups sugar, juice and 1 cup water. Bring to a boil. Reduce heat and simmer until thick, about 20 minutes. Remove from heat. Add remaining 1 cup cranberries and stir to combine. Serve warm or chilled with cake.

CRANBERRY WALNUT POUND CAKE

Since this recipe calls for dried cranberries, it can be made any time of the year. Once baked during the holidays, expect it to become a wintertime tradition.

- 1 cup butter, softened
- 2½ cups sugar
- 6 eggs, room temperature
- ⅔ cup jellied cranberry sauce, whisked until smooth
- 3 cups flour
- ¼ teaspoon salt
- 1 teaspoon baking soda
- ½ cup buttermilk, room temperature
- 1 Tablespoon finely grated orange zest (about 3 oranges)
- ½ teaspoon orange extract
- ¾ cup chopped walnuts
- 1½ cups dried cranberries, divided

Butter and flour a 10-inch tube pan. Cream the butter for 2 minutes, until lightened in color. Gradually add the sugar and beat on high speed for 5 minutes. Add the eggs, one at a time, beating well after each addition. Mix the cranberry sauce well into the batter. Sift together the flour, salt and soda. Add ½ of the flour to the batter, blending well, then add the buttermilk. Add the remaining flour. Blend the zest and orange extract well into batter. Fold in the chopped walnuts and 1 cup of the cranberries. Pour the batter into the prepared pan. Sprinkle the remaining ½ cup cranberries on top of the cake and lightly push into the batter with a rubber spatula. Bake at 325° for about 1 hour and 5 to 10 minutes, or until the cake tests done. Cool in the pan for 15 minutes, then turn out onto a rack and cool completely.

POUND CAKES MADE WITH CURRANTS

GRANDMA'S CURRANT POUND CAKE

Currants can be found at the supermarket with the raisins and other dried fruit. They are delicious in this big, moist cake, made the old-fashioned way.

    1½ cups currants
    2 cups butter or margarine
    2 cups sugar
    1 teaspoon mace
    9 eggs, separated
    4¼ cups plain flour, sifted
    1 teaspoon lemon extract
    1 teaspoon vanilla extract

Rinse currants in hot water, drain and dry on a towel. Cream butter until fluffy, add sugar and spice and cream thoroughly. Beat egg yolks until thick and creamy; add to butter mixture and blend well. Add one-half of the flour and mix until smooth; add remainder of flour and mix until smooth again. Mix in stiffly beaten egg whites. Pour batter into a well-greased and floured 10-inch tube pan OR 2 prepared loaf pans. Bake at 350° for 1 hour and 25 minutes, or until cake tests done. Cool 15 minutes; remove from pan and cool completely on wire rack.

BUTTERMILK BROWN SUGAR POUND CAKE

This recipe includes anise flavoring, orange rind and currants, which come together to create a unique taste. An extra nice touch can be added by brushing the still warm cake with orange marmalade; garnish with orange zest.

- 1 cup unsalted butter
- 2 cups light brown sugar
- 3 eggs
- 2½ cups plain flour
- 1 teaspoon baking powder
- ½ teaspoon baking soda
- ⅛ teaspoon salt
- 1 cup buttermilk
- 1 teaspoon vanilla extract
- ¼ teaspoon anise extract
- grated rind of 1 orange
- ½ cup plumped currants

Note: To plump currants, cover with boiling water in small cup and let stand 10 minutes. Drain.

Stir together flour, baking powder, baking soda and salt in large bowl. Beat the butter and brown sugar in a large bowl until light and fluffy, for about 3 minutes, scraping down the bowl as needed. Add eggs, one at a time, beating 1 minute after each addition. Beat in vanilla and anise extracts. Reduce speed to lowest setting; add one-third flour mixture, beating just until blended. Pour in ½ cup buttermilk, beating until combined. Repeat with the remaining flour mixture and buttermilk, ending with the flour mixture; mix well after each addition. Fold in orange rind and the drained currants. Spoon batter into a greased and floured 10-inch tube pan. Rotate pan briskly to even and settle batter. Bake at 350° for 1 hour or until wooden pick inserted in center comes out clean. Transfer pan to rack to cool 30 minutes. Run thin knife around side of pan and tube. Invert cake onto rack; re-invert cake onto serving plate. Cool to room temperature.

POUND CAKES MADE WITH DATES

DATE NUT POUND CAKE

This cake is reminiscent of another holiday favorite, date nut bread. With generous amounts of butter, sugar and eggs, it's anything but bread.

- 2 cups butter
- 2 cups sugar
- 6 eggs
- 4 cups plain flour
- 1 oz. lemon extract
- 1 pound dates, chopped
- 1 pound (4 cups) pecans or walnuts, chopped

Cream butter until light and fluffy. Add sugar and continue beating until light and fluffy. Add eggs, one at a time, beating thoroughly after each addition. Stir in flavoring. Coat dates and nuts with one cup of flour. Add remaining flour (3 cups) to egg and butter mixture and mix well. Fold in dates and nuts. Spoon mixture into a well-greased and floured 10-inch tube pan. Bake at 300° for 2 hours, or until cake tests done. Remove from oven and cool 10 minutes in pan; remove from pan and cool completely on wire rack.

POUND CAKES MADE WITH FIGS

FIG POUND CAKE

Fig-lovers get ready for a tasty treat. This is a small cake, suitable for a loaf pan – or, double the recipe for a 10-inch tube pan.

    1 cup butter or margarine
    3 eggs
    ½ cup honey
    ½ cup sugar
    1 Tablespoon vanilla
    1 Tablespoon grated fresh lemon peels
    2 cups all purpose flour
    1 teaspoon baking powder
    ¼ teaspoon salt
    ¼ teaspoon baking soda
    1 cup chopped fresh figs
    ½ cup broken pecans

In large mixer bowl, beat butter on medium speed of electric mixer about 1 minute. Gradually add honey, then sugar; beat 5 to 7 minutes after all honey and sugar are added. Add vanilla and lemon peel; mix well. Add eggs one at a time; beat after each addition. Scrape bowl frequently. Combine, flour, baking powder, salt and baking soda; mix well. Add flour mixture to egg mixture; beat on low speed only until ingredients are blended. Gently stir in figs and pecans. Pour batter into a 9×5×3 inch greased and floured loaf pan. Bake at 325° for 60 minutes or until a cake tester comes out clean. Cool 15 minutes in pan. Remove from pan; cool completely on a wire rack.

POUND CAKES MADE WITH HAZELNUTS

HAZELNUT POUND CAKE WITH ALMOND CHOCOLATE GLAZE

This makes a small loaf pan, but it's a delicious cake that's fairly easy to prepare.

- 1 cup butter
- 1 cup sugar
- 2 eggs
- 1½ cups flour
- 3 oz. hazelnuts, chopped
- 2 teaspoons baking powder
- ½ cup half and half

Combine butter and sugar in large bowl. Beat with electric mixer until fluffy. Add eggs, one at a time, beating well after each addition. Combine flour, nuts and baking powder. Add flour mixture to butter mixture alternately with half and half, beginning and ending with flour mixture. Pour into greased 9×5×3-inch loaf pan and bake at 325° for 60 minutes.

Almond Chocolate Glaze

- ¼ cup almond liqueur
- 8 oz chocolate chips

Place chocolate chips in microwave-safe container and melt by heating on high (100%) power for 3 minutes, stirring halfway through cooking time. Blend in liqueur. Drizzle over cooled cake.

POUND CAKES MADE WITH LEMON

LEMON CREAM POUND CAKE

This basic lemon pound cake is made with evaporated milk, but the recipe will work quite nicely with regular milk.

- 1 cup butter
- ½ cup shortening
- 3 cups sugar
- 5 eggs
- 3 cups plain flour, sifted
- ½ teaspoon baking powder
- ½ teaspoon salt
- 1 cup evaporated milk
- 2 teaspoons lemon extract

Cream butter and shortening until light and fluffy. Add sugar and beat well. Add eggs, one at a time, beating after each addition. Sift dry ingredients together, and then add to sugar and egg mixture, alternating with milk. Mix well after each addition, adding flour mixture first and last. Pour into a well-greased and floured 10-inch tube pan. Bake at 350° for 1 hour and 10 minutes, or until cake tests done. Cool in pan 10 minutes; remove from pan and cool completely on wire rack.

LEMON BUTTERMILK POUND CAKE

This moist buttermilk pound cake is delightful plain, or dress it up with the lemon sauce and fresh seasonal berries to garnish.

    1 cup vegetable shortening
    ½ cup margarine
    2½ cups sugar
    4 eggs
    3½ cups plain flour
    ½ teaspoon salt
    1 cup buttermilk
    1 teaspoon lemon extract
    ½ teaspoon baking soda dissolved in 1 Tablespoon hot water

Cream shortening and margarine together. Add sugar gradually and cream until light and fluffy. Add eggs, one at a time, beating well after each addition. Sift flour and salt together and add alternately with buttermilk. Mix well after each addition. Add lemon extract and blend. Stir in soda and water mixture. Pour batter into a greased and floured 10-inch tube pan. Bake at 325° for 1¼ hour, or until cake tests done. Remove cake from pan immediately to serving plate.

Lemon Sauce

    1 cup sugar
    ½ cup hot water
    juice of 2 lemons

Mix ingredients and bring to a boil. Reduce heat and simmer 10 to 12 minutes. Pour sauce over hot cake.

LEMON SOUR CREAM POUND CAKE WITH LEMON GLAZE

This cake is a great one when you're pressed for time. It takes only about 10 minutes to mix, but a large heavy-duty mixer is the secret to this one-step mixing method.

>   3 cups sugar
>   3 cups all purpose flour
>   ¼ teaspoon salt
>   ¼ teaspoon baking soda
>   1 cup butter, softened
>   1 (8 oz) container sour cream
>   6 eggs
>   2 Tablespoons lemon juice
>   ½ teaspoon vanilla extract

Place ingredients in a 4-quart mixing bowl (in order given). Beat at low speed with a heavy-duty mixer for 1 minute; scraping sides frequently. Beat at medium speed for 2 minutes. Spoon batter into a greased and floured 10-inch tube pan. Bake at 325° for 1 hour and 30 minutes or until a cake tester comes out clean. Cool cake in pan on a wire rack. Drizzle with Lemon Glaze.

Lemon Glaze

>   1 cup powdered sugar
>   2 Tablespoons fresh lemon juice
>   ½ teaspoon vanilla extract
>   1 teaspoon grated lemon rind (optional)

Stir together first 3 ingredients and, if desired, lemon rind, until glaze is smooth. Makes about ⅓ cup glaze. Drizzle on cooled cake.

LEMON POPPY SEED POUND CAKE

This recipe uses separated eggs as well as baking powder to produce a big, tall cake.

- 1 cup softened unsalted butter
- 2 cups sugar
- 10 eggs, separated
- 2 Tablespoons lemon juice
- 2 Tablespoons grated lemon peel
- 1 teaspoon vanilla extract
- ½ cup poppy seeds
- 4½ cup sifted cake flour
- 4 teaspoons baking powder
- ¾ teaspoon salt

Butter well a 10-inch tube pan and dust with flour, shaking out the excess. Cream the butter, then add 1½ cups of the sugar, a little at a time, and beat the mixture until light and fluffy. Beat in the egg yolks, one at a time, the lemon juice, lemon peel, vanilla extract, and poppy seeds. In a bowl, sift the flour, baking powder, and salt. Beat the flour mixture into the butter mixture. In another bowl with an electric mixer, beat the egg whites until they form very soft peaks. Add the remaining sugar, a little at a time, and then continue to beat the egg whites until they are stiff but not dry. Stir in one-fourth of the egg-white mixture, and then fold in the remaining whites gently but thoroughly into the batter. Spoon the batter into the prepared pan and bake at 325° for 1¼ hours, or until a cake tester inserted in the center comes out clean. Let cool in the pan for 5 minutes and invert onto rack to cool completely.

POPPY SEED POUND CAKE WITH LEMON GLAZE

A moist buttermilk pound cake with poppy seeds and grated lemon peel. The lemony glaze adds a nice touch.

- 1 cup butter, softened
- 2 cups granulated sugar
- 1 cup buttermilk
- 4 eggs
- 3 cups flour
- ¼ cup poppy seeds
- ½ teaspoon baking soda
- ½ teaspoon baking powder
- ½ teaspoon salt
- 4 teaspoons grated lemon peel
- ½ teaspoon vanilla extract

In large bowl, combine butter, sugar, buttermilk and eggs. Mix at medium speed with an electric mixer until smooth. In a separate bowl, combine flour, poppy seeds, baking soda, baking powder, and salt. Add flour mixture to liquid ingredients, beating on high speed until thoroughly mixed. Add lemon peel and vanilla, and beat 1 minute more or until mixture is smooth. Pour batter into greased and floured 10-inch tube pan. Bake at 325° for 1 hour or until cake tests done. Allow cake to cool in pan; invert onto serving plate.

Glaze

- 1 cup confectioners' sugar
- ½ Tablespoon lemon juice

Mix confectioners' sugar with lemon juice; spoon over cake.

SOUTHERN LEMON RIND POUND CAKE

This citrus cake has the lemon rind in the cake, not in a glaze.

>   1½ cups butter, room temperature
>   3 cups sugar
>   1 teaspoon vanilla extract
>   1 teaspoon lemon extract
>   1 Tablespoon fresh lemon juice
>   1 Tablespoon grated lemon rind
>   6 eggs
>   3 cups all purpose flour
>   1 teaspoon baking powder
>   ¼ teaspoon salt
>   ½ cup evaporated milk

Grease and flour a 10-inch tube pan. Beat butter in large mixing bowl until light and fluffy. Add sugar ½ cup at a time, creaming well after each addition. Stir in vanilla, lemon extract, juice and rind. Add eggs, one at a time, blending well after each addition. Sift together flour, baking powder and salt; add to creamed mixture alternately with milk. Stir thoroughly after each addition. Pour into prepared pan and bake at 325° for 1 hour and 20 minutes or until wooden pick inserted near center comes out clean. Cool 20 minutes, and then remove from pan.

LEMON POUND CAKE WITH NUTS AND RAISINS

This recipe brings together an interesting mix of tastes—lots of lemon flavor, with pecans and the white raisins.

> 2 cups butter or margarine
> 2 cups sugar
> 6 eggs
> 4 cups plain flour
> 2 cups white raisins, dredged lightly in flour
> 2 cups chopped pecans
> 1 (2 oz.) bottle of lemon extract

Cream butter and sugar until light and fluffy. Add eggs, one at a time, beating well after each addition. Add flour and mix well. Fold in raisins, then nuts and flavoring. Pour batter into a greased and floured 10-inch tube pan. Bake at 325° for 1 hour and 30 minutes or until cake tests done. Cool 10 minutes in pan; remove from pan and cool completely on wire rack.

LEMON-THYME POUND CAKE

Fresh thyme gives this cake a delightful aroma and blends with lemon for an unforgettable taste. This is a small recipe, suitable for a Bundt pan.

2¾ cups all-purpose flour
2 Tablespoons chopped fresh thyme
½ teaspoon baking soda
½ teaspoon cinnamon
½ teaspoon salt
1 cup unsalted butter, softened
2 cups sugar
1 teaspoon lemon extract
6 eggs
1 cup plain low-fat yogurt
¼ cup fresh lemon juice
2 teaspoons lemon zest

Grease and flour a 10-inch Bundt pan. In a bowl, mix flour, thyme, baking soda, cinnamon and salt. In another, large bowl, beat butter, sugar and extract until fluffy, about 3 minutes. Beat in eggs, one at a time, beating well after each. In bowl, combine yogurt, lemon juice and zest. On low speed, alternately beat in flour mixture with yogurt mixture in 3 additions, beginning and ending with flour mixture. Pour into pan. Bake at 350° for 55 minutes, until tester comes out clean. Cool on rack 10 minutes. Remove cake from pan and cool completely.

Glaze

½ cup lemon juice
½ cup sugar
1 Tablespoon fresh thyme

In small saucepan, combine lemon juice, sugar and thyme. Over medium-high heat, stir until sugar is dissolved. Boil, without stirring, until syrupy, about 10 minutes. Strain, let cool for 5 minutes. Brush over cooled cake.

LEMON YOGURT POUND CAKE

This recipe calls for lots of beating - ten minutes to cream the butter and sugar. Extra beating ensures lots of air in the batter, thus a taller, lighter cake. Note that this is a COLD oven recipe.

    1 cup butter
    2½ cups sugar
    6 eggs
    3 cups plain flour
    ½ teaspoon salt
    ½ teaspoon baking soda
    1 cup lemon yogurt
    1 teaspoon lemon extract

Cream together butter and sugar until light and fluffy, about 10 minutes. Add eggs one at a time, beating for 1 minute after each addition. Combine the dry ingredients and add alternately (in three additions) with the yogurt, scraping the bowl and beating well after each addition. Add lemon extract and mix well. Pour batter into a greased and floured 10-inch tube pan. Place in cold oven and set oven temperature to 325°. Bake for 1 hour 15 minutes or until cake tests done. Cool 45 minutes before removing from pan. Cool completely on wire rack

Glaze

    1 cup confectioners' sugar
    2 teaspoons lemon juice

Beat confectioners' sugar and lemon juice until smooth. Drizzle over cooled cake.

LIGHT AND LEMONY POUND CAKE

This "healthy" pound cake has reduced saturated fat and cholesterol by using frozen egg substitute and yogurt as the liquid. It's low on fat, but big on taste.

- ¾ cup margarine
- 2 cups sugar
- 1½ cups frozen egg substitute, thawed
- 2¾ cups plain flour
- ½ teaspoon baking soda
- 1 Tablespoon lemon juice
- ½ teaspoon lemon extract
- 1 cup low-fat plain yogurt
- 2 Tablespoons grated, fresh lemon peel

Combine flour and soda; set aside. Cream margarine about 30 seconds in large bowl. Add sugar gradually and cream 5 to 7 minutes. Gradually add egg substitute, beating well. Stir in lemon juice and lemon extract. Add flour mixture in 3 parts, alternating with 2 parts yogurt. Beat at low speed after each addition just until combined. Do not overmix. Fold in lemon peel. Pour batter into a greased and floured 10-inch tube pan. Bake at 325° for 1 hour or until toothpick inserted near center comes out clean. Cool on wire rack for 10 minutes before removing from pan. Finish cooling on wire rack.

OATMEAL-LEMON POUND CAKE

The oatmeal gives this cake an extra smooth texture. Sprinkle it with powdered sugar and serve with raspberry sauce made from a 10-oz. package of frozen red raspberries, thawed and blended in a blender.

- 2 cups margarine or butter, softened
- 2½ cups sugar
- 6 eggs
- 3½ cups plain flour
- 2 teaspoons baking powder
- 1 teaspoon salt (optional)
- 2 cups oatmeal, uncooked
- 1½ cups milk
- 4 Tablespoons grated lemon peel (about 5 lemons)

In a blender, blend oats about 1 minute. Combine with flour, baking powder and salt; set aside. Beat sugar and margarine, or butter, until fluffy. Add eggs and lemon peel; mix well. Add dry ingredients alternately with milk, mixing well after each addition. Pour into a greased and floured 10-inch tube pan. Bake at 350° for 1 hour and 10 minutes or until wooden pick inserted in center comes out clean. Cool 10 minutes in pan. Remove to wire rack; cool completely.

OATMEAL-LEMON POUND CAKE

The oatmeal gives this cake an extra smooth texture. Sprinkle it with powdered sugar and serve with raspberry sauce made from a 10-oz. package of frozen red raspberries, thawed and blended in a blender.

- 2 cups margarine or butter, softened
- 2½ cups sugar
- 6 eggs
- 3½ cups plain flour
- 2 teaspoons baking powder
- 1 teaspoon salt (optional)
- 2 cups oatmeal, uncooked
- 1½ cups milk
- 4 Tablespoons grated lemon peel (about 5 lemons)

In a blender, blend oats about 1 minute. Combine with flour, baking powder and salt; set aside. Beat sugar and margarine, or butter, until fluffy. Add eggs and lemon peel; mix well. Add dry ingredients alternately with milk, mixing well after each addition. Pour into a greased and floured 10-inch tube pan. Bake at 350° for 1 hour and 10 minutes or until wooden pick inserted in center comes out clean. Cool 10 minutes in pan. Remove to wire rack; cool completely.

POUND CAKES MADE WITH LIME

FLORIBBEAN POUND CAKE

Serve with slices of tropical fruit and whipped cream. May substitute regular milk for the coconut milk.

- 3 cups plain flour
- 1½ teaspoons baking powder
- 1½ cups butter, softened
- 1½ cups sugar
- 6 eggs
- 4½ teaspoons lime peel, finely shredded (takes about 3 limes)
- ⅓ cup canned coconut milk, unsweetened

Stir together the flour and baking powder; set aside. In a large mixing bowl, beat butter with electric mixer on medium speed for 30 seconds. Gradually add sugar (about 2 tablespoons at a time), beating on medium-high for about 6 minutes or until very light and fluffy. Add eggs, one at a time, beating 1 minute after each addition, scraping bowl often. Beat in lime peel. Gradually add flour mixture, beating on medium-low speed until just combined. Beat in milk. Spread batter evenly in a greased and floured 10-inch tube pan. Bake at 325° for 55-60 minutes, or until toothpick inserted near center comes out clean. Cool cake in pan on wire rack for 10 minutes; invert cake onto cooling rack. Prick top and sides of cake with a toothpick and top immediately with topping and coconut (below).

TOPPING

½ cup sugar
⅓ cup lime juice
½ - 1 cup toasted coconut

In a small saucepan, combine sugar and lime juice; heat over medium heat to dissolve sugar. Brush warm cake with syrup. Immediately sprinkle with coconut.

KEY LIME POUND CAKE

Key lime lovers, here is a cake to satisfy your cravings. In summer, serve it with vanilla ice cream or frozen yogurt and fresh berries.

- 1 cup butter
- ½ cup shortening
- 2 cups sugar
- 2 Tablespoons Key lime juice
- 2 teaspoons lime rind, finely grated
- 1 teaspoon vanilla
- 5 eggs
- ¼ cup sour cream
- 3 cups plain flour
- 1 teaspoon baking soda

Cream together butter, shortening and sugar; beating until light and fluffy. Add Key lime juice, lime rind and vanilla. Add eggs, one at a time, mixing well after each addition. Mix in sour cream. Add flour and baking soda and mix thoroughly to blend. Spoon batter into a greased and floured 10-inch tube pan. Bake at 350° for 1 hour and 5 minutes or until cake tests done. Cool on wire rack for 15 minutes; turn cake out of pan to glaze.

Glaze

- ½ cup confectioners' sugar
- 1 Tablespoon Key lime juice

Mix until smooth. Pour glaze over warm cake. Let cool before serving.

POUND CAKES MADE WITH MACADAMIA NUTS

MACADAMIA-COCONUT POUND CAKE

This cake is a bit of an investment, in time and money, but it's well worth the effort.

> 2 cups (6-oz.) sweetened flaked coconut
> 1 jar (7-ounce) macadamia nuts
> 1 cup unsalted butter, softened
> 1½ cups firmly packed light brown sugar
> 8 ounces cream cheese, softened
> 4 large eggs
> 1 Tablespoon vanilla
> 2⅔ cups all-purpose flour
> 2½ teaspoons baking powder
> 1 teaspoon salt

Butter and flour a 10-inch Bundt pan. Spread coconut in a shallow baking pan and toast in oven, stirring occasionally and watching carefully to avoid burning, until golden, 10 to 12 minutes. Transfer coconut to a bowl and cool. Spread nuts in pan and toast in oven until pale golden, 8 to 10 minutes. Cool nuts and chop coarse. In a bowl with an electric mixer beat together butter and brown sugar until light and fluffy and beat in cream cheese. Add eggs, 1 at a time, beating well after each addition, and beat in vanilla. Sift flour, baking powder, and salt into bowl. Add to batter and beat just until combined well. Stir in coconut and chopped nuts. Spread batter evenly in pan and bake at 350° for 1 hour to 1 hour and 10 minutes, or until tester comes out clean. Cool cake in pan on a rack 5 minutes and invert onto rack to cool completely.

GLAZE

¼ cup of water
¾ cup sugar
¼ cup amber or dark rum

In a small heavy saucepan bring water with sugar to a boil, stirring until sugar is dissolved. Stir in rum. Brush hot glaze evenly over outside of warm cake until absorbed. Cool cake completely.

POUND CAKES MADE WITH MIXED FRUITS

CANDIED FRUIT POUND CAKE

This cake contains the same candied fruits and nuts as holiday fruitcake, but with a pound (or more) of the four main ingredients, there's no mistaking this one for anything but a pound cake.

- 2 ⅓ cups sugar
- 2 cups butter
- 10 eggs
- 6 cups flour
- 3 teaspoons baking powder
- ½ cup pineapple juice
- 1 lb candied cherries, chopped
- 2 cups chopped walnuts
- ¼ lb candied pineapple, chopped

Cream sugar and butter together until light and fluffy. Add eggs, one at a time, mixing well after each addition. Add flour, baking powder and pineapple juice; beat until well mixed. Add chopped cherries, nuts and pineapple; mix well. Spoon batter into a greased and floured 10-inch tube pan. Bake at 350° for 2 hours, or until cake tests done. Cool in pan for 10 minutes; remove from pan and cool completely on wire rack.

POUND CAKES MADE WITH ORANGES

ORANGE POUND CAKE

Orange juice and grated orange rind give this cake a zesty flavor, a tad sweeter than the more traditional lemon.

- 1½ cups butter or margarine, softened
- 3 cups sugar
- 5 eggs
- 3½ cups plain flour
- 1 teaspoon cream of tartar
- 1½ teaspoons baking powder
- ¼ teaspoon salt
- ¾ cup plus 2 Tablespoons milk
- ¼ cup orange juice
- 1 teaspoon vanilla extract
- 1 teaspoon almond extract
- 2 Tablespoons grated orange rind

Cream butter; gradually add sugar, beating at medium speed until light and fluffy. Add eggs, one at a time, beating after each addition. Combine flour, cream of tartar, baking powder, and salt; add to creamed mixture alternately with milk and orange juice, beginning and ending with flour mixture. Mix just until blended after each addition. Stir in flavorings and orange rind. Pour batter into a greased and floured 10-inch tube pan. Bake at 325° for 1 hour and 25 minutes or until a wooden pick inserted near center comes out clean. Cool cake in pan 10 minutes. Remove from pan and cool completely on a wire rack.

Glaze

½ cup water
½ cup granulated sugar
⅓ cup orange juice
¼ teaspoon orange flavored liqueur
2 teaspoons vanilla extract

Combine water and sugar in saucepan. Bring to a boil. Remove from heat and add remaining ingredients. Brush glaze evenly over outside of cake. Cool and cover or wrap in plastic wrap for storage.

CANDIED ORANGE POUND CAKE

This is an all time favorite, with its cool, clean citrus flavor. And, since it is a smaller, loaf cake, it is perfect for gift giving or for packing in a picnic basket.

- ¾ cup butter, room temperature
- 1½ cups sugar
- 4 eggs, room temperature
- 1½ cups flour
- ¾ teaspoon orange extract
- 2 Tablespoons orange juice
- ¾ cup chopped candied orange rind*

Butter and flour a 9×5×3-inch loaf pan. Cream the butter until lightened in color. Slowly add the sugar and continue beating about 5 minutes. Add eggs, one at a time, mixing well after each addition. Gradually add the flour, mixing well. Fold in the orange extract, orange juice, and candied orange rind. Turn the batter into the loaf pan and bake at 350° for 50 to 60 minutes or until a tester comes out clean. Allow the cake to cool in pan on a wire rack for about 10 minutes, and then turn out on rack and the cake cool completely.

*Candied orange rind can be found at specialty cook stores or the local supermarket.

AMBROSIA POUND CAKE

This cake is orange-flavored, using orange extract, while the cream cheese icing is made with orange rind, raisins and coconut.

>   1 cup margarine
>   ½ cup shortening
>   3 cups sugar
>   6 eggs
>   1 cup milk
>   3 cups plain flour
>   ½ teaspoon salt
>   ½ teaspoon baking powder
>   3 teaspoons orange extract

In a large bowl, mix well margarine, shortening, sugar, and eggs. Add milk and stir. Add flour that has been sifted with salt and baking powder; mix well. Stir in orange extract. Pour into a greased and floured tube pan. Bake at 350° for 1 hour and 30 minutes or until cake tests done. Cool in pan 10 minutes; remove from pan and cool completely on wire rack.

Icing

>   8 oz. cream cheese, softened
>   2 Tablespoon grated orange rind
>   1 pound box powdered sugar
>   2 cups raisins
>   1 cup flaked coconut

Mix thoroughly cream cheese, orange rind, and sugar. Fold in raisins and coconut. Frost cooled cake.

LOW-FAT ORANGE POUND CAKE

This version is just as moist and tasty as the 'regular' recipes, but definitely is lower in fat and calories.

> 2½ cups white flour
> 1¼ cups sugar
> 3¾ teaspoons baking powder
> ¾ teaspoon salt
> ¾ cup canola oil
> 1 cup applesauce
> 1 teaspoon lemon extract
> 2½ teaspoons orange juice concentrate
> 1 Tablespoon orange zest
> 9 egg whites
> 3 ⅓ Tablespoon sugar

In a large bowl, sift together flour, first amount of sugar, baking powder and salt. Set aside. In a separate bowl, whisk together canola oil, applesauce, lemon extract, orange juice concentrate and orange zest. Set aside. In a small bowl, whip egg whites until foamy. Add in second amount of sugar and whip until stiff, not dry. Combine wet ingredients with dry and stir. Gently fold egg whites into batter until just incorporated. Pour batter into a Bundt pan sprayed with nonstick vegetable coating. Bake at 375° for 45 minutes to 1 hour, until cake is baked through. Remove from heat and let cool.

ORANGE POPPY SEED POUND CAKE

An orange-rum glaze makes this cake extra moist—and extra appetizing. It's a good recipe to make ahead; cover tightly and store at room temperature up to 2 days or freeze up to one month.

- 1 cup butter or margarine, softened
- 1¼ cups sugar
- 4 large eggs
- 3 cups plain flour
- ⅓ cup poppy seeds
- 1 Tablespoon baking powder
- ½ teaspoon salt
- ¾ cup milk
- ⅓ cup orange juice
- 2 teaspoons grated orange peel
- 1 teaspoon vanilla extract

Beat butter and sugar together in mixer bowl at medium-high speed until light and fluffy. Add eggs, one at a time, beating well after each addition. Combine flour, poppy seeds, baking powder and salt in medium bowl. Stir together milk, orange juice, orange peel and vanilla in small bowl.

With mixer at low speed, alternately add flour mixture and milk mixture, beginning and ending with flour. Pour batter into a greased and floured Bundt pan. Bake at 350° for 50 minutes or until toothpick inserted in center comes out clean. Cool in pan 10 minutes; remove cake from pan and cool completely on wire rack.

Orange-Rum Glaze

⅔ cup sugar
½ cup water
1 Tablespoon orange juice
¼ teaspoon grated orange peel
2 Tablespoons dark rum

Combine sugar, water, orange juice and peel in saucepan. Bring to boil over medium heat. Boil 5 minutes until mixture thickens slightly. Remove from heat; stir in rum. Brush warm mixture over cake, allowing glaze to soak into cake completely.

POLENTA POUND CAKE

This densely textured pound cake is flavored with orange-flower water, a fragrant distillate made from bitter-orange blossoms. Orange-flower water is available at Middle Eastern grocery stores and specialty food shops. This is a small cake, suitable for a loaf pan.

- 3 cups all purpose flour
- 1 cup polenta
- ½ teaspoon salt
- 2 cups sugar
- 1½ cups unsalted butter, softened
- 6 eggs
- ½ cup orange-flower water (see note)
- 1 Tablespoon finely grated orange zest

Butter and flour a 2-quart loaf pan (10×5×3 inches). In a bowl, sift together the flour, polenta and salt. In a standing electric mixer fitted with the paddle, beat the sugar and butter at medium speed until light and fluffy. Add the eggs, one at a time, beating just until each is incorporated. Add the orange-flower water and orange zest and beat until blended. Mix in the dry ingredients at low speed until thoroughly moistened, scraping the side and bottom of the bowl as necessary. Spread the batter in the prepared pan and smooth the surface. Bake at 325° in the center of the oven for about 2 hours, or until a cake tester comes out clean. Let cool in the pan for 10 minutes, then turn it out onto a wire rack to cool completely. The cake can be wrapped in plastic and stored in an airtight container for several days.

POUND CAKES MADE WITH PEACHES

PEACHY POUND CAKE

This recipe works best with fresh peaches. A generous sprinkling of sugar in the bottom of the pan gives this cake a nice crunchy top. It's just peachy!

    1 cup plus 2 Tablespoons butter
    2¼ cups granulated sugar, divided
    4 eggs
    1 teaspoon vanilla
    3 cups plain flour, divided
    1 teaspoon baking powder
    ½ teaspoon salt
    2 cups peeled and chopped fresh peaches

Grease 10-inch tube pan with 2 tablespoons of butter; sprinkle pan with ¼ cup sugar. Cream remaining butter; gradually add remaining sugar, beating well. Add eggs, one at a time, beating well after each addition. Add vanilla and mix well. Combine 2¾ cups flour, baking powder and salt; gradually add to creamed mixture, beating until well blended. Dredge peaches with remaining ¼ cup flour. Fold peaches into batter. Pour batter into prepared pan. Bake at 325° for 1 hour and 10 minutes or until cake tests done. Cool in pan 10 minutes; remove from pan and cool completely on wire rack.

PEACH POUND CAKE

This cake is fun to make in summertime when fresh peaches are at their peak, but it will work just as well with frozen peaches that have been thawed and chopped.

    1 cup butter or margarine, softened
    3 cups sugar
    6 eggs
    3 cups plain flour
    ¼ teaspoon baking soda
    ¼ teaspoon salt
    ½ cup sour cream
    2 cups fresh peaches, peeled and finely chopped
    1 teaspoon vanilla extract
    1 teaspoon almond extract

Cream together butter or margarine and sugar until light and fluffy. Add eggs, one at a time, beating well after each addition. Combine flour, soda and salt in separate bowl. Mix together sour cream and chopped peaches. Add dry ingredients to creamed mixture alternately with sour cream and peaches, beginning and ending with dry ingredients. Add these ingredients with a minimum of beating. Fold in to evenly distribute through batter. Stir in vanilla and almond extract. Pour batter into a greased and floured 10-inch tube pan. Bake at 350° for 1 hour and 15 minutes or until cake tests done. Cool in pan 10 minutes; remove from pan and let cool completely on wire rack.

POUND CAKES MADE WITH PEANUTS

PEANUT BUTTER POUND CAKE

Peanut butter in the batter gives a nutty flavor to this cake. For variation, sprinkle ⅓ cup finely chopped peanuts onto the batter to give the cake a crunchy topping.

- 1¼ cups butter
- 2 cups sugar
- 6 eggs
- 1 teaspoon vanilla extract
- ½ cup peanut butter, smooth or crunchy
- 2 cups flour
- 1 teaspoon baking powder
- ¼ teaspoon salt

Cream butter and sugar until light yellow. Beat in eggs, one at a time, until thoroughly blended. Add vanilla extract and slowly beat in peanut butter. Sift flour with baking powder and salt. Add flour mixture, a little at a time, until well blended. Spoon batter into a greased and floured 10-inch tube pan. Bake at 350° for 45 minutes; reduce heat to 325° and bake 15 to 20 minutes longer, or until cake tests done. Cool in pan on wire rack for 10 minutes, then remove from pan and cool completely on wire rack.

PEANUT BUTTER BROWN SUGAR POUND CAKE

Brown sugar and peanut butter keep this one moist for a week. It's also delicious with the chocolate glaze. NOTE that this is a recipe for loaf pan or small Bundt pan.

> 2 cups flour
> 2 teaspoons baking powder
> ¾ cup creamy peanut butter
> ½ cup butter or margarine, softened
> 1 cup granulated sugar
> ½ cup packed brown sugar
> 2 eggs
> 2 teaspoons vanilla extract
> ⅔ cup milk

Grease 10-cup loaf pan or 10-cup fluted baking pan; dust with flour. On waxed paper, combine flour and baking powder, set aside. In a large bowl, beat peanut butter and butter with sugars until blended, scraping bowl often with rubber spatula. Increase speed to medium-high; beat until creamy, about 3 minutes, occasionally scraping bowl. Reduce speed to low; add eggs, one at a time, beating well after each addition. Beat in vanilla. Alternately add flour mixture and milk, beginning and ending with flour mixture; beat just until smooth. Spoon batter into prepared pan and spread evenly. Bake at 325° for 60 to 65 minutes of until toothpick inserted near center comes out clean. Cool cake in pan on wire rack for 15 minutes. Loosen cake from side of pan; invert onto wire rack to cool completely.

RICH CHOCOLATE GLAZE

> 3 oz milk chocolate, broken into pieces
> 3 Tablespoons butter or margarine
> 1 Tablespoon light corn syrup
> 1 Tablespoon milk

In 1-quart glass measure, heat chocolate with remaining ingredients in microwave on High for 1½ to 2 minutes until smooth, stirring twice during cooking. Immediately pour glaze over top of cooled cake, allowing it to run down sides. Let cake stand at least 30 minutes to allow glaze to set before serving.

POUND CAKES MADE WITH PECANS

PECAN POUND CAKE

This crunchy top cake is chock full of nuts.

    1½ cups butter
    1 box (1 lb) 4-X powdered sugar
    6 eggs
    3½ cups plain flour, sifted
    1 teaspoon vanilla extract
    1 teaspoon lemon extract
    3 cups chopped pecans

Cream butter and powdered sugar. Add eggs, one at a time, beating after each addition. Fold in flour, extracts and pecans. Pour into a greased and floured 10-inch tube pan. Bake at 300° for 40 minutes and then at 325° for 30 minutes, or until cake tests done. Cool in pan 10 minutes, then remove from pan and cool completely on wire rack.

PECAN SOUR CREAM POUND CAKE

This cake is perfect with strawberry sauce or fresh strawberries and cream. It is even better when made a day ahead.

- 2 sticks (1 cup) butter
- 2¾ cups sugar
- 6 eggs
- 3 cups plain flour
- 1 teaspoon baking powder
- ½ teaspoon salt
- 1 cup sour cream
- 1 Tablespoon vanilla
- 1 Tablespoon lemon extract
- 1 cup finely chopped pecans

Cream butter and sugar until light and fluffy. Add eggs, one at a time, blending well after each one. Add the dry ingredients (flour, baking powder, salt mixed together) alternately with the sour cream. Blend in the flavorings and the nuts. Pour the batter into a greased and floured 10-inch tube pan or Bundt pan. Bake at 325° for 1 hour and 30 minutes or until cake tests done.

Strawberry Sauce

- 3 quarts strawberries
- ½ cup sugar

Wash, hull and slice berries into a container. Mash berries and add the sugar. Stir and chill until ready to use. Pour over pound cake and top with whipped cream.

PECAN HAZELNUT POUND CAKE

If you love a nutty flavored cake, then this one is for you! Try the glazes, white chocolate over dark chocolate, for an especially festive cake.

2½ cups plain flour
½ cup finely ground pecans
1 Tablespoon baking powder
½ teaspoon salt
¾ cup unsalted butter, softened
2 cups sugar
4 eggs
¾ cup buttermilk
¼ cup hazelnut liqueur
1 teaspoon vanilla
Garnish (Optional): ¼ cup pecans, coarsely chopped

Coat a 12-cup Bundt pan with nonstick cooking spray. Dust with flour. Combine flour, pecans, baking powder and salt in medium sized bowl. Beat butter and sugar in large bowl until creamy, about 4 minutes. Beat in eggs, one at a time, beating well after each addition. Alternately beat in flour mixture and buttermilk, hazelnut liqueur and vanilla, beginning and ending with flour mixture, until well blended and smooth. Pour into prepared pan. Bake at 350° for 50 minutes or until tester inserted comes out clean. Let cake cool in pan 15 minutes. Remove cake from pan to rack; let cool completely.

DARK CHOCOLATE GLAZE

⅓ cup evaporated milk
⅛ teaspoon salt
5 squares (1 ounce each) bittersweet chocolate, chopped

Combine milk and salt in small saucepan. Bring just to a boil over medium heat. Add chocolate; stir until melted and smooth. Spoon over cake; let stand until set.

White Chocolate Glaze

5 squares (1 ounce each) white baking chocolate, chopped
3 Tablespoons solid vegetable shortening
1/8 teaspoon salt

Combine chocolate, shortening and salt in small heavy saucepan. Place over very low heat, stirring occasionally, until melted and smooth. Let cool slightly, about 8 minutes. Spoon over top of Dark Chocolate Glaze; let set. Garnish with chopped pecans, if desired.

TOASTED PECAN- BROWN SUGAR POUND CAKE WITH CARAMEL SAUCE

This is a wonderful cake with a surprisingly light texture. It's perfect for a make-ahead dessert that is dressy enough to serve anywhere.

½ cup butter, room temperature
2½ cups light brown sugar
2 Tablespoons lemon juice
6 eggs, room temperature
2¾ cups cake flour
½ teaspoon baking soda
½ teaspoon salt
1 cup sour cream, room temperature
1 Tablespoon vanilla extract
2 cups pecan halves, toasted at 325° for 10 minutes, then coarsely chopped

Butter and flour a 10-inch tube pan. Cream the butter and sugar on high speed for 5 minutes, then add lemon juice and beat for two more minutes. Add eggs, one at a time, mixing well after each addition. Sift the flour with the soda and salt. Combine the cream and vanilla extract. Add half of the flour to the batter, blending well, then add all of the sour cream, again mixing well. Blend in the remaining flour. Fold in the prepared pecans. Transfer the batter to the pan and bake at 325° for approximately 60 to 70 minutes, or until a cake tester comes out clean. Let cool completely. For serving, give each person a generous slice of cake and pass the bowl of chilled Caramel Sauce (below).

Caramel Sauce

1½ cups sugar
¾ cup water
¾ cup cream

Place sugar and water in a small heavy saucepan; stir over medium high heat. After sugar has dissolved, let the syrup boil until it turns a gold brown color. Be careful not to let it burn or turn too dark. Remove saucepan from heat and gradually add the cream. Whisk until smooth and return to low heat and cook until it thickens slightly, about 5 minutes. After the sauce has cooled, place in refrigerator.

PECAN CREAM CHEESE POUND CAKE

For a little extra zip, try substituting bourbon for the milk in this recipe.

1½ cups butter or margarine, softened
1 8-oz package cream cheese, softened
3 cups sugar
6 eggs
3 cups all-purpose flour
½ teaspoon salt
¼ cup milk
1½ teaspoons vanilla extract
1½ cups pecans, chopped and toasted*

*Heat the pecans in microwave and then coat them with a little flour before folding them into the batter.

Beat butter and cream cheese at medium speed about 2 minutes or until creamy. Gradually add sugar beating 5 minutes. Add eggs one at a time beating just until yellow disappears. Combine flour and salt and add to butter mixture alternately with bourbon or milk. Beginning and ending with flour mixture. Beat at low speed just until blended after each addition. Stir in vanilla and chopped pecans. Pour batter in to a greased and floured 10-inch tube pan. Bake at 325° for 1 hour and 30 minutes or until a long wooden pick inserted in center comes out clean. Cool in pan on a wire rack 10 to 15 minutes. Remove from pan and cool completely on a wire rack.

Cream Cheese Icing:

1 box 4-X confectioners' sugar
1 (3-oz.) package cream cheese, softened
¼ cup butter, softened
2 teaspoons vanilla extract

Cream all ingredients together and ice completely cooled cake.

MISSISSIPPI PRALINE POUND CAKE WITH BOURBON GLAZE

This recipe has all the elements of the old South – it tastes best on a long, low veranda.

- 1½ cups butter
- 1¾ cups lightly packed brown sugar
- 6 eggs, separated
- ½ teaspoon salt
- ½ teaspoon baking powder
- ½ teaspoon baking soda
- 3 cups flour
- 7/8 cup buttermilk
- 1 teaspoon vanilla extract
- 1 tablespoon bourbon
- 1 cup chopped pecans
- ½ cup sugar

Beat butter until very light and gradually beat in the brown sugar. Add egg yolks one by one. Sift salt, baking powder, baking soda and flour together. Add to the butter mixture in 3 parts, alternating with the buttermilk. Stir in vanilla extract, bourbon and pecans. Beat the egg whites until frothy and slowly add the granulated sugar. Beat until stiff peaks form. Fold into the batter, turn into a greased and floured tube pan. Bake at 325° for about 1 hour and 15 minutes, or until a clean straw inserted in the middle of the cake comes out clean. Let cool 15 to 20 minutes then invert to turn out.

BOURBON GLAZE

- ½ cup light brown sugar
- ¼ cup butter
- 2 Tablespoons water
- ¼ cup bourbon

Mix ingredients and pour over warm cake.

POUND CAKES MADE WITH PINEAPPLE

PINEAPPLE POUND CAKE

Pineapple gives this pound cake a tangy-sweet flavor. Serve with a dollop of whipped cream topped with a sprinkle of pecans. Note that this is a cold oven pound cake.

- 1 cup butter
- 2 cups sugar
- 6 large eggs
- 3½ cups plain flour
- 2 teaspoons baking powder
- ½ teaspoon salt
- 1 cup evaporated milk
- 2 teaspoons vanilla extract
- 1 cup canned crushed pineapple, drained

Beat the butter and sugar together until light and fluffy. Beat in the eggs one at a time, beating well after each addition. Add the combined dry ingredients alternately with the milk, beating just until smooth. Add the vanilla. Fold in the drained pineapple. Pour the batter into a greased and floured 10-inch tube pan and place in cold oven. Set the temperature to 350° and bake for 1 hour, or until cake tests done. Cool the cake in the pan for 30 minutes before turning onto wire rack to cool completely. For a finished look, dust the cake with sifted confectioners' sugar.

GLAZE

- ¼ cup butter or margarine
- 1½ cups powdered sugar
- 1 cup crushed pineapple, drained

Combine ingredients and pour over cake while it is still hot.

HAWAIIAN POUND CAKE

What's more Hawaiian than pineapple? Add some coconut for a totally tropical pound cake.

- 1 cup shortening or margarine
- 3 cups sugar
- 6 eggs
- 4 cups sifted plain flour
- 1 teaspoon baking powder
- ¼ teaspoon salt
- 1 cup milk
- 1 small can crushed pineapple, undrained
- 1 small can flaked coconut (or 6 to 8 oz. package of frozen coconut)
- 1 teaspoon lemon extract or lemon juice
- 1 teaspoon vanilla extract (optional)

Cream shortening or margarine until fluffy. Add sugar and blend until fluffy. Add eggs, one at a time, beating well after each addition. Add mixture of flour, baking powder, and salt, alternating with additions of milk; mixing well after each addition. Add flour first and last. Stir in pineapple and coconut until well mixed. Add flavorings and blend. Place in a large tube pan that has been greased and floured. Bake at 350° for 1 hour and 30 minutes or until golden brown. Cool in pan 5 minutes and invert on serving dish; allow to cool completely before glazing.

Glaze

- ½ cup butter, softened
- juice of one lemon
- 1 cup confectioners' sugar

Mix all ingredients together and spread on cooled cake.

MOTHER'S POUND CAKE

This cake is flavored by using pineapple juice as the liquid in the recipe. We don't know whose mother came up with the idea, but it was a good one.

    1 cup butter
    ½ cup margarine
    1 pound box powdered sugar
    6 eggs
    1 powdered box filled with plain flour
    ⅛ teaspoon salt
    1 cup pineapple juice
    ½ teaspoon vanilla extract
    ½ teaspoon almond extract

Cream butter and margarine; add sugar ¼ at a time and mix well. Add eggs, one at a time, beating after each addition. Add flour and juice alternately, beginning and ending with flour; mix well after each addition. Add flavorings and blend well. Pour into a greased and floured 10-inch tube pan. Bake at 325° for 1 hour and 20 minutes, or until cake tests done. Cool 10 minutes in pan; remove and cool completely on wire rack.

KENTUCKY SOUR MASH POUND CAKE

This cake contains not a drop of sour mash, so who knows how it got its name? It's a somewhat unusual recipe, but the combination of pineapple, nuts and cinnamon is a mouth-watering delight.

> 1½ cups cooking oil
> 2 cups sugar
> 4 eggs
> 2½ cups self- rising flour
> 1 small can crushed pineapple and juice
> 2½ teaspoons cinnamon
> 1 cup pecans, chopped

Cream oil and sugar. Add eggs, one at a time, beating after each addition. Add flour, alternating with pineapple; mix well after each addition. Stir in cinnamon and nuts. Pour batter into a greased and floured 10-inch tube pan. Bake at 350° for 1 hour or until cake tests done. Cool in pan for 10 minutes; remove from pan and cool completely on wire rack.

Brown Sugar Frosting

> ½ cup margarine
> 1 cup light brown sugar
> ½ cup evaporated milk

Mix all ingredients together and boil for 5 to 6 minutes. Beat and cool. Spread on cake.

PINA COLADA POUND CAKE

This tropical delight is made without alcohol. Garnish it with shredded sweetened coconut and thin strips of lime rind.

- 2½ cups all-purpose flour
- ½ teaspoon baking soda
- ½ teaspoon salt
- 1 cup unsalted butter, softened
- 2 cups sugar
- 4 eggs
- 1 container (8 ounces) vanilla yogurt
- ¼ cup canned crushed pineapple
- 1 teaspoon grated lime rind
- 1 teaspoon coconut extract
- ½ teaspoon vanilla

Grease a 12-cup Bundt pan and lightly dust with flour; tap out excess flour. Whisk together flour, baking soda and salt in a medium-size bowl until well mixed. Beat together butter and sugar in second bowl until light and fluffy, about 3 minutes. Beat in eggs, one at a time, beating well after each addition. Mix together yogurt, pineapple and lime rind in small bowl. On low speed, beat flour mixture into butter mixture in 3 additions, alternating with the yogurt mixture, starting and ending with the flour mixture. Add coconut extract and vanilla, and beat on medium speed for 3 minutes. Pour the batter into prepared pan. Bake at 325° for 60 minutes or until a wooden pick inserted in the center of the cake comes out clean. Transfer pan to wire rack and cool for about 15 to 20 minutes. Turn out cake onto rack; turn right side up. Cool completely.

Glaze

- 2 teaspoons fresh lime juice
- ½ cup confectioners' sugar

Whisk together lime juice and confectioners' sugar in small bowl until good drizzling consistency. Drizzle over cake.

PINEAPPLE MACADAMIA NUT POUND CAKE

To the combination of pineapple and macadamia, a vanilla bean is added to create a cake that is as stunning and exotic as the lands from which the ingredients come.

    1½ cups crushed pineapple (in heavy syrup)
    1 vanilla bean, cut in thirds and split
    1 teaspoon vanilla extract
    ¾ cup butter, room temperature
    1 cup light brown sugar
    ½ cup sugar
    3 eggs, room temperature
    2¼ cups flour
    ½ teaspoon salt
    ½ teaspoon baking powder
    2 egg whites (room temperature)
    ⅓ cup sugar
    1 cup macadamia nuts, sliced in chunks

Butter and flour a 10-inch tube pan. Mix the crushed pineapple with the cut vanilla bean, scraping out as many seeds as possible. Add the vanilla extract. Leave the bean in the pineapple while preparing the cake. In a large mixing bowl, cream the butter, slowly adding both the sugars. Add the eggs, one at a time, mixing well after each addition. Whisk the flour in a bowl with the salt and baking powder to mix. Gently blend the flour into the cake batter. Beat the egg whites until soft peaks form and slowly add the ⅓ cup sugar. Beat for 2 minutes. Remove the vanilla bean from the pineapple and then mix the pineapple with the cake batter. Add the macadamia nuts and then gently but thoroughly fold the egg whites into the batter. Fill the prepared pan with the mixture. Sprinkle with the topping and bake at 350° for 55 to 60 minutes or until a cake tester comes out clean. Cool the cake on a wire rack for 15 minutes, then turn out onto a rack and cool completely.

TOPPING

2 Tablespoons sugar mixed with 1 teaspoon cinnamon; sprinkle on cake.

POUND CAKES MADE WITH PISTACHIO NUTS

PISTACHIO POUND CAKE

This cake was created especially for pistachio lovers but, with its unique taste and texture, it will be a hit with everyone who tries it.

- 1 cup butter
- 1½ cups sugar
- 6 eggs
- 3 cups flour
- ½ teaspoon salt
- ½ cup cream
- ¾ teaspoon almond extract
- 2 teaspoons vanilla extract
- 1½ teaspoons lemon extract
- 1½ cups chopped pistachios

Butter and flour a 10-inch tube pan. Cream butter on high speed for 2 to 3 minutes. Slowly add sugar and continue beating for 5 minutes. Add eggs, one at a time, mixing well after each addition. Sift together the flour and salt. Add ½ the flour to the batter. Mix in the cream and then the remaining flour. Beat in the extracts. Fold in the chopped pistachios. Pour batter into the prepared pan and bake at 325° for 1 hour and 15 minutes or until cake tests done. Cool cake in pan on a wire rack for about 15 minutes, then turn out onto a rack to cool completely.

POUND CAKES MADE WITH PLUMS

PLUM POUND CAKE

If you love the taste of plums, you don't have to wait until they are in season. This recipe uses baby food. This cake is a delicious blend of fruit and spices.

- 2 cups self-rising flour
- 2 cups sugar
- 1 cup cooking oil
- 3 eggs, beaten
- 2 small jars plum baby food
- 1 teaspoon cinnamon
- 1 teaspoon cloves
- 1 cup nuts, chopped and floured

Mix flour and sugar well in a mixing bowl. Add oil and eggs. Stir well to mix. Add spices, plums and nuts. Bake in a well-greased Bundt pan at 350° for 45 minutes to 1 hour. Cool for 5 minutes in pan and then invert onto a wire rack to cool completely.

POUND CAKES MADE WITH POPPY SEEDS

LEMON POPPY POUND CAKE

This is a rich, lemony cake, soaked with a rich lemon glaze after baking. Note that this is a small recipe, for a loaf pan. It tastes best if it sits a day before serving.

    2 cups unsalted butter
    2 cups sugar
    6 eggs
    4 cups flour
    1 teaspoon salt
    2 Tablespoon lemon zest
    6 Tablespoon poppy seeds

Cream together the butter and sugar until light and fluffy. Beat in the eggs, one at a time. Stir in the combined dry ingredients. Pour into a greased and floured 10-inch tube pan. Bake at 350° for 1 hour and 20 minutes or until cake tests done. Place the pan on a wire rack with a cookie sheet underneath for glazing.

LEMON GLAZE

    ¾ cup sugar
    ¾ cup lemon juice

Combine sugar and lemon juice in a small saucepan, bring to a boil, then remove from heat and set aside to cool. Prick the top of the cake several times with a toothpick. Brush the top of the cake with the glaze, allowing it to run down the sides and soak into the cake. Allow cake to cool slightly before removing from pan to the wire rack to cool completely. When completely cooled, wrap the cake in foil or heavy plastic wrap and let it sit for a day before serving.

LOW CHOLESTEROL POPPY SEED POUND CAKE

It is difficult to find a tasty pound cake that is low in fat and cholesterol, but this light and airy cake is a nice surprise for those who normally have to say no to baked goods.

> non-stick cooking spray
> ¼ cup poppy seeds
> ½ cup margarine, room temperature
> ¾ cup granulated sugar
> 3 egg whites, room temperature
> 1 Tablespoon vanilla extract
> ¾ teaspoon lemon extract
> 2½ cups flour
> ¾ teaspoon baking soda
> ¼ teaspoon salt
> 1 cup low-fat lemon yogurt
> 1½ teaspoons finely grated lemon zest

Spray non-stick cooking spray on the bottom and sides of a loaf pan 8½ x 4½ inches and approximately 3 inches deep. Dust lightly with flour and set aside. In a dry, non-stick skillet, carefully toast the poppy seeds until lightly toasted and fragrant. Cream together the margarine and sugar. Add egg whites and beat 4 minutes. Add vanilla and lemon extracts. Combine the flour, soda and salt. Combine the yogurt and lemon zest. Add the dry ingredients alternately with the yogurt, beginning and ending with the flour mixture. Fold in the poppy seeds, being certain to incorporate well. Pour into the prepared pan and bake at 325° for 40 to 55 minutes. Note: check the cake after 40 minutes of cooking. Although in some ovens the cooking time may be longer, it is important not to overcook this cake, as it will be too dry. After cooking, let the cake rest in the pan for 5 to 10 minutes, and then turn out onto a wire rack to cool completely.

POUND CAKES MADE WITH POTATOES

POTATO CHOCOLATE ORANGE POUND CAKE

Whoever heard of putting potatoes in a pound cake? Don't knock it 'til you've tried it!

- 1½ cups butter
- 3 cups sugar
- 5 eggs
- 3 cups plain flour
- ½ cup unsweetened cocoa
- 1 teaspoon baking soda
- ¼ teaspoon salt
- 1 8-oz. container sour cream
- 1 large potato cooked and mashed (about 1 cup)
- ½ cup unsweetened orange juice
- 2 teaspoons orange extract

Cream butter and sugar together until light and fluffy, scraping down sides of bowl frequently. Add eggs, one at a time, beating thoroughly after each addition. Combine dry ingredients (flour, cocoa, soda and salt) and add alternately with sour cream, beginning and ending with flour mixture. Blend in other ingredients and mix well. Spoon batter into a greased and floured 10-inch tube pan. Bake at 350° for 1 hour and 30 minutes, or until cake tests done. Cook cake on a wire rack for 15 minutes. Loosen cake from pan with a knife, turn pan upside down and remove cake. Place on wire rack to cool completely.

CREAM CHEESE ICING

- 3 oz. cream cheese
- 2 Tablespoons milk
- 2 cups confectioners' sugar
- 1 teaspoon vanilla extract

In small bowl, beat cream cheese and milk until smooth. Beat in vanilla. Gradually beat in confectioners' sugar until well blended, with a good spreading consistency. Add additional milk if necessary. Spread frosting over top of cooled cake.

POUND CAKES MADE WITH PRUNES

PRUNE POUND CAKE WITH WALNUT ICING

Don't be put off by the prunes; they make a moist, rich and absolutely delicious cake!

- ¾ cup butter, room temperature
- 2 cups sugar
- 3 eggs
- 2 cups flour
- 1 teaspoon baking soda
- 1 teaspoon salt
- 1 teaspoon cinnamon
- 1 teaspoon cloves
- 1 teaspoon freshly grated nutmeg
- 1 cup buttermilk, room temperature
- 1 teaspoon vanilla extract
- 1 cup cooked mashed prunes

Butter and flour a 9-inch Bundt pan. Cream the butter until it lightens in color. Add the sugar and continue to beat for 3 minutes. Beat in the eggs, one at a time, and mix well. In another bowl, whisk together the flour, soda, salt and spices. Alternately add the flour and buttermilk to the batter in the following manner: ⅓ flour; ½ buttermilk; ⅓ flour; ½ buttermilk; then the remaining ⅓ flour. Fold in the vanilla and prunes. Transfer to the prepared pan and bake at 300° for 55-60 minutes. Let cool on rack for about 15 minutes then turn out onto plate to be iced. Let cake cool completely before slicing and serving.

Walnut Icing

¼ cup butter
1 cup sugar
½ teaspoon baking soda
½ cup buttermilk
2 teaspoons white Karo syrup
1 cup finely shopped walnuts
½ teaspoon vanilla extract

As soon as the cake is in the oven, combine the icing ingredients in a saucepan, except the vanilla, and allow to simmer about 45 minutes to an hour, until it becomes darker in color and thicker. Remove pan from heat and let the icing cool as the finished cake cools in the pan on the rack (about 15 minutes). Slowly spoon icing onto the warm cake.

POUND CAKES MADE WITH PUMPKIN

PUMPKIN POUND CAKE

At first glance this will remind you of a pumpkin pie, but watch out for the rum added to the cake batter. For variation, add 1 teaspoon almond extract and omit the cinnamon, cloves, apple pie spice and rum. For less pumpkin flavor, the amount of pumpkin can be reduced to 1 cup.

1 cup butter or margarine, softened
3 cups sugar
5 large eggs
3 cups plain flour
2 teaspoons baking powder
½ teaspoon baking soda
½ teaspoon salt
2 teaspoons ground cinnamon
¼ teaspoon ground cloves
⅛ teaspoon apple pie spice
2 cups mashed pumpkin, canned or cooked
⅓ cup rum

Beat butter at medium speed with an electric mixer about 2 minutes or until soft and creamy. Gradually add sugar, beating at medium speed 5 to 7 minutes. Add eggs, one at a time, beating just until yellow disappears. Combine flour and next 6 ingredients. Combine pumpkin and rum. Add flour mixture to creamed mixture alternately with pumpkin mixture, beginning and ending with flour mixture. Mix at lowest speed just until blended after each addition. Pour batter into a greased and floured 10-inch tube pan. Bake at 325° for 1 hour and 25 minutes or until a wooden pick inserted in center of cake comes out clean. Cool cake in pan on a wire rack 10 minutes; remove from pan and let cool completely on wire rack.

Walnut Sauce

1 cup light brown sugar
¼ cup dark corn syrup
½ cup whipping cream
2 Tablespoons butter
1 dash salt
½ teaspoon vanilla extract
½ cup chopped walnuts

In medium saucepan, combine brown sugar, corn syrup, whipping cream, butter and salt. Bring to a boil over medium heat, stirring constantly. Reduce heat to low; simmer 5 minutes, stirring constantly. Remove from heat; stir in vanilla and walnuts. Serve warm sauce over cake. Refrigerate any leftover sauce.

PUMPKIN PIE POUND CAKE

This cake has all the seasoning and flavors associated with a traditional pumpkin pie, but it is a wonderful and welcome change from the ubiquitous dessert commonly served at Thanksgiving and Christmas.

1 cup Crisco shortening
1 cup sugar
½ cup dark brown sugar
5 eggs, room temperature
1 cup canned pumpkin
2¼ cups flour
2 teaspoons cinnamon
1 teaspoon freshly grated nutmeg
½ teaspoon mace
½ teaspoon salt
1 teaspoon baking soda
½ cup orange juice, room temperature
2 teaspoons vanilla
1¼ cups chopped pecans

Butter and flour a 10-½ inch decorative Bundt pan. Cream the shortening to lighten it, then gradually add both sugars, continuing to cream for about 5 minutes on high speed. Add the eggs, one a time, mixing well after each addition. Blend the pumpkin into the batter. In a bowl, whisk together the flour, spices, salt, and baking soda, mixing well. Gradually beat the dry ingredients into the batter until well incorporated. Fold in the orange juice, vanilla and chopped pecans. Pour the batter into the prepared pan, smoothing the tope of the cake. Bake at 325° for 55-60 minutes, or until a tester comes out clean. Allow the cake to rest in the pan on a wire rack for 10-15 minutes, then turn out onto a rack and cool completely before icing.

Icing

1 cup confectioners' sugar
4 Tablespoons butter, melted
2 Tablespoons orange juice
¼ teaspoon orange extract

Sift the sugar and then thorough mix with the remaining ingredients. Allow the icing to rest and thicken somewhat before icing the cooled cake. The icing will run down the sides of the cake when poured over the top.

POUND CAKES MADE WITH QUINCE

QUINCE POUND CAKE

This is a great way to do something else with quince besides traditional jam or jelly, and it's a nice change from other "autumn" cakes and pies. It will keep in an airtight container at room temperature for about 4 days.

Quince

2 medium quinces (about 1 pound total)
2 cups water
¾ cup sugar
½ cup honey
2 teaspoons fresh lemon juice
½ teaspoon cinnamon

Cake

1¾ cups all-purpose flour
¼ teaspoon cinnamon
¼ teaspoon salt
½ cup unsalted butter
1½ cups sugar
1 large egg yolk
3 eggs
½ cup heavy cream
1 teaspoon vanilla

For quince: Peel, quarter, and core quinces. Cut quarters crosswise into ⅛-inch-thick slices. In a 3-quart heavy saucepan bring quince, water, sugar, honey, lemon juice, and cinnamon to a boil. Reduce heat and simmer mixture, stirring occasionally, 2½ hours (quince will be deep pinkish orange). Drain quince in a large sieve and transfer to paper towels. Pat quince dry and cool. Chill quince, covered, at least 1 hour and up to 3 days.

For cake: Butter and flour a 9-inch tube pan, knocking out excess flour. Into a bowl sift together twice flour, cinnamon, and salt. In another bowl, beat together butter and sugar until combined well. Add yolk and whole eggs, 1 at a time, to butter mixture, beating well after each addition. Beat in half of flour mixture and all of cream until just combined. Add remaining flour mixture and vanilla, beating until just combined. Fold cooked quince slices into batter until combined well and spread batter evenly in pan. Bake at 350° for 1¼ hours, or until a tester comes out clean, and cool in pan on a rack 20 minutes. Turn cake out onto rack and cool completely.

POUND CAKES MADE WITH RAISINS

NUT AND RAISIN POUND CAKE

This is basic plain pound cake recipe, with nuts and raisins to make it fancy enough for a special occasion.

- 3 cups sugar
- 1 cup butter
- ½ cup vegetable shortening
- 6 eggs
- 3¼ cups plain flour
- ¼ teaspoon salt
- ½ teaspoon baking powder
- 1 cup milk
- 1 cup raisins (chopped)
- 1 cup chopped nuts

Combine sugar, butter, and shortening; cream until light and fluffy. Add eggs, one at a time, beating well after each addition. Add flour mixed with salt and baking powder to creamed mixture, alternating with milk; beat well after each addition. Stir in raisins and nuts. Pour batter into a greased and floured 10-inch tube pan. Bake at 300° for 1 hour and 40 minutes, or until cake tests done. Cool 10 minutes in pan; remove from pan and let cake cool completely on wire rack.

RAISIN HONEY POUND CAKE

This nut and raisin cake is sweetened with honey and flavored with a touch of lemon extract. The raisin and lemon combination is unusual, but very tasty.

- 1 cup raisins, chopped
- 1 cup shortening
- 1 cup honey
- 4 eggs, well-beaten
- 3 cups sifted plain flour
- 3 teaspoons baking powder
- ½ teaspoon salt
- 1 teaspoon vanilla extract
- 1 teaspoon lemon extract
- ¾ cup chopped walnuts

Rinse, drain, and dry raisins; cut fine with scissors. Set aside. Cream shortening; gradually add honey. Add beaten eggs and blend. Gradually mix in dry ingredients, sifted 3 times, then beat until smooth. Add raisins, extracts and nuts, and blend. Pour into a greased and floured 10-inch tube pan. Bake at 300° for 2 hours or until cake tests done. Cool in pan for 10 minutes; cool completely on wire rack.

DOUBLE-TROUBLE POUND CAKE

A king-size pound cake with two kinds of flour, two kinds of dairy products and two cups each of nuts and raisins. It's big on taste, too!

- 1 cup butter
- 1 Tablespoon vegetable shortening
- 2½ cups sugar
- 6 eggs
- 1½ cups plain flour
- 1½ cups self-rising flour
- 8 ounces whipping cream
- 8 ounces sour cream
- 1 teaspoon vanilla extract
- 2 cups raisins, chopped and floured
- 2 cups nuts, chopped and floured

Cream butter and shortening with sugar. Add eggs, one at a time, mixing well after each addition. Mix the two flours together in a separate bowl. Mix whipping cream and sour cream together in a separate bowl. Add flour and cream mixtures alternately, beginning and ending with flour mixture. Stir in vanilla, raisins and nuts. Pour batter into a greased and floured 10-inch tube pan. Bake at 325° for 1 hour and 20 minutes or until cake tests done. Cool 10 minutes in pan; remove from pan and cool completely on wire rack.

POUND CAKES MADE WITH RASPBERRIES

RASPBERRY SWIRL POUND CAKE

This recipe makes a cake with a traditional pound cake texture and weight but with an unexpected and delicate flavor. It's also a beautiful and delicious cake, suitable for the most special occasions.

Raspberry Swirl

2 cups fresh raspberries
2 Tablespoons red currant jelly
2 Tablespoons framboise (raspberry liqueur)
1 Tablespoon cornstarch

Cake

1 cup butter, room temperature
6 oz cream cheese, room temperature
2½ cups sugar
6 eggs, room temperature
3 cups sifted flour
pinch salt
2 teaspoons vanilla extract
3 Tablespoons grated or finely minced lemon zest

For raspberry swirl, put raspberries through a food mill or puree in a food processor, being sure to strain out any seeds. Melt jelly in a small saucepan. Add the raspberry puree and warm over low heat. Dissolve cornstarch in the framboise and add to the saucepan. Bring to a simmer, whisking until thickened. Remove from heat and cool completely.

For cake, cream together the butter and cream cheese until fluffy. Gradually add sugar, beating until lighter and fluffier. Add eggs, one at a time, beating well after each addition. Sift the flour with the salt and then slowly add to the batter, in three additions, being careful not to overbeat. Fold in the vanilla and lemon with a spatula. Place ⅓ batter in pan, smoothing it evenly. In a circle, add ½ of the raspberry puree, not allowing it to touch the sides of the pan. Add ⅓ of the batter, gently covering the puree. Add the remaining puree in the same fashion, and finish with the remaining batter. Pour batter into a buttered and floured 9-inch tube pan. Bake at 325° for 1 hour and 5-10 minutes, until a tester comes out clean. Allow to cool in the pan for 15 minutes before unmolding. Cool completely on a rack.

POUND CAKES MADE WITH STRAWBERRIES

STRAWBERRY POUND CAKE

This large and colorful cake is one of the old-fashioned recipes that calls for separating the eggs. Don't let that stop you—this is a good one.

> 2 cups margarine
> 2¾ cups sugar
> 8 eggs, separated
> 3½ cups plain flour
> 1 cup strawberries, mashed (fresh or frozen)
> 1 teaspoon red food coloring

Beat egg whites and add 6 Tablespoons of the sugar; let set in refrigerator while mixing the cake. Cream margarine and add remaining sugar; mix well. Add egg yolks, one at a time, beating well after each one. Add flour and strawberries alternately; mix well after each addition. Stir in food coloring. Fold in beaten egg whites. Pour batter into greased and floured 10-inch tube pan. Bake at 350° for 1 hour and 30 minutes or until cake tests done. Cool 10 minutes in pan; remove from pan and cool completely on wire rack.

FROSTING

> ½ cup melted butter
> 1 box (1 lb) confectioners' sugar
> ½ cup frozen strawberries, thawed

Mix ingredients thoroughly and spread on cooled cake.

STRAWBERRY PECAN POUND CAKE

This colorful cake has strawberries and pecans in the batter and a sweet strawberry glaze on top.

> 1 package (16 oz.) frozen sweetened sliced strawberries
> 1 cup butter-flavored shortening
> 2 cups sugar
> 4 eggs
> 3 cups flour
> 1 teaspoon baking soda
> ½ teaspoon baking powder
> ½ teaspoon salt
> ⅔ cup buttermilk
> ½ cup chopped pecans
> 1 teaspoon vanilla extract
> ¼ teaspoon almond or strawberry extract

Drain strawberries, reserving ½ cup juice. Chop the strawberries; set juice and berries aside. Cream shortening and sugar together. Add eggs, one at a time, beating well after each addition. Combine the dry ingredients; add to creamed mixture alternately with buttermilk. Stir in the pecans, chopped strawberries and extracts. Pour into greased and floured tube pan. Bake at 325° for 1 hour and 15 minutes or until cake tests done. Cool for 10 minutes; remove from pan to a wire rack.

STRAWBERRY GLAZE AND SAUCE

> 1 cup sugar
> juice reserved from frozen strawberries (above)
> ½ cup sliced fresh strawberries
> ½ teaspoon vanilla extract
> ½ teaspoon almond or strawberry extract

In small saucepan, combine the sugar and reserved strawberry juice. Add the sliced strawberries. Bring to a boil; cook and stir for 1 minute. Remove from the heat; stir in extracts. Brush some of the sauce over the warm cake. Serve cake with remaining sauce.

POUND CAKES MADE WITH SWEET POTATOES

SWEET POTATO POUND CAKE

This version is a spicy, aromatic cake that is especially good when served with the Spiced Whipped Cream.

- 1 cup butter, softened
- 2 cups sugar
- 4 eggs
- 2 cups cooked, mashed sweet potatoes
- 2½ cups flour
- ¼ teaspoon salt
- 1 teaspoon baking powder
- 1 teaspoon baking soda
- ½ teaspoon freshly grated nutmeg
- 1 teaspoon cinnamon
- ⅛ teaspoon ground cloves
- ¼ cup orange juice
- 1 teaspoon finely grated lemon zest

Butter and flour a 9½- inch Bundt pan. Cream butter at high speed and mix in sugar at medium speed. Continue to beat until light in color and texture. Add eggs, one at a time, beating well after each addition. Thoroughly mix in the mashed sweet potatoes. Whisk the flour, salt, baking powder, baking soda and spices together in a bowl. Gently fold in the flour, just until mixed. Next, fold in the orange juice and lemon zest. Pour into prepared pan. Bake at 325° for 55-60 minutes. Cool in pan on rack for 10 to 15 minutes, then turn out and let cool completely. Serve with Spiced Whipped Cream.

Spiced Whipped Cream

2 cups cream
¼ cup sugar or to taste
¼ teaspoon nutmeg
½ teaspoon cinnamon

Whip chilled cream with chilled beaters until soft peaks start to form, then add the sugar and spices and whip until desired consistency.

SWEET POTATO COCONUT POUND CAKE

This is a tasty combination of sweet potatoes, spices, coconut and pecans. It can be served plain or glazed.

- 1 cup butter or margarine, softened
- 2 cups sugar
- 4 eggs
- 2½ cups cooked, mashed sweet potatoes
- 3 cups plain flour
- 2 teaspoons baking powder
- 1 teaspoon baking soda
- 1 teaspoon ground cinnamon
- ½ teaspoon ground nutmeg
- ¼ teaspoon salt
- 1 teaspoon vanilla extract
- ½ cup flaked coconut
- ½ cup chopped pecans

Cream butter or margarine; gradually add sugar, beating well. Add eggs, one at a time, beating well after each addition. Add sweet potatoes; beat well. Combine flour, baking powder, soda, cinnamon, nutmeg, and salt; gradually add to sweet potato mixture, beating well after each addition (batter will be stiff). Stir in vanilla, coconut, and pecans. Spoon batter into a greased and floured 10-inch tube pan. Bake at 350° for 1 hour and 15 minutes or until cake tests done. Cool in pan 15 minutes; remove from pan and let cool completely on wire rack.

GLAZE

- 1¼ cups sifted powdered sugar
- ¼ cup orange juice
- 1 teaspoon orange extract

Mix all ingredients until smooth; add more sugar if too thin. Spread on warm cake.

SWEET POTATO STREUSEL POUND CAKE

A delicious cake, with crunchy nuts and brown sugar inside and out.

Streusel:
    1 cup brown sugar
    ½ cup low fat margarine, melted
    ½ cup chopped pecans

Cake:
    1 cup shortening
    ½ cup butter, softened
    1½ cups granulated sugar
    1½ cups brown sugar
    5 large eggs
    1 cup cooked, mashed sweet potatoes
    ¼ cup milk
    2 teaspoons vanilla
    3 cups plain flour
    1 teaspoon cinnamon
    1 teaspoon nutmeg
    ¼ teaspoon cloves
    ½ teaspoon salt
    1 teaspoon baking powder

For Streusel topping: Mix brown sugar, margarine, and chopped pecans in a bowl. Stir ingredients together and set aside.

For cake: Beat together shortening and butter for about 2 minutes or until well blended. Gradually add granulated sugar and brown sugar, beating 5 to 7 minutes or until creamy. Add eggs, one at a time, beating just until yellow disappears. In small bowl, combine sweet potato, milk and vanilla; set aside. In large bowl, combine flour, cinnamon, nutmeg, cloves, salt and baking powder; add to shortening mixture alternately with sweet potato mixture, beginning and ending with flour mixture. Beat at low speed just until blended after each addition. Pour ½ of batter into a greased and floured 10-inch tube pan. Spread ½ of streusel topping over batter, then top with remaining half of batter and remaining streusel topping. Bake at 350° for 1 hour and 20 minutes or until cake tests done. Cool in pan on wire rack for 10-15 minutes; remove cake from pan and let cool completely on wire rack.

SUGAR-FREE SWEET POTATO POUND CAKE

This recipe uses Splenda artificial sweetener, greatly reducing the calorie level without any harm to the taste.

½ cup walnuts
3 cups flour
2 cups Splenda granular sweetener
1 teaspoon baking powder
½ teaspoon salt
¼ teaspoon baking soda
1 cup butter, softened
1 cup cooked and mashed sweet potato
1 cup low-fat buttermilk
1 teaspoon lemon extract
1 teaspoon vanilla extract
6 eggs

Grease and flour a 10-inch tube pan. Sprinkle walnuts in pan and set aside. Combine flour, Splenda, baking powder, salt and soda in a large bowl; set aside. Beat butter a medium speed about two minutes or until creamy. Add sweet potatoes, buttermilk and extracts, beating until blended. Add flour mixture in thirds, beating until batter is smooth after each addition. Add eggs, one at a time, beating just until yellow disappears. Spoon batter into prepared pan. Bake at 350° for 50 to 60 minutes or until wooden pick inserted in center comes out clean. Cool in pan on a wire rack 10-15 minutes; remove from pan and cool on wire rack. Remove from pan, nut side up.

POUND CAKES MADE WITH TANGERINES

TANGERINE POUND CAKE

Tangerine juice, citrus zest and tangerine oil make this cake a winner. Yes, two cups of butter is correct.

- 2 cups unsalted butter
- 2 cups sugar
- 1 Tablespoon tangerine zest, finely minced
- 4 eggs
- 2 teaspoons vanilla extract
- ½ teaspoon tangerine or orange oil or orange extract (optional)
- 4 teaspoons baking powder
- 1½ teaspoons baking soda
- ½ teaspoon salt
- 4 cups all purpose flour
- 1 cup sour cream
- 1 cup orange, tangerine, or Clementine juice
- Non-stick cooking spray

Generously spray a 10-inch tube pan with non-stick cooking spray. In a mixing bowl, cream the butter, sugar and zest. Blend in eggs, vanilla and orange oil or orange extract. In a separate bowl, stir together baking powder, baking soda, salt and flour. Blend into batter, adding sour cream and orange juice as mixtures combines. Mix on low speed, scraping bottom of bowl frequently to ensure ingredients are incorporated and no fat and sugar are stuck to the bottom. Spoon batter into prepared pan. Bake at 350° for 55-60 minutes or until cake tests done and springs back when lightly pressed with fingertips. Remove from oven and let cool 15-20 minutes, and then cool completely on a wire rack.

Glaze

2-4 Tablespoons orange, tangerine, or Clementine juice
1½ cups confectioners' sugar
¼ teaspoon tangerine oil (optional)

Stir juice and confectioners' sugar together. Drizzle over cake. Allow glaze to set, then repeat. Garnish cake with long shreds of citrus zest.

POUND CAKES MADE WITH WALNUTS

BLACK WALNUT POUND CAKE

This elegant cake can be made even better by the addition of 1 teaspoon of rum extract or black walnut flavoring.

- 1 cup butter
- ½ cup shortening
- 3 cups sugar
- 5 eggs
- 3 cups plain flour
- 1 teaspoon baking powder
- 1 cup half-and-half
- 1 cup black walnuts, chopped fine
- 1 teaspoon vanilla extract

Cream butter and shortening, add sugar and beat well. Add eggs, one at a time, beating well after each addition. Add vanilla and beat well. Mix ¼ cup flour with nuts. Add remaining flour with baking powder alternately with milk, starting and ending with flour. Mix well after each addition. Fold floured nuts into the batter. Bake in a greased and floured 10-inch tube pan at 325° for 1 hour and 20 minutes, or until cake tests done. Do not open oven during first hour of baking. Turn onto wire rack for cooling.

BLACK WALNUT - COCONUT POUND CAKE

If you love black walnuts, then you'll love this cake that also has the delightful taste of coconut, both in the cake and in the syrup.

- 2 cups sugar
- 1 cup oil
- 4 eggs, beaten
- 3 cups plain flour
- ½ teaspoon salt
- ½ teaspoon baking soda
- 1 cup buttermilk
- 1 cup chopped black walnuts
- 1 cup flaked coconut
- 2 teaspoons coconut flavoring

Combine sugar, oil and eggs. Beat well. Combine all dry ingredients; add to sugar mixture with buttermilk. Beat until smooth; stir in coconut, flavoring and walnuts. Pour into Bundt pan and bake 1 hour 15 minutes at 325°. Remove from oven and pour hot syrup over it. (See below).

SYRUP

- 1 cup sugar
- ½ cup water
- 2 teaspoons margarine
- 1 teaspoon coconut extract

Combine sugar, water and margarine in saucepan. Bring to a boil. Boil 5 minutes. Remove from heat and add extract. Pour hot coconut syrup over hot cake. Leave cake in pan and cover tightly with aluminum foil and then cover with towel and let set for four hours.

MAPLE WALNUT POUND CAKE

Here's another delicious variation for walnut lovers.

    1 cup butter or margarine, softened
    1½ cups granulated sugar
    ½ cup packed brown sugar
    2¼ cups flour
    1 teaspoon baking powder
    ½ teaspoon salt
    ¼ cup milk
    1 Tablespoon maple flavoring
    5 eggs
    1½ cups chopped walnuts
    maple glaze
    chopped walnuts for garnish

In a mixing bowl, cream butter and sugars until fluffy. In another bowl combine flour, baking powder and salt. In a measuring cup combine milk and maple flavoring; beat into butter mixture alternately with flour mixture. Beat in eggs one at a time. Mix in 1½ cups chopped walnuts. Turn into greased 10-inch tube pan. Bake at 300° oven for 1 hour to 1 hour 15 minutes, just until pick inserted near center comes out clean. Cool in pan 15 minutes, then turn out onto rack to cool completely. Drizzle with maple glaze and garnish with walnuts.

Maple Glaze

    1 cup powdered sugar
    1 to 1½ Tablespoon milk
    ¼ teaspoon maple flavoring

In a small bowl, mix sifted powdered sugar with milk to make a glaze of thick pouring consistency. Stir in maple flavoring. Drizzle over cake.

CHAPTER 6

POUND CAKES MADE WITH WINES, LIQUEURS AND OTHER SPIRITS

The 30 recipes in this chapter use a variety of alcoholic beverages to add a distinctive flavor as part of the liquid in the recipe. These include cakes made with sherry, whiskey, rum, tequila, brandy, and liqueurs. These recipes will keep your spirits up!

POUND CAKES MADE WITH SHERRY

HARVEY'S BRISTOL CREAM POUND CAKE

Delicious and elegant for a formal dessert served with a scoop of ice cream or a spoonful of whipped cream. It goes well with a glass of the real stuff.

- 1 cup butter
- 2 cups sugar
- 6 eggs
- 2 teaspoons baking powder
- ⅛ teaspoon ground nutmeg
- ½ teaspoon salt
- 3 cups plain flour
- ¾ cup Harvey's Bristol cream sherry
- 1 teaspoon vanilla extract
- ¾ cup pecans, finely chopped

Cream butter and sugar until fluffy. Add eggs, one at a time, mixing well after each addition. Sift together dry ingredients. Add dry ingredients alternately with sherry, mixing well after each addition. Stir in vanilla and nuts. Pour batter into a greased and floured 10-inch tube pan. Bake at 325° for 1 hour and 30 minutes, or until cake tests done. Cool 10 minutes in pan; remove from pan and cool completely on wire rack.

CHOCOLATE-SHERRY POUND CAKE

There's sherry flavoring in the cake batter, but the frosting contains the real thing. Chocolate and sherry is an exquisite combination.

1½ cups margarine
3 cups sugar
5 eggs
3 cups plain flour
½ teaspoon baking powder
½ teaspoon salt
½ cup cocoa
1 cup milk
½ teaspoon sherry flavoring

Cream margarine and sugar together. Add eggs, one at a time, beating well after each addition. Add flour, baking powder, salt and cocoa alternately with milk; mix well after each addition. Stir in flavoring. Spoon batter into a greased and floured 10-inch tube pan. Bake at 325° for 1 hour and 15 minutes or until cake tests done. Cool for 10 minutes in pan; remove from pan and cool on wire rack.

Frosting

1½ cup sugar
⅓ cup cocoa
6 Tablespoons butter
3/8 cup milk
1 teaspoon sherry
pinch salt

Mix together first four ingredients; bring to a boil and cook for 1 minute. Remove from heat, stir in sherry and salt; spread on cake.

POUND CAKES MADE WITH WHISKEY

OLD KENTUCKY BROWN SUGAR POUND CAKE

For those who like their dessert with a kick. For total decadence, dress it up with a bourbon-flavored glaze.

- 1½ cups unsalted butter, softened
- 1 lb box light brown sugar
- ½ cup granulated sugar
- 5 large eggs
- 3 cups plain flour
- ½ teaspoon baking powder
- ½ teaspoon baking soda
- ½ teaspoon salt
- ¾ cup buttermilk
- ¼ cup bourbon whiskey, preferably Kentucky sour mash
- 2 teaspoons vanilla extract
- 1 cup pecans, toasted (See below)

Toasted pecans: Spread pecan pieces on a baking sheet. Bake 5 to 7 minutes or until nuts are lightly browned. Cool, and then chop coarsely.

Beat butter and sugars 2 minutes, or until light and fluffy. Add eggs, one at a time, beating well after each addition. In another bowl, sift together flour, baking powder, baking soda and salt; set aside. In glass measuring cup, mix buttermilk, bourbon and vanilla. At low speed, beat in one-fourth of the flour mixture alternately with buttermilk mixture (in thirds), beginning and ending with flour mixture and beating just until blended. Stir in chopped toasted pecans. Spoon batter into a greased and floured 10-inch tube pan. Bake at 350° for 1 hour and 15 minutes or until toothpick inserted in center comes out clean. Cool in pan on wire rack for 15 minutes. Invert cake onto wire rack to cool.

Bourbon Glaze

½ cup sugar
¼ cup bourbon

Combine sugar and bourbon in a small saucepan. Cook until sugar dissolves. Brush warm glaze over warm cake.

Chocolate-Bourbon Glaze

4 ounces semi-sweet chocolate, cut up
2 Tablespoons heavy cream
¼ cup unsalted butter, cut up
2 Tablespoons bourbon whiskey

Place chocolate in medium glass bowl. In small saucepan, heat butter, cream and bourbon to boiling. Pour over chocolate. Whisk until chocolate melts and glaze is smooth. Allow to cool. Drizzle glaze on top of cake.

BOURBON-PECAN POUND CAKE

This sour cream pound cake packs a punch plain or with bourbon glaze.

- 1 cup butter
- 2½ cups sugar
- 6 eggs
- 3 cups plain flour
- 2 teaspoons baking powder
- ½ teaspoon salt
- ½ teaspoon ground nutmeg
- 1 (8 oz.) carton sour cream
- ½ cup bourbon whiskey
- 1-1½ cup chopped pecans

Beat butter at medium speed and gradually add sugar, beating well. Add eggs, one at a time, beating after each addition. Combine flour and next 3 ingredients. Combine sour cream and bourbon; add to creamed mixture alternately with flour mixture, beginning and ending with flour mixture. Mix just until blended after each addition. Stir in pecans. Pour batter into a greased and floured 10-inch tube pan. Bake at 325° for 1 hour and 10 minutes or until a wooden pick inserted near center comes out clean. Cool in pan on wire rack 15 minutes; remove from pan and invert onto serving plate.

Bourbon Glaze

- 2¼ cups sifted powdered sugar
- 1-2 Tablespoons bourbon whiskey
- 2 Tablespoons water

Combine sugar and bourbon; stir while gradually adding water. Add only enough water to make a pourable glaze without allowing mixture to become too thin. Pour glaze over top of warm cake and let it dribble down sides.

WILD TURKEY POUND CAKE

Wild Turkey is the bourbon of choice for this recipe, but it'll work with your favorite as well. Why not go all the way with turkey at your next Thanksgiving feast?

- 2 cups butter
- 3 cups sugar
- 8 eggs
- 2 teaspoons vanilla extract
- 2 teaspoons almond extract
- 6 Tablespoons bourbon whiskey
- 3 cups plain flour
- 1½ cups pecans, chopped

Cream butter and sugar until fluffy. Add eggs one at a time, beating well after each addition. Combine vanilla, almond extract, and whiskey. Add alternately with flour to creamed mixture; mix well after each addition. Put one half of the pecans on the bottom of a greased and floured 10-inch tube pan. Add all of the batter, and put the remaining nuts on the top of the batter. Bake at 350° for 1 hour and 30 minutes or until cake tests done. Cool 10 minutes in pan; remove to wire rack and cool completely.

BOURBON NUT POUND CAKE

Get ready for big flavor. This one is brimming with bourbon and tastes even better after it mellows for a week.

    4 cups sifted flour
    1 teaspoon baking powder
    4 teaspoons ground nutmeg
    1 cup butter or margarine
    2 cups sugar
    6 eggs
    4 ounces bourbon
    4 cups coarsely chopped pecans
    1 pound dark raisins
    ½ pound candied cherries, sliced or chopped
    powdered sugar

Sift flour with baking powder and nutmeg. Cream butter well, then gradually add sugar and continue to cream until fluffy. Beat in eggs, one at a time. Add sifted dry ingredients alternately with bourbon. Stir in nuts, raisins and cherries. Turn batter into well-greased 10-inch tube pan lined on bottom with waxed paper. Bake at 300° for 2 hours, or until cake tester inserted near center comes out clean. If top of cake begins to brown before it is done, cover loosely with foil. Remove cake from oven and let stand 10 to 15 minutes, and then turn out onto rack to cool completely. When cool, sprinkle with additional bourbon and wrap. Use more bourbon if fragrant cake is desired. Let cake mellow 1 week or longer for best flavor. Sift powdered sugar over top.

POUND CAKES MADE WITH RUM

RUM POUND CAKE

Top this delectable cake with whipped cream and rum frosting; garnish with sliced almonds.

- 1 cup plus 2 Tablespoons butter, divided
- 1 cup sliced almonds, toasted
- 4 eggs
- 1½ cups sugar
- 2¼ cups plain flour, sifted
- 2 teaspoons baking powder
- ¼ cup milk
- ½ cup rum
- 1 teaspoon vanilla extract

Toasted almonds: Melt 2 Tablespoon butter in a heavy skillet over medium heat. Add 1 cup almonds and stir constantly until nuts are golden. Watch carefully; almonds burn easily. Spread on absorbent paper and cool to room temperature.

Cream remaining butter. Add sugar and beat for 2 minutes. Add eggs, one at a time, beating for 1 minute after each addition. Combine flour and baking powder; set aside. Combine milk, rum and vanilla. Turn mixer to low speed and add flour mixture alternately with milk mixture, mixing 1 minute after each addition. Reduce mixer to low speed and add toasted almonds, mixing just until blended. Pour batter into greased and floured Bundt pan or 10-inch tube pan. Bake at 350° for 50 to 60 minutes or until cake tests done. Cool in pan for 10 minutes; remove cake from pan and cool completely on wire rack.

Whipped Cream and Rum Frosting

1 cup heavy cream, chilled
2 Tablespoons sugar
2 Tablespoons rum

Place all ingredients in a chilled bowl. Whip until stiff peaks form, about 2 minutes. Do not overbeat. Spread frosting on cooled cake.

MARBLE RUM POUND CAKE

This cake is pleasing to the eye and to the taste, with toasted pecans adding an extra flavor. Just before serving, mix together 1½ Tablespoons powdered sugar and 1½ Tablespoons cocoa and sift lightly over cake.

- 1 cup unsalted butter, softened
- 2½ cups powdered sugar, sifted
- 5 large eggs
- 2 cups plain flour, sifted
- ½ teaspoon salt
- ¼ teaspoon baking soda
- ⅓ cup cocoa
- 2 teaspoons light rum
- ¼ cup boiling water
- ½ cup toasted pecans, coarsely chopped

Toasted pecans: Place pecans on a baking sheet and toast for 7 to 10 minutes at 350° until browned. Remove from oven and let cool.

Sift flour and salt together; set aside. Place butter in mixing bowl and beat on medium speed until smooth and creamy. Reduce speed and gradually beat in sugar until light and fluffy, 3 to 4 minutes. Add eggs, one at a time, beating after each addition. Stir in rum. Gently fold in flour mixture in 3 additions, incorporating just until smooth. Fold in pecans. Sift cocoa and baking soda into medium bowl. Stir in boiling water until smooth. Add 1½ cups cake batter to cocoa mixture, stirring until well blended. Spread remaining batter in a greased and floured Bundt pan or 10-inch tube pan. Spoon chocolate batter on top. Using small metal spatula, swirl batters gently to form marbled design. Bake at 325° for 1 hour and 20 minutes or until toothpick inserted in center of cake comes out clean and cake springs back when lightly touched near center. Remove from oven and let cool in pan 10 minutes. Invert onto wire rack, remove pan, and re-invert onto second wire rack to cool completely.

RUM RUNNER POUND CAKE

This small cake contains plenty of eggs to make it extra rich. You can vary the amount of rum to suit your taste.

> 1 cup butter
> 2 cups sugar
> 4 whole eggs
> 5 egg yolks
> 3 cups plain flour
> 1 teaspoon vanilla
> 1 oz. rum (or more)

Cream butter and sugar with electric mixer. Add the remaining ingredients. Beat only until smooth, and then pour into a greased and floured 10-inch tube pan. Bake at 300° for 1 hour and 30 minutes, or until cake tests done. Cool in pan 10 minutes; remove from pan and cool completely on wire rack.

ALLSPICE POUND CAKE

This delicious cake is full of the flavor of ginger, allspice and nutmeg. It's extra good when warm from the oven (or warm a slice for 15 seconds in the microwave).

- 2 cups sugar
- 2/3 cup butter
- 2 eggs
- 1 large egg white
- 3 cups flour
- 2 teaspoons baking powder
- 1 teaspoon baking soda
- ½ teaspoon ground ginger
- ½ teaspoon ground allspice
- ½ teaspoon ground nutmeg
- ¼ teaspoon salt
- 1¼ cups buttermilk
- ¼ cup dark rum
- 1 Tablespoon grated orange rind
- 1 teaspoon vanilla

Beat sugar and butter at medium speed of a mixer until well-blended. Add the eggs and egg white, 1 at a time, beating well after each addition. Combine flour and the next 6 ingredients (flour through salt). Combine buttermilk, rum, orange rind, and vanilla. Add flour mixture to sugar mixture alternately with buttermilk mixture, beginning and ending with flour mixture. Pour batter into a 10-inch tube pan coated with cooking spray. Bake at 375° for 50 minutes or until cake tests done. Cool in pan 10 minutes; remove from pan. Cool completely on a wire rack.

BUTTERED RUM POUND CAKE

Buttery flavor, nuts and rum make a great combination—try it warm from the oven, with buttered rum glaze or bananas foster sauce.

    1 cup butter, softened
    2½ cups sugar
    6 eggs, separated
    3 cups plain flour
    ¼ teaspoon baking soda
    1 carton (8 oz.) sour cream
    1 teaspoon vanilla extract
    1 teaspoon lemon extract
    ½ cup sugar (for egg whites)

Cream butter and gradually add in sugar. Add egg yolks, one at a time, beating well after each addition. Combine flour and soda and add to creamed mixture alternately with sour cream; begin and end with flour. Mix well after each addition. Stir in flavorings. Beat egg whites, until stiff peaks form, with ½ cup sugar. Fold egg whites into cake batter. Pour batter into a greased and floured 10-inch tube pan; bake at 325° for 1 hour and 30 minutes, or until cake tests done. Cool in pan for 10 minutes; invert onto serving dish for glazing.

Buttered Rum Glaze

    ¼ cup butter plus 2 tablespoons
    3 Tablespoons dark rum
    ¾ cup sugar
    3 Tablespoons water
    ¼ cup coarsely chopped walnuts

Combine first four ingredients in a small saucepan; bring to a boil. Boil for 3 minutes, stirring constantly. Remove from heat and stir in walnuts. While cake is still warm, prick with a meat fork at 1 inch intervals. Pour hot glaze over warm cake.

Bananas Foster Sauce

½ cup firmly packed brown sugar
¼ cup butter, melted
¼ teaspoon ground cinnamon
⅓ cup banana liqueur
4 bananas, peeled and sliced
⅓ cup light rum

Combine the first four ingredients in a large skillet; cook over medium heat, stirring constantly, until bubbly. Add bananas and cook 2 to 3 minutes or until thoroughly heat. Remove from heat. Heat rum in a small saucepan over medium heat (do not boil). Quickly pour rum over bananas mixture, and immediately ignite with a long match just above the liquid mixture to light the fumes (not the liquid itself). Let flames die down; serve immediately with cake.

BUTTERMILK RUM POUND CAKE

This rich cake is made extra moist by the infusion of a warm butter sauce, flavored with rum. For variation, try the butter rum glaze.

- 1 cup butter, softened
- 2 cups sugar
- 2 teaspoons rum extract
- 4 eggs
- 3 cups plain flour
- 1 teaspoon salt
- 1 teaspoon baking powder
- ½ teaspoon baking soda
- 1 cup buttermilk

Combine butter and sugar and beat well. Add flavoring and eggs; blend well. Add flour and all remaining ingredients; blend at low speed until moistened. Beat 3 minutes at medium speed. Pour batter into a greased and floured 10-inch tube pan. Bake at 325° for one hour or until toothpick inserted in center comes out clean. Invert cake onto serving plate and allow it to cool completely. Just before serving, sprinkle with 2-3 teaspoons of powdered sugar. Or, try one of these glazes.

Butter Rum Sauce

- ¾ cup sugar
- ⅓ cup butter
- 3 Tablespoons butter
- 1½ teaspoon rum extract

In small saucepan, combine all sauce ingredients. Cook over low heat, stirring occasionally, until butter melts. Do not boil. With long-tined fork, pierce cake 10-12 times. Slowly pour hot sauce over warm cake. Let stand 5 to 10 minutes.

Butter Rum Glaze

½ cup butter
1 cup sugar
¼ cup light rum
¼ cup water

Melt butter in small saucepan. Add remaining ingredients and boil for 3 minutes. Pour hot glaze over hot cake.

RUM BROWN SUGAR POUND CAKE

Rum, brown sugar and pecans are a perfect combination. This buttery, golden-brown cake is even better the next day, so make it ahead, wrap and store at room temperature overnight.

- 1½ cups butter, softened
- 1 box (1 lb) light brown sugar
- 1 cup granulated sugar
- 5 large eggs, at room temperature
- ¾ cup milk
- ¼ cup dark rum
- 2 teaspoons vanilla extract
- 3 cups plain flour
- 1 teaspoon baking powder
- ½ teaspoon salt
- 1 cup chopped pecans

Beat butter in mixer bowl until light. Gradually add sugars and continue beating until very light and fluffy. Beat in eggs one at a time, beating well after each addition. Combine milk, rum and vanilla; add to batter alternately with dry ingredients that have been sifted together. Begin and end with dry ingredients and mix well after each addition. Fold in nuts. Pour into a greased and floured 10-inch tube pan. Bake at 325° for 1 hour and 45 minutes, or until cake tests done. Cool in pan on wire rack 30 minutes; remove from pan and cool completely on wire rack.

ORANGE RUM POUND CAKE

A taste of the tropics—with a potent orange and rum-flavored glaze. This is another recipe that tastes better with a day's aging; wrap it well and store overnight before serving.

- 2 cups unsalted butter, softened
- 2 cups granulated sugar
- 8 large eggs
- 1 Tablespoon grated orange peel
- 4 teaspoons orange juice
- 2 teaspoons lemon juice
- 3 cups plain flour
- 1 teaspoon cream of tartar
- 1 teaspoon salt

Beat butter at medium-high speed until creamy. Gradually add sugar and continue beating until light and fluffy, about 5 minutes. Beat in eggs, one at a time, beating well after each addition. Stir in lemon juice, orange juice and peel. Add dry ingredients (mixed together) and beat 1 minute more. Spoon batter into a greased and floured 10-inch tube pan. Bake at 325° for 1 hour and 30 minutes, or until cake tests done. Remove cake from oven and brush top with 2 teaspoons of liqueur mixture (before adding sugar to make glaze). Cool in pan on wire rack for 30 minutes, then invert onto rack set over wax paper and cool completely.

Glaze

- 2/3 cup dark rum
- 1/4 cup orange-flavored liqueur
- 1/4 cup orange juice
- 2 cups granulated sugar

Combine rum, liqueur, and orange juice in small bowl. Stir sugar into liqueur mixture and brush over entire cake. Cool.

RUM RAISIN POUND CAKE

1½ cups brown raisins
2¼ cups all-purpose flour, sifted
1 teaspoon baking powder
½ teaspoon salt
1¼ cups unsalted butter, softened
1⅔ cups sugar
5 eggs
7 Tablespoons dark rum
2 teaspoons vanilla extract
½ cup powdered sugar
2 teaspoons whipping cream

Butter and flour a 12-cup Bundt pan. Toss raisins with 2 tablespoons flour in a small bowl. Combine remaining flour, baking powder and salt in a medium bowl. Beat butter in a large bowl until light. Add 1⅔ cups sugar and beat until fluffy. Add eggs 2 at a time; beat after each addition until well blended. Beat in 6 Tablespoons rum and vanilla. Mix in flour mixture; fold in raisin mixture and spoon batter into prepared pan. Bake at 350° until top is golden and tester comes out clean, about 1 hour. Cool in pan on rack for 10 minutes. Turn out cake onto rack and cool completely. Stir powdered sugar and 1 tablespoon rum in bowl until smooth; mix in cream and spoon over cake. Let stand until glaze is set, about 30 minutes.

RUM PECAN POUND CAKE

2 Tablespoons coarse chopped pecans
1 cup butter, softened
3 cups sugar
6 eggs
3 cups flour
1 cup heavy cream
2 teaspoons rum extract

Butter and flour a 9-inch tube pan. Sprinkle pecans on bottom of pan. Cream butter and sugar in bowl. Add eggs, one at a time, beating well after each addition. Add flour, 1 cup at a time, mixing just until blended. Stir in cream and extract. Pour batter into prepared pan. Bake at 300° for 90 minutes of until cake tests done. Cool on rack 10 minutes. Remove from pan to cool completely.

SAUCE

1 cup heavy cream, chilled
½ cup powdered sugar
¼ cup dark rum

Combine cream, powdered sugar and rum. Whip until soft peaks form. Spoon over cake slices.

DAIQUIRI POUND CAKE

Daiquiri glaze, poured over the top of the warm cake, makes for a tart and tangy surprise.

    1 cup butter or margarine, softened
    ½ cup shortening
    3 cups sugar
    5 large eggs
    3 cups plain flour
    ½ teaspoon baking powder
    1 cup milk
    1-2 Tablespoons rum
    1 Tablespoon grated lime rind
    2 teaspoons lime juice
    1½ teaspoons vanilla extract
    ½ teaspoon lemon juice

Beat butter and shortening at medium speed with an electric mixer about 2 minutes or until soft and creamy. Gradually add sugar, beating at medium speed 5 to 7 minutes. Add eggs, one at a time, beating just until yellow disappears. Combine flour and baking powder; add to creamed mixture alternately with milk, beginning and ending with flour mixture. Mix at lowest speed just until blended after each addition. Stir in rum and remaining ingredients. Spoon batter into a greased and floured 10-inch tube pan. Bake at 325° for 1 hour and 30 minutes or until cake test done. Cool in pan on a wire rack 15 minutes; remove from pan. While warm, prick top of cake with a wooden pick; pour glaze over cake. Cool completely on a wire rack.

Daiquiri Glaze

¼ cup sugar
¼ cup butter or margarine
2 Tablespoons lime juice
3 Tablespoons rum

Combine sugar, butter, and lime juice in a small saucepan; bring to a boil. Boil 1 minute, stirring constantly. Remove from heat, stir in rum and drizzle warm glaze over cake.

PINA COLADA POUND CAKE

Here's another tropical creation using rum, coconut and pineapple in the special "pina colada" combination. A delight from the islands.

1 cup margarine
½ cup shortening
3 cups sugar
6 eggs
3 cups plain flour
½ teaspoon salt
½ teaspoon baking powder
½ cup milk
½ cup rum
1 teaspoon vanilla extract

Beat margarine and shortening together until creamy. Gradually add sugar, beating until mixture is light and fluffy. Add eggs one at a time, mixing well after each addition. Sift flour with salt and baking powder. Add rum and vanilla to milk. Alternately add flour mixture and milk mixture, beginning and ending with flour mixture; mixing well after each addition. Pour into a greased and floured 10-inch tube pan. Bake at 350° for 1 hour and 30 minutes, or until cake tests done. Cool 10 minutes in pan; remove from pan and cool completely on wire rack.

FROSTING

8 oz. cream cheese
¼ cup rum
1 pound box powdered sugar
1 (8-oz.) can crushed pineapple, drained
1 cup flaked coconut

Mix cream cheese, rum, sugar and pineapple. Fold in coconut. Frost cake.

Glaze

2 cups sifted powdered sugar
3 Tablespoons brandy
2 Tablespoons milk

Combine all ingredients; mix well. Spread glaze on top and sides of warm cake and then cool.

POUND CAKES MADE WITH BRANDY

APRICOT BRANDY POUND CAKE

Try this recipe for an unusual and exotic blend of flavors—apricot, orange and rum.

    1 cup butter, softened
    3 cups sugar
    6 large eggs
    1 cup sour cream
    ½ cup apricot brandy
    1 teaspoon dark rum
    1 teaspoon vanilla extract
    1 teaspoon orange extract
    3 cups plain flour
    ½ teaspoon salt
    ¼ teaspoon baking soda

Cream butter until light and fluffy. Gradually add sugar; beat until mixture is light. Add eggs, one at a time, beating after each addition. Add sour cream, brandy, rum and extracts; continue beating. Sift dry ingredients together and gradually stir into batter mixture until well blended. Spoon batter into a greased and floured 10-inch tube pan. Bake at 325° for one hour or until a wooden pick inserted in center comes out clean. Cool in pan for 15 minutes; remove from pan and let cool completely on a wire rack.

CANDIED GINGER AND BRANDY POUND CAKE

Candied ginger and the hint of brandy combine to make a flavor that is different from any other pound cake you're likely to find. It's delicious!

- 1 cup butter, softened
- 1½ cups sugar
- 5 eggs, room temperature
- 2½ cups cake flour
- 1½ teaspoons dried ginger
- ¼ teaspoon salt
- ½ cup cream, room temperature
- ⅓ cup brandy
- 1 cup small diced crystallized ginger (about 20 large pieces)
- 1½ teaspoons orange extract

Butter and flour a 9½-inch Bundt pan. Cream together butter and sugar until light and fluffy. Add the eggs to the batter, one at a time, beating well after each addition. In a bowl, whisk together the cake flour, ginger and salt. Add half of the flour to the batter. Then add the ½ cup cream. Gently but thoroughly blend in the remaining flour. Fold in the brandy, chopped ginger, and orange extract. Be sure to fold in thoroughly, but do no over beat. Pour the batter into the prepared pan and bake at 325° for 50-60 minutes, or until a tester comes out clean.

PEACH BRANDY POUND CAKE WITH CRÈME ANGLAISE

Try this delicious cake topped with the very rich crème anglaise.

    1 cup butter or margarine, softened
    3 cups sugar
    6 large eggs
    3 cups all-purpose flour
    ¼ teaspoon baking soda
    ¼ teaspoon salt
    1 (8 oz) carton sour cream
    ½ cup peach brandy
    2 teaspoons dark rum
    1 teaspoon orange extract
    1 teaspoon vanilla extract
    ½ teaspoon lemon extract
    ¼ teaspoon almond extract

Beat butter or margarine at medium speed for 2 minutes, or until creamy. Gradually add sugar, beating 5 minutes. Add eggs, one at a time, beating just until yellow disappears. Combine flour, soda and salt; add to butter mixture alternately with sour cream, beginning and ending with flour mixture. Beat at low speed just until blended after each addition. Stir in brandy and remaining ingredients. Spoon batter into a greased and floured 10-inch tube pan. Bake at 350° for 1½ hours or until a wooden pick inserted in center comes out clean. Cool in pan on a wire rack for 10-15 minutes; remove from pan, and cool completely on a wire rack.

CRÈME ANGLAISE

    2 cups whipping cream
    6 large egg yolks
    ½ cup sugar
    2 teaspoons vanilla extract

Heat whipping cream in heavy saucepan until bubbles just form at edge. In bowl, whisk together yolks and sugar. Slowly whisk a little of hot cream into egg mixture and return all to saucepan. Continue to heat over low heat, stirring constantly with wooden spoon, until slightly thickened. Stir in vanilla. Makes 2½ to 3 cups.

TEXAS BRANDY POUND CAKE

If Texas means "big," then this one is aptly named.

- 2 cups butter, softened
- ½ teaspoon cream of tartar
- 2 cups sugar
- 9 eggs
- 4 cups plain flour
- ½ teaspoon salt
- 2 Tablespoons brandy

Cream butter; gradually add sugar, beating well. Add eggs, one at a time, beating well after each addition. Combine the flour, cream of tartar, and salt; add to creamed mixture, mixing well. Stir in the brandy. Pour batter into a greased and floured 10-inch tube pan. Bake at 325° for 1 hour and 10 minutes or until cake tests done. Cool in pan for 10 minutes; remove from pan and let cool completely on wire rack.

WHITE CORNMEAL POUND CAKE

This is another textured cake due to the addition of corn meal, but it is light in color and full of flavor from nutmeg, cinnamon and a touch of brandy.

- 6 Tablespoons butter
- 1 cup sugar
- 4 eggs
- 1¼ cups sifted plain flour
- ¾ teaspoon baking powder
- ¼ cup sifted plain white corn meal
- ¼ teaspoon nutmeg
- ¼ teaspoon cinnamon
- 2 teaspoons brandy
- ½ teaspoon vanilla extract

Thoroughly cream butter and sugar until fluffy. Add one egg at a time, beating after each addition. Sift flour with baking powder and corn meal; combine spices with flour mixture. Blend flour mixture into batter alternately with brandy and vanilla. Pour into a greased and floured 10- × 6-inch loaf pan. Bake at 325° for 1 hour and 30 minutes. Remove from oven; cool for 10 minutes. Invert onto wire rack and cool completely.

POUND CAKES MADE WITH LIQUEURS

AMARETTO POUND CAKE

This one is made with Italy's finest liqueur, so dress it up with a dusting of powdered sugar or drizzle it with Amaretto glaze and serve with sweetened whipped cream.

- 1 cup butter, softened
- 3 cups sugar
- 6 eggs
- 3 cups plain flour
- 1 cup sour cream
- ¼ teaspoon baking soda
- ½ teaspoon salt
- ½ cup Amaretto liqueur

Cream butter and gradually add sugar. Add eggs, one at a time, beating well after each addition. Add flour and mix well. Fold in sour cream to which the baking soda and salt have been added. Add Amaretto, stirring well. Pour batter into a greased and floured 10-inch tube pan. Bake at 300° for 1 hour and 30 minutes, or until cake tests done. Top warm cake with glaze below.

AMARETTO GLAZE

- ½ cup butter
- ¼ cup water
- 1 cup sugar
- ½ cup Amaretto Liqueur

Combine all ingredients in saucepan and bring to a boil, stirring until sugar dissolves. Prick cake with a fork while still in pan; drizzle with half of glaze. Invert onto serving plate. Prick top with fork and top with remaining glaze.

FRANGELICO BROWN SUGAR POUND CAKE

Toasted hazelnuts, toasted coffee, vanilla berries, rhubarb root and sweet orange flowers give Frangelico liqueur the rich, smooth flavor that makes this an outstanding cake. Dust it with powdered sugar and serve it with whipped cream and sliced strawberries.

- 1½ cups butter
- 1 pound brown sugar
- 1 cup white sugar
- 5 eggs
- ¾ cup milk
- ¼ cup Frangelico liqueur
- 2 teaspoons vanilla extract
- 3 cups plain flour
- 1 teaspoon baking powder
- ¼ teaspoon salt
- 1 cup chopped hazelnuts

Cream butter and sugars together until light and fluffy. Add eggs one at a time, beating well after each addition. Combine milk, vanilla and Frangelico. Combine dry ingredients and add to batter alternately with the milk mixture, beginning and ending with flour mixture. Blend well. Fold in the nuts and pour into a greased and floured 10-inch tube pan. Bake at 325° for 1 hour and 20 minutes or until cake tests done. Cool in pan on wire rack for 10 minutes, then invert and cool completely.

IRISH CREAM AND COFFEE POUND CAKE

If you like Irish coffee, you'll surely love this tasty cake. Add green food coloring and go all the way for St. Patrick's Day. You'll have the luck of the Irish.

> 1½ cups butter or margarine, softened
> 3 cups sugar
> 6 large eggs
> 4 cups plain flour
> 1½ Tablespoon instant coffee granules
> ½ cup Irish cream liqueur
> ¼ cup boiling water
> 1 teaspoon vanilla extract
> 1 teaspoon almond extract

Beat butter at medium speed about 2 minutes or until soft and creamy. Gradually add sugar, beating at medium speed 5 to 7 minutes. Add eggs, one at a time, beating just until yellow disappears. Dissolve coffee granules in boiling water; stir in liqueur. Add flour to butter mixture alternately with coffee mixture, beginning and ending with flour mixture. Mix at low speed until just blended after each addition. Stir in flavorings. Pour batter into a greased and floured 10-inch tube pan. Bake at 300° for 1 hour and 40 minutes or until a wooden pick inserted in center of cake comes out clean. Cool in pan on a wire rack 10 to 15 minutes; remove from pan, and let cool 30 minutes on wire rack.

Irish Cream Glaze

> 1 teaspoon instant coffee granules
> 2 Tablespoons boiling water
> 1½ Tablespoons Irish cream liqueur
> ⅔ cup sifted powdered sugar

Dissolve coffee granules in water; add liqueur and powdered sugar, stirring until blended. Brush glaze over warm cake and let cool completely.

COFFEE POUND CAKE

Here's another coffee-flavored favorite, with coffee liqueur for punch!

- 1 cup butter
- 3 cups sugar
- 6 eggs, room temperature
- 3 cups flour
- ¼ teaspoon baking soda
- ½ teaspoon almond extract
- ½ teaspoon vanilla
- 1 cup sour cream
- ½ cup coffee liqueur

Grease and flour 10-inch tube pan. In large mixing bowl, cream together butter and sugar. Add the eggs, one at a time, beating until very fluffy. Add flour, ½ cup at a time. Beat until all flour is absorbed. Beat in baking soda, almond extract, vanilla, sour cream and coffee liqueur. Pour batter into prepared ban and bake at 325° for 1½ hours. Cool in pan.

CAPPUCINO-KAHLUA POUND CAKE

This cake is a delicious blend of coffee, chocolate, spices and kahlua.

- ¾ cup vegetable oil
- ½ cup honey
- 4 eggs
- ½ cup milk
- ½ cup sour cream
- 1 Tablespoon crème de cacao
- 1 Tablespoon kahlua
- 1 cup sugar
- 2 cups self-rising flour
- 2 teaspoons cocoa powder
- 1 Tablespoon instant coffee granules
- 2 teaspoons ground cinnamon
- ¼ teaspoon ground nutmeg
- ¼ teaspoon ground cloves

Spray a 10-inch tube pan with non-stick vegetable spray. In a large mixing bowl, combine oil, honey, eggs, milk, sour cream, crème de cacao, and kahlua; beat until well blended. Add sugar, flour, cocoa powder, coffee granules, cinnamon, nutmeg, and cloves; beat until well blended and smooth. Pour into prepared tube pan, smooth the top. Bake at 325° for 1 hour and 10 minutes or until a tester inserted near the center comes out clean. Cool in pan for 20 minutes. Remove from pan; cool completely on a wire rack.

Coffee Kahlua Cream Glaze

- 1 cup heavy cream
- 1 teaspoon instant coffee granules
- 2 Tablespoons sugar
- 1 Tablespoon kahlua

In a medium bowl, combine all ingredients; beat until stiff. Spread over cooled cake.

KAHLUA FUDGE POUND CAKE

This coffee flavored cake has chocolate, too. It's more work than an ordinary pound cake, but the final product is worth it!

Kahlua Fudge

½ cup powdered cocoa
¼ cup sugar
¼ cup light corn syrup
¼ cup coffee-flavored liqueur
¼ cup water

Cake

2 cups unsalted butter, softened
2½ cups sugar
6 large eggs
4 cups plain flour
¼ teaspoon baking soda
¾ cup milk
1 Tablespoon vanilla extract

Kahlua Glaze

4 oz. semi-sweet chocolate
4 Tablespoons unsalted butter
2 Tablespoons heavy cream
2 Tablespoons coffee-flavored liqueur

For fudge: In saucepan, over low heat, mix all glaze ingredients. Heat to boiling over medium heat while stirring; cool.

For cake: In small glass measure, mix milk and vanilla. In large bowl of electric mixer, at high speed, beat butter and sugar 3 minutes or until fluffy. Add eggs, one at a time, beating after each addition. Add flour (in fourths), alternately with milk mixture (in thirds), beginning and ending with flour. Mix well after each addition. Spoon one third of batter (about 2½ cups) into medium bowl. Stir baking soda into fudge; stir into batter in medium bowl. Pour half of remaining plain batter into a greased and floured 10-inch tube pan. Top with fudge batter; add remaining plain batter. Bake at 300° for 1 hour and 40 minutes or until tester inserted in cake comes out clean. Cool cake in pan on wire rack 15 minutes; invert onto rack and cool completely.

For glaze: In food processor, chop chocolate. In saucepan, heat butter, cream and liqueur to boiling. Pour mixture into chocolate while processor is on. Continue process until chocolate melts and mixture is smooth. Cool completely; drizzle over cake.

PEACH SCHNAPPS POUND CAKE

This moist pound cake is irresistible. It is wonderful served with fresh peaches and ice cream.

>   3 cups sugar
>   1 cup butter
>   6 eggs
>   3 cups all-purpose flour
>   ¼ teaspoon baking soda
>   ½ teaspoon salt
>   1 cup sour cream
>   ¼ cup apricot brandy
>   1 teaspoon lemon zest

Grease and flour a 10-inch tube pan. In a large bowl, cream together the butter and sugar until light. Beat in the eggs, one at a time. Stir in the lemon zest and sour cream. Sift together the flour, baking soda and salt, stir into the creamed mixture alternately with the brandy. Put the batter into the prepared tube pan. Bake at 325° for 1 hour and 15 minutes in the preheated oven. Cake will spring back to the touch when done. Turn the cake out onto a wire rack. Place cake in the upside down position, and place a cookie sheet under the wire rack. Poke holes in the bottom of the cake with a fork. Pour the syrup (recipe below) over the entire cake, until all of the syrup is absorbed. Let cake stand for a few minutes. Turn the cake over onto a serving plate, drizzle the warm glaze (recipe below) over the top. Serve warm or cooled.

Syrup

>   1 cup white sugar
>   1 cup water
>   ½ cup peach schnapps
>   1 teaspoon lemon zest

Combine the sugar, water, peach schnapps, and lemon zest in a small saucepan over medium high heat. Bring to a boil for 1 minute.

GLAZE

1 cup peach preserves
1 teaspoon lemon zest
½ cup apricot brandy

In a small saucepan, combine the peach preserves, apricot brandy and lemon zest. Bring to a boil over medium heat. Let the mixture boil for 1 minute.

CHAPTER 7

SPICY POUND CAKES

The 25 recipes in this chapter are made with all sorts of herbs and spices – some common, some uncommon, and some just crazy mixed-up flavors.

ANISE HYSSOP POUND CAKE

This herb gives a light anise flavor, like licorice, to this dessert. The herb's purple blossoms create purple flecks throughout the cake.

>   3 cups cake flour, sifted
>   1½ teaspoons baking powder
>   ⅛ teaspoon salt
>   1 cup butter
>   1½ Tablespoons anise hyssop blossoms – snipped fresh OR
>   1½ Tablespoons licorice basil – snipped fresh OR
>   1½ Tablespoons lemon thyme – snipped fresh OR
>   1½ Tablespoons nasturtium blossoms – snipped fresh

Grease and flour the bottom and sides of a 10-inch tube pan. Set aside. In a medium mixing bowl, stir together cake flour, baking powder and salt. Set aside. In a large mixing bowl, beat butter, granulated sugar and vanilla with a mixer on medium speed until well combined. Add the 3 eggs; beat until the mixture is light and fluffy. With mixer at low speed, add flour mixture alternately with milk, beating well after each addition. Fold in anise hyssop blossoms (or herbs). Spoon the batter into the prepared pan. Bake at 350° for about 40 minutes or until a wooden toothpick inserted near the center comes out clean. Cool the cake on a wire rack for 10 minutes. Loosen sides of cake from pan. Remove cake from pan and cool completely. Sift powdered sugar over cake to garnish.

Note: As a rule, you may substitute 1 teaspoon dried herbs for 1 Tablespoon fresh herbs.

BLACK PEPPER POUND CAKE

This is a cake with a different taste. The pepper and nutmeg combine for an unexpected twist. It does best if wrapped and stored 24 hours before serving.

- 2 cups unsalted butter, softened
- 2 cups sugar
- 8 large eggs
- 3 cups plain flour
- 1½ teaspoons freshly ground pepper
- ½ teaspoon salt
- ½ teaspoon nutmeg
- 1 teaspoon cream of tartar
- 1 teaspoon vanilla extract
- 1 Tablespoon lemon juice

In mixing bowl, cream butter until light. Gradually add sugar and beat until very light and fluffy. Add eggs, one at a time, beating 1 minute after each addition. Stir in vanilla and lemon juice. Combine flour, pepper, salt, nutmeg and cream of tartar; fold into creamed mixture. Gradually add to batter, mixing until just blended. Pour batter into a greased and floured 10-inch tube pan. Bake at 325° for 1 hour and 30 minutes or until toothpick comes out clean. Cool in pan 15 minutes; remove from pan and cool completely on wire rack.

CARAWAY SEED POUND CAKE

This plain cake becomes unique with the addition of caraway seeds and nutmeg. Note that this is a small cake for a loaf pan.

- 2 cups all purpose flour
- 1 teaspoon baking powder
- ½ teaspoon salt
- 1½ teaspoons caraway seeds
- ¼ teaspoon ground nutmeg
- 1 cup butter or margarine, softened
- 1 cup sugar
- 3 eggs
- 1 Tablespoon vanilla extract
- ⅓ cup whole milk

Grease a metal loaf pan, 8½ by 4½ inches. Line pan with foil; grease and flour foil. On waxed paper, combine flour, baking powder, salt; caraway seeds and nutmeg; set aside. In large bowl, with mixer at low speed, beat butter with sugar until blended, scraping bowl often with rubber spatula. Increase speed to medium high; beat until creamy, about 3 minutes, occasionally scraping bowl. Reduce speed to low, add eggs, one at a time, beating well after each addition. Beat in vanilla. Alternately add flour mixture and milk, beginning and ending with flour mixture; beat just until smooth. Spoon batter into pan and spread evenly. Bake at 325° for 1 hour and 10 minutes to 1 hour and 15 minutes or until cake tester comes out clean. Cool cake in pan on wire rack for 15 minutes. Invert cake onto wire rack; immediately turn loaf top side up to cool completely. Makes 16 servings.

CARDAMOM-WALNUT POUND CAKE

Of all the Eastern spices, none rivals cardamom in aroma and flavor. This pungent spice is used in many cuisines, but is not usually found in Southern cooking, let alone pound cakes!

- 2 cups plain flour
- 1 Tablespoon ground cardamom
- ½ teaspoon salt
- 2 cups finely chopped walnuts
- 1 cup unsalted butter, softened
- 2 cups sugar
- 1 Tablespoon vanilla
- 7 eggs
- ½ cup milk

Combine ½ cup flour, cardamom, salt, and walnuts in a bowl; set aside. Beat butter in large bowl on medium speed for about 2 minutes. Add sugar; beat until fluffy, about 5 minutes. Beat in vanilla. Beat in eggs, one at a time, alternately with 1 tablespoon flour, beating about 30 seconds after each addition. Fold in remaining flour, nut mixture and milk. Pour batter into a greased and floured 10-inch tube pan. Bake at 325º for 1 hour and 25 minutes or until wooden toothpick inserted in center comes out clean. Remove to wire rack and cool 15 minutes. Invert cake onto wire rack and cool completely.

GLAZE

- 1½ cups powdered sugar
- 2 Tablespoons milk

Beat ingredients together in bowl until smooth. Pour over cake.

CAROB POUND CAKE

Carob, also known as locust bean, comes from the fruit of the carob tree, an evergreen believed to have originated in Syria and cultivated since ancient times. Carob powder is made from the bean pods; it is somewhat sweet and is often used as a substitute for cocoa.

- 3 cups butter or margarine, softened
- 1½ cups honey
- 6 eggs
- 3 cups whole wheat flour
- ½ cup carob powder
- 2 teaspoons baking powder
- 1 cup milk
- 1 teaspoon vanilla

Cream butter or margarine and honey together. Beat in eggs well. Sift dry ingredients together and add alternately with the milk and vanilla. Pour in a greased and floured tube pan. Bake at 325° for 1¼ to 1½ hours or until it tests done.

Note: White flour may be substituted for part of the whole-wheat flour.

FRESH GINGER POUND CAKE

Fresh ginger adds a warm, bright flavor. Glaze with ½ cup heated apricot jam drizzled on top and sides of cake.

- ¾ cup butter
- 1¾ cups firmly packed brown sugar
- 2 eggs, plus 3 egg whites
- 3 Tablespoons grated fresh ginger
- 3 cups plain flour
- ½ teaspoon baking soda
- 1 cup buttermilk

Beat butter and sugar together until fluffy. Beat in eggs and egg whites until smooth, scraping bowl often. Stir in ginger. In small bowl, combine flour and baking soda. Add flour mixture alternately with buttermilk, beginning and ending with flour mixture, mixing well after each addition. Pour batter into a greased and floured 10-inch tube pan. Bake at 350° for 1 hour and 10 minutes, or until cake tests done. Cool 15 minutes on wire rack. Remove from pan and cool completely on wire rack.

FIVE FLAVOR POUND CAKE

There's something here for everyone—a wild mixture of flavors in the cake and in the glaze.

>   1 cup margarine, softened
>   ½ cup shortening
>   3 cups sugar
>   5 eggs
>   3 cups plain flour
>   ½ teaspoon baking powder
>   1 cup milk
>   1 teaspoon each coconut, rum, butter, lemon, and vanilla extract

Cream margarine, shortening and sugar. Add eggs, one at a time, beating after each. Sift baking powder with flour. Add flour mixture and milk alternately to the creamed mixture, beginning and ending with flour mixture; mixing well after each addition. Stir in flavorings. Pour into a greased and floured 10-inch tube pan. Bake at 325° for 1 hour and 30 minutes, or until cake tests done. Immediately remove from pan and pour glaze over warm cake.

Glaze

>   1 cup sugar
>   ½ cup water
>   1 teaspoon each: almond, coconut, rum, butter, lemon, and vanilla extract

Bring sugar and water mixture to a boil until sugar dissolves. Stir in flavorings. Pour glaze over warm cake and let it set for about 2 hours before removing it from pan. When cake is turned out of the pan, re-invert it so that glaze will continue to run down through the cake.

FOUR-FLAVOR POUND CAKE

This "healthy" pound cake calls for egg whites, vegetable oil and skim milk. Fat and cholesterol are reduced, but there is plenty of flavor in this delightful cake.

- 1¾ cups sifted plain flour
- ¾ cup sugar
- 2 teaspoons baking powder
- ¼ teaspoon salt
- ½ cup vegetable oil
- ½ cup skim milk
- ½ teaspoon grated lemon rind
- ¼ teaspoon each almond extract, rum extract, lemon extract, and vanilla extract
- 4 egg whites, stiffly beaten

Combine flour and next 3 ingredients in a large bowl. Add oil and milk; beat at medium speed of an electric mixer until batter is smooth (batter will be thick). Add lemon rind and next 4 ingredients; fold in about one-third of egg whites. Gently fold in remaining egg whites. Pour batter into a greased and floured 10-inch tube pan. Bake at 350° for 1 hour and 15 minutes or until a wooden pick inserted in center comes out clean. Cool in pan 10 minutes; remove from pan and cool on a wire rack.

GERANIUM POUND CAKE

Try scented or unscented geranium leaves for a different taste and aroma. Sift powdered sugar over the top of the cake to dress it up.

- 1 cup butter or margarine, softened
- 2 cups sugar
- 3 eggs
- 3 cups plain flour
- 2 teaspoons baking powder
- 1 cup milk
- 1 teaspoon vanilla extract
- 8-10 geranium leaves (or enough to cover bottom of pan)

Cream butter; gradually add sugar, beating well. Add eggs, one at a time, beating well after each addition. Combine flour and baking powder; add to creamed mixture alternately with milk, beginning and ending with flour mixture; mix well after each addition. Stir in vanilla. Line a well-greased 10-inch tube pan with geranium leaves; pour batter into pan. Bake at 350° for 1 hour or until cake tests done. Cool in pan 15 minutes; remove from pan and let cool completely on wire rack. (Remove leaves.)

GINGER POUND CAKE

Sweet and moist crystallized ginger gives this recipe a different taste. Delicious served with vanilla ice cream.

¾ cup milk
1 (2.7 oz.) jar crystallized ginger, finely minced
2 cups butter or margarine
3 cups sugar
6 eggs
4 cups all-purpose flour
1 teaspoon vanilla extract

Cook milk and ginger in a saucepan over medium heat until thoroughly heated (do not boil). Remove from heat and let stand 10 to 15 minutes. Beat butter at medium speed with an electric mixer until creamy; gradually add sugar, beating 5 to 7 minutes. Add eggs, 1 at a time, beating after each addition just until yellow disappears. Add flour to butter mixture alternately with milk mixture, beginning and ending with flour. Beat at low speed just until blended after each addition. Stir in vanilla. Pour batter into a greased and floured 10-inch tube pan. Bake at 325° for 1 hour and 25 minutes or until a wooden pick inserted in center comes out clean. Cool in pan on a wire rack for 10 minutes. Remove from pan and cool completely on a wire rack.

GINGERBREAD POUND CAKE

The delightful flavors of old-timey gingerbread come together in this cake, which is best served with lemon sauce.

- 1 cup butter
- 1 cup sugar
- 5 eggs
- 2 cups plain flour
- ½ teaspoon baking soda
- 1 teaspoon ginger
- 1 teaspoon cinnamon
- 1 teaspoon cloves
- ½ teaspoon ground nutmeg
- 1 cup molasses
- ½ cup sour cream

Cream butter and gradually add sugar, beating at medium speed until smooth. Add eggs, one at a time, beating after each addition. Combine flour, baking soda and spices. Set aside. Combine molasses and sour cream. Add flour mixture to creamed mixture, alternating with molasses mixture, beginning and ending with flour mixture. Mix just until blended after each addition. Pour batter into a greased and floured 10-inch tube pan. Bake at 325° for 1 hour or until toothpick inserted in center comes out clean. Cool in pan for 15 minutes; remove from pan and let cool completely on wire rack. Serve with lemon sauce.

Lemon Sauce

½ cup sugar
2 Tablespoons cornstarch
1 cup water
1 Tablespoon butter
2 teaspoons lemon rind, grated
⅓ cup lemon juice

Combine sugar, cornstarch and water; stir until smooth. Cook over medium heat, stirring until smooth and thickened. Add butter, lemon rind and juice. Cook until heated through, stirring constantly.

JASMINE GINGER POUND CAKE

Try this cake for an interesting mix of flavors – jasmine tea, ginger and lime. Note that it is a small recipe, suitable for a loaf pan. You may substitute unflavored green tea, but do not use tea from tea bags.

> Canola oil spray
> ¼ cup loose jasmine tea leaves
> 2 cups plain flour
> 2 teaspoons ground ginger
> 1 teaspoon baking powder
> 1 teaspoon salt
> ¼ teaspoon baking soda
> zest of 1 small lime
> 4 eggs
> 1 cup sugar
> ¾ cup canola oil
> 2 Tablespoons fresh lime juice
> 2 teaspoons vanilla extract

Lightly oil a 9-inch loaf pan with canola oil spray, then line bottom with waxed paper or parchment paper. Using a blender or food processor, pulverize tea leaves as fine as possible. In a large bowl, sift together the flour with the powdered tea, ginger, baking powder, salt and baking soda. Stir in the lime zest. In a separate large bowl, beat the eggs, first at low-medium speed until light in color. Slowly add sugar, beating after each addition, until mixture becomes thick, pale and creamy. At high speed, gradually beat in the oil, limejuice and vanilla. Fold in the dry ingredients, one-third at a time, just until well blended. Pour batter into prepared pan and bake at 350° for 50-55 minutes or until a toothpick inserted in the center comes out clean. Cool pan on rack for 10-15 minutes. Remove loaf from pan, peel of paper and allow to cool on rack.

LAVENDER LEMON POUND CAKE

Lavender is widely grown for use in dried flower arrangements; it's known for its fresh fragrance. It blends nicely with lemon in this small cake, suitable for a loaf pan.

- 1 cup unsalted butter
- 4 Tablespoons dried lavender, divided
- 5 eggs
- 1 cup sugar
- 1½ cups plus 2 Tablespoons flour
- ¼ teaspoon salt
- 1 Tablespoon grated lemon zest
- 1 teaspoon vanilla extract

Butter and flour a 9×5-inch loaf pan. Melt the butter with 1 Tablespoon of the lavender in a small saucepan. Let the mixture steep 10 minutes, then strain, discarding the lavender. Set aside to cool. Beat the eggs and 1 cup of the sugar in the bowl of a mixer until thick and pale, about 5 minutes. Sift together the flour and salt into a bowl. Using a whisk, fold the lemon zest and one-third of the flour mixture into the eggs until thoroughly combined. Fold in the rest of the flour in 2 batches. In a separate bowl, whisk 1 cup of the batter with the melted butter and the vanilla. Add this to the remaining batter and fold to combine. Pour the batter into the prepared pan. Bake at 350° for 40-45 minutes, or until a toothpick inserted in the middle comes out clean. Transfer the cake to a wire rack. Using a cake tester or skewer, poke the cake all over. Brush the loaf with half of the glaze and let cool for 10 minutes. Invert the cake onto the rack, remove the pan and brush the syrup over the bottom and sides of the cake. Turn the cake back over and brush with the remaining syrup. Let cool completely.

GLAZE

½ cup sugar
¼ cup strained lemon juice
¼ cup water
3 Tablespoons lavender

Combine the sugar, lemon juice, water and the lavender in a saucepan. Bring the mixture to a simmer and cook, stirring, until the sugar dissolves.

LEMON GERANIUM POUND CAKE

Use lemon geranium leaves to add a hint of lemon to this classic recipe.

> 4 to 6 large fresh lemon geranium leaves
> Vegetable oil
> 1 cup butter or margarine, softened
> 3 cups sugar
> 6 eggs
> 3 cups all-purpose flour
> ½ teaspoon salt
> ¼ teaspoon baking soda
> 1 (8 oz) container sour cream
> 2 teaspoons vanilla extract
> Garnish: fresh lemon geranium leaves

Brush both sides of leaves with oil. Arrange leaves, dull side up, around the sides of a greased and floured 10-inch tube pan; set aside. Beat butter at medium speed with an electric mixer until creamy; gradually add sugar, beating well. Add eggs, 1 at a time, beating until blended after each egg. Combine flour, salt, and baking soda; add to butter mixture alternately with sour cream, beginning and ending with flour mixture. Beat at low speed until blended after each addition. Stir in vanilla. Spoon batter into prepared pan. Bake at 325° for 1 hour and 20 minutes or until a wooden tester comes out clean. Cool in pan on wire rack for 15 minutes. Remove from pan. Garnish, if desired, with fresh lemon geranium leaves.

LEMON-PEPPER POUND CAKE

You can taste the lemon as soon as you bite into this cake – the pepper's spark comes as a lively aftertaste. This is a small cake, suitable for a loaf pan.

> 2 cups flour
> ¾ teaspoon baking powder
> ¾ teaspoon white pepper
> ¼ teaspoon salt
> ⅔ cup butter
> ⅔ cup sugar
> 3 eggs
> 1 teaspoon vanilla
> 2 teaspoon grated lemon rind
> ⅓ cup milk

Butter and flour an 8-½-inch loaf pan. In a medium bowl, stir together the flour, baking powder, pepper and salt; set aside. In a large bowl, cream the butter and sugar. Beat in the eggs, one at a time, then beat in vanilla and lemon rind. Alternating between the two, gradually add the dry ingredients and the milk, beating just until combined. Do not overbeat! Spread the batter evenly in the prepared pan. Rap the pan once or twice on the counter to remove any air pockets. Bake at 350° for 40-50 minutes, or until toothpick inserted in center of cake comes out clean and dry. Let cake cool in pan on a rack for 5 minutes, and then turn it out onto the rack to cool completely.

LEMON ROSEMARY MINI-POUND CAKES

This recipe makes 3 mini-loaves that are great for gift giving. Wrap them in plastic wrap; store at room temperature for up to 1 day, refrigerate for up to 4 days, or freeze for up to 1 month.

- 1 cup butter
- 2½ teaspoons freshly grated lemon peel
- 2 teaspoons fresh rosemary, finely chopped
- 1 teaspoon baking powder
- ¼ teaspoon salt
- ¾ cup sugar
- 4 eggs
- 1 teaspoon vanilla extract
- 2 cups plain flour

Coat three 5¾ × 3¼ × 2-inch disposable foil baby-loaf pans with nonstick spray. Have a baking sheet ready to hold filled pans so they can be moved in and out of oven easily. Beat butter, lemon peel, rosemary, baking powder and salt in a large bowl with mixer on medium high speed until creamy. Gradually beat in sugar; beat 2 minutes or until fluffy. Beat in eggs, one at a time, then vanilla. On low speed, beat in flour until just blended. Half fill each prepared pan. Smooth tops and place pans on baking sheet. Bake at 325° for 35 – 40 minutes or until a wooden pick inserted in centers comes out clean. Cool in pans on a wire rack 5 minutes before inverting on a rack. Turn cakes right side up and apply topping before cake cools completely.

LEMON-SUGAR TOPPING

½ cup sugar
¼ cup fresh lemon juice

Mix sugar and lemon juice in a cup. While cakes are still warm, pierce tops all over with a wooden pick. Gently brush or spoon on topping, letting it soak in before adding more. Let cakes cool completely. Garnish with rosemary and lemon peel.

RED PEPPER POUND CAKE

They say some like it hot, and this recipe proves that anything goes with pound cakes. Note that this is a small cake, suitable for a loaf pan.

> 1 cup butter or margarine
> 1 cup granulated sugar
> 1 cup light brown sugar, firmly packed
> 4 eggs
> 3 cups sifted cake flour
> 2 teaspoons baking powder
> ½ teaspoon allspice
> ¼ teaspoon salt
> 1 cup milk
> 3 teaspoons vanilla
> ½ teaspoon Tabasco brand pepper sauce
> Confectioners' sugar (optional)

Cream butter or margarine, and sugars together. Beat in eggs one at a time, beating well after each addition. In another medium bowl, sift together cake flour, baking powder, allspice and salt. Beat flour into creamed mixture alternately with milk, beat in vanilla and Tabasco© brand pepper sauce. Turn into lightly buttered 9-inch tube pan. Bake at 350°f or 50 to 60 minutes or until cake tester inserted near center comes out clean. Cool in pan on wire rack 20 to 30 minutes; remove from pan, cool completely. Before serving, dust with confectioners' sugar, if desired. Makes 8 to 10 servings.

ROSE PETAL POUND CAKE

This cake calls for rosewater, which is a very sweet clear liquid that you can obtain in Middle Eastern grocery stores and other specialty markets.

- 1 cup butter
- 1 2/3 cups sugar
- 5 eggs
- 2 cups plain flour
- 1-2 drops red food coloring
- ½ teaspoon salt
- 1 teaspoon almond extract
- 3 Tablespoons finely ground almonds
- 1 teaspoon rosewater

Cream butter well. In a separate bowl, beat sugar and eggs together until doubled in volume. Add flour and salt gradually. Fold in creamed butter and beat thoroughly. Divide batter into two equal parts. Into one part, add the almond extract and the ground almonds. To the other part, add the rosewater and the red food coloring. Spoon batters alternately into a greased and floured 10-inch tube pan. Bake at 350° for 50 to 60 minutes or until cake tests done. Let cake cool for 30 minutes in pan on wire rack. Remove from pan and dust with confectioners' sugar.

ROSEMARY POUND CAKE

Fresh rosemary, orange flower water and a taste of honey! Top it with orange glaze and garnish with a few sprigs of fresh rosemary. You can find orange flower water in Middle Eastern grocery stores and other specialty food markets.

> 2 cups butter, softened
> 2 cups sugar
> ½ cup honey
> 8 eggs
> 4 cups sifted plain flour
> 2 teaspoons baking powder
> 2 Tablespoons snipped fresh rosemary OR 2 teaspoons dried rosemary
> 1 Tablespoon orange flower water OR ½ teaspoon orange extract
> 2½ teaspoons shredded orange peel
> 1 Tablespoon orange juice

Beat butter and sugar with an electric mixer on medium speed for 6 minutes or until light and creamy. Beat in honey. Add eggs, one at a time, beating for 1 minute after each addition. (Batter may look slightly curdled.) Stir together flour and baking powder. Gradually add the flour mixture to the sugar mixture, beating on low speed just until blended. Gently stir in the rosemary, orange water or extract, peel, and orange juice. Pour into greased and floured 10-inch tube pan. Bake at 325° for 1 hour and 30 minutes or until toothpick inserted near center comes out clean. Cool in pan 10 minutes. Remove from pan and cool completely on wire rack.

ORANGE GLAZE

> 1 cup sifted powdered sugar
> 1 Tablespoon orange juice

Stir together powdered sugar and orange juice. Drizzle over cooled cake.

SPICE POUND CAKE WITH RUM GLAZE

This is a delicious spicy cake made even more so by the addition of the rum glaze.

- 2 teaspoons baking powder
- 3 cups all-purpose flour
- 1½ Tablespoons ground cinnamon
- 1 teaspoon nutmeg
- 1 cup margarine, softened
- 3 cups granulated sugar
- 1 teaspoon vanilla
- ½ teaspoon butter flavoring
- 1 cup sour cream
- 6 eggs

Grease and flour a 10-inch tube pan. Sift together baking powder, flour, cinnamon, and nutmeg. Set aside. Cream margarine and gradually beat in sugar. Add vanilla and butter flavoring to sour cream. Mix well. Add to sugar mixture. Beat in eggs one at a time to mixture. Blend in flour mixture, 1 cup at a time, beating after each addition. Bake at 325° for 1 hour and 30 minutes, or until tester come out clean.

Rum Glaze

- ½ cup water
- 1 cup sugar
- 2 Tablespoons Jamaican Rum Flavor

Combine water and sugar. Bring to a boil while stirring. Cool for 15 minutes. Stir in rum flavor. With a pastry brush, <u>slowly</u> apply glaze to top and sides of warm cake as if painting the cake.

SPICED PEACH POUND CAKE

This tasty cake could quickly become a family favorite.

- ½ cup shortening
- 2 cups sugar
- 4 eggs
- 2 cups self-rising flour
- 1 teaspoon ground cinnamon
- ¼ teaspoon ground nutmeg
- ¼ teaspoon ground cloves
- 5 jars (2½ ounces each) peach baby food
- 1 cup chopped walnuts

In a large mixing bowl, cream shortening and sugar. Add eggs, one at a time, beating well after each addition. Combine the flour, cinnamon, nutmeg and cloves; add to creamed mixture alternately with baby food. Fold in the walnuts. Pour batter into greased and floured 10-inch tube pan. Bake at 325° for 60-65 minutes or until a toothpick inserted near the center comes out clean. Cool in pan for 10 minutes before removing from pan to a wire rack.

Glaze:

- ¾ cup confectioners' sugar
- 1 to 2 Tablespoons lemon juice

Combine the glaze ingredients and drizzle over warm cake. Cool completely before serving.

SPICED POUND CAKE

This is another warm and cozy spice cake, with a couple of options for sauces.

½ cup chopped pecans
1½ cups butter, softened
1½ cups packed brown sugar
1 cup sugar
3 eggs
2 teaspoons vanilla extract
1 teaspoon ground cinnamon
½ teaspoon ground allspice
½ teaspoon ground cloves
¼ teaspoon ground ginger
3½ cups cake flour
¼ teaspoon baking soda
1 teaspoon salt
1 cup buttermilk

Prepare a Bundt pan with an even coating of shortening and flour. Place chopped pecans evenly in the bottom of the Bundt pan. In the bowl of a mixer, cream butter and sugars together, beating until fluffy, about 3 minutes. Add eggs, 1 at a time, beating well after each addition. Add vanilla, cinnamon, allspice, cloves, and ginger. Sift together flour, baking soda, and salt; add flour mixture to egg mixture alternating the buttermilk, and beginning and ending with the flour. Pour into prepared pan and bake at 325° for 1 hour and 15 minutes. Cool in the pan for 15 minutes, turn out onto wire rack to cool partially, and then place on a cake plate.

Orange Rum Glaze

½ cup sugar
2 tablespoons cornstarch
Pinch salt
1 medium orange, juiced, strained, and combined with water to yield 1 cup
½ teaspoon orange zest
¼ cup rum
1 tablespoon butter
1 teaspoon vanilla extract

Stir together the sugar, cornstarch, and salt in small saucepan. Add juice and water mixture, zest, and rum. Cook over medium heat until bubbly, stirring constantly. Remove from heat and add butter and vanilla; stir. Pour approximately half of the glaze over the warm cake. Reserve remaining glaze for serving with the cake.

Chocolate Sauce

¾ cup clear corn syrup
1 tablespoon butter
3 ounces semisweet chocolate, chopped
1 teaspoon vanilla extract

Place corn syrup and chocolate in a microwave-safe container. Microwave for 1 minute on high and then stir to melt chocolate. Add butter and vanilla and whisk until chocolate is thoroughly combined. Drizzle over cooled cake and serve.

TEA POUND CAKE

This cake carries blends the best of two Southern traditions - iced tea and pound cake.

    1 cup butter, softened
    ½ cup shortening
    3 cups sugar
    5 eggs
    3 cups plain flour
    ½ teaspoon baking powder
    ¼ teaspoon salt
    ½ cup unsweetened instant tea powder
    1 cup milk
    1 teaspoon vanilla extract

Beat butter and shortening at medium speed for two minutes or until creamy. Gradually add sugar, beating 5 to 7 minutes. Add eggs, one at a time, beating just until yellow disappears. Combine flour and next 3 ingredients; add to butter mixture alternately with milk, beginning and ending with flour mixture. Beat at low speed just until blended after each addition. Stir in vanilla. Pour batter into a greased and floured 10-inch tube pan. Bake at 325º for 1 hour and 35 minutes or until a toothpick inserted in center comes out clean. Let cool in pan 10 minutes; remove from pan and cool completely on a wire rack.

THREE-FLAVOR POUND CAKE I

Here's another interesting mix of flavors—lemon, orange and vanilla.

- 1 cup shortening
- ¼ lb (½ cup) margarine
- 3 cups sugar
- ¼ teaspoon salt
- 1 teaspoon baking powder
- 1 cup milk
- 7 eggs
- 3 cups plain flour
- 1 Tablespoon each vanilla extract, lemon extract, and orange extract

Cream sugar, shortening and margarine in a large mixing bowl. Stir in salt, flavorings and baking powder. Blend eggs and milk in blender at high speed for 1 minute. Add egg and milk mixture alternately with flour to ingredients in mixing bowl; mixing well after each addition. Pour batter into a greased and floured 10-inch tube pan. Bake at 325° for 1 hour and 30 minutes or until cake tests done. Cool 10 minutes in pan; remove and cool completely on wire rack.

THREE-FLAVOR POUND CAKE II

Here's a different twist—using orange, coconut and pineapple flavors

- 1 cup solid shortening
- 2 cups sugar
- 6 eggs
- 2 cups sifted flour
- ¼ teaspoon baking powder
- ½ teaspoon salt
- 1 teaspoon orange extract
- 2 teaspoons coconut extract
- 2 teaspoons pineapple extract
- ⅛ cup milk

Cream shortening and sugar together. Add eggs one at a time, mixing well after each addition. Add dry ingredients together and mix with creamed mixture. Add extracts and milk and blend well. Pour into a well-greased and floured tube pan and bake 1 hour at 350° or until cake tests done. Cool 10 minutes before removing from pan. Cool completely on wire rack.

CHAPTER 8

CAKE MIX CAKES

The 31 recipes in this chapter can be characterized as quick and easy. All use a commercial cake mix as the starting point.

PLAIN POUND CAKES

LOW-FAT SOUR CREAM POUND CAKE

Quick, easy and low-fat, too!

> Vegetable cooking spray
> Plain flour
> 1 (18.25 ounce) package low-fat yellow cake mix
> ½ cup sugar
> 1 (8-ounce) container fat-free sour cream
> 1 cup egg substitute
> ¾ cup applesauce
> 1 teaspoon almond or vanilla extract

Beat cake mix and next 5 ingredients at medium speed for 4 minutes. Spoon into 10-inch tube pan that has been coated with vegetable cooking spray and flour. Bake at 325° for 45 minutes or until a wooden toothpick inserted in center comes out clean. Cool in pan on a wire rack 10 minutes. Remove from pan and cool completely on wire rack. Serve with Raspberry Sauce.

RASPBERRY SAUCE:

> 4 (10-ounce) packages frozen raspberries, thawed
> 4 teaspoons sugar

Process both ingredients in a blender until smooth. Pour through a wire-mesh strainer, discarding seeds. Chill one hour.

DUNCAN HINES POUND CAKE

This is a quick and easy recipe that uses cake mix and instant pudding to create a pretty passable pound cake.

> 1 package (2-layer) deluxe yellow cake mix
> 1 small package (4 ½ oz.) instant vanilla pudding mix
> ½ cup vegetable oil
> 1 cup water
> 4 eggs

Blend all ingredients in large bowl and beat at medium speed for 2 minutes. Pour into greased and floured Bundt pan or 10-inch tube pan. Bake at 350° for 50 minutes or until cake tests done. Cool in pan 10 minutes; remove from pan and cool completely on wire rack.

CHOCOLATE POUND CAKES

MILK CHOCOLATE POUND CAKE

This version requires milk chocolate bars but also includes a cake mix and instant pudding. It makes a big cake with easy preparation.

- 4 bars (1.55 ounces each) milk chocolate
- 1 package (18.25 ounces) plain yellow cake mix
- 1 package (3.4 ounces) vanilla instant pudding mix
- 1 cup sour cream
- ½ cup vegetable oil
- 4 eggs
- 1 teaspoons vanilla
- 1 Tablespoon confectioners' sugar

Lightly coat 12 cup Bundt pan with nonstick cooking spray. Dust with flour; shake off excess. Break chocolate bars into 1 inch pieces, place in food processor. Pulse 12 to 15 times, until candy is grated, but not a powder. Combine cake mix, pudding mix, sour cream, oil, eggs and vanilla in a large bowl. Beat on low speed for 1 minute. Stop mixing to scrape down the sides of the bowl. With speed at medium, beat 2 minutes. Fold in chocolate. Pour batter into prepared pan. Bake at 350° for 55 minutes or until golden and top springs back when lightly pressed. Remove pan to wire rack to cool 20 minutes. Run long knife along edge of cake; invert onto rack to cool completely. Place cake on serving plate and sift confectioners' sugar on top. Makes 16 servings.

CHOCOLATE CHIP POUND CAKE

This is a quick and easy recipe. It's simple to put together since it relies on pre-packaged cake mix and instant pudding. You don't even need to use an electric mixer.

- 1 package (two-layer) yellow cake mix
- 2 packages instant chocolate pudding mix (4½ oz.-size)
- ¾ cup oil
- ¾ cup water
- 5 eggs
- 1 (6 oz.) package chocolate chips
- 1 cup chopped nuts

Mix dry cake mix and pudding mix. Add oil and water; mix well. Add one egg at a time and beat well after each addition. Stir in chocolate chips and chopped nuts. Pour batter into a greased and floured Bundt pan. Bake at 350° for 1 hour or until cake tests done. Cool 10 minutes in pan; remove from pan and cool completely on wire rack.

CHOCOLATE CHIP AMARETTO POUND CAKE

This is a super-easy, double-chocolate delight. It works best in Bundt pan.

3 eggs
1 (18.25 ounce) box devil's food cake mix
⅓ cup vegetable oil
1 cup water
2 Tablespoons almond extract
1 cup semisweet chocolate chips
Confectioners' sugar

Mix eggs, cake mix, oil, water and almond extract with electric beater or mixer. Stir in chocolate chips. Pour into greased Bundt pan. Bake at 350° for 1 hour or until cake tests done. Cool 10 minutes in pan on wire rack; remove from pan to cool completely. Dust with confectioners' sugar.

PISTACHIO CHOCOLATE POUND CAKE

It's green and crunchy and chocolate and delicious!

- 1 box yellow cake mix
- 1 box pistachio instant pudding mix
- ½ cup oil
- ½ cup sugar
- 1 cup water
- 1 teaspoon vanilla extract
- 5 eggs
- 5½ oz. chocolate syrup
- ½ cup chopped nuts
- ½ cup chocolate chips

Combine cake mix and pudding mix in large mixing bowl. Add oil, sugar, water, vanilla and eggs. Beat well for 2 minutes. Take out 1 cup of batter and mix with chocolate syrup. Sprinkle nuts and chips on bottom of greased and floured 10-inch tube pan (or Bundt pan). Pour green batter in the pan. Swirl chocolate batter on top. Bake at 350° for 1 hour, cool for 10 minutes and remove from pan.

CHOCOLATE FUDGE POUND CAKE

This is a quick and easy recipe, made with pre-packaged cake mix and instant pudding. Sour cream makes it rich; chocolate fudge icing makes it downright sinful.

    1 package (two-layer) yellow cake mix
    1 package (4 ½ oz.) instant chocolate pudding mix
    1¾ cups margarine, melted
    ½ cup sour cream
    ½ cup milk
    4 eggs
    1 cup cocoa
    1 cup sugar

Mix together cake mix, pudding mix, margarine, sour cream and milk, and then add eggs, one at a time and beat well after each addition. Sift sugar and cocoa together, then add to cake mix and beat well. Pour batter into a greased and floured Bundt pan or a 10-inch tube pan. Bake at 300° for 1 hour and 35 minutes or until cake tests done. Cool 10 minutes in pan; remove from pan and cool completely on wire rack.

Old Timey Fudge Frosting

    3 cups sugar
    ⅔ cup cocoa
    ½ teaspoon salt
    1½ cups milk
    ½ cup margarine
    2 teaspoons vanilla extract

Mix all ingredients, except margarine and vanilla, bring to a boil, then turn down to low and cook until a small amount forms a soft ball when dropped into cup of cold water. Normally, it should cook for about 50 minutes. Remove from heat; add margarine and vanilla and beat. Cool fudge for 10-15 minutes, and then use it to fill the hole in the middle of the cake. Spread the remaining fudge over the entire cake.

DEVIL'S FOOD POUND CAKE

This is a quick and easy recipe using pre-packaged cake mix and instant pudding. It's a double chocolate treat that can be made fancier with a chocolate glaze.

>1 package (two-layer) devil's food cake mix
>1 package (4½ oz.) chocolate instant pudding mix
>½ cup vegetable oil
>1 cup water
>4 eggs

Blend all ingredients in large bowl; beat at medium speed for 2 minutes. Pour into well-greased and floured 10-inch tube pan and bake at 350° for 50 to 60 minutes, or until done. Cool right side up for 20 minutes, then remove from pan and cool completely on wire rack.

GLAZE

>2 Tablespoons cocoa
>1 Tablespoon plus 2 teaspoons water
>1 Tablespoon vegetable oil
>1 Tablespoon corn syrup
>1 cup confectioners' sugar

Combine first four ingredients. Cook and stir over low heat until mixture is smooth. Remove from heat and beat in sugar. Add a few drops of water if needed to get proper spreading consistency. Spread on cooled cake.

CAJUN POUND CAKE

Easy to make, this exotic blend of flavors will tickle your taste buds.

- 1 package devils food cake mix
- 1 package instant chocolate pudding
- 4 eggs
- ½ cup oil
- 1 teaspoon cinnamon
- 3 Tablespoons rum or brandy extract
- 1 cup water
- 1 cup chocolate chips

Combine all ingredients. Pour into greased and floured 10-inch tube pan. Bake at 350° for 45-50 minutes, or until cake tests done. Do not remove from pan until ready to glaze.

Glaze

- 2 tablespoons cocoa
- 5 teaspoons water
- 1 Tablespoon margarine
- 1 Tablespoon corn syrup
- 1 cup confectioner's sugar

Cook all ingredients except the sugar until the margarine is melted. Add the sugar and glaze the cake.

EASY MARBLE POUND CAKE

This is a quick and easy recipe that makes a pretty little cake for elegance in a hurry.

> 1 package (two-layer) yellow cake mix
> 1 package (4½ oz.) chocolate instant pudding mix
> 4 eggs
> ½ cup vegetable oil
> ¾ cup water

Dump all ingredients, except pudding, mix, into large bowl. Mix well. Pour half of batter into a greased and floured 10-inch tube pan. Add pudding mix to remaining batter; mix well. Drop spoonfuls of chocolate batter over batter in cake pan. With a knife, swirl the chocolate batter into the yellow batter. Bake at 350° for 60 minutes or until cake tests done. Cool in pan 10 minutes; remove from pan and cool completely on wire rack.

BROWN SUGAR, BUTTERSCOTCH, AND BUTTERNUT POUND CAKES

BUTTERSCOTCH RUM POUND CAKE

This easy recipe starts with a cake mix. Sour cream and nuts make it rich and a touch of rum makes it special.

- 1 (11 oz) pkg butterscotch morsels
- 1 (18.25 oz) pkg yellow cake mix
- 4 eggs
- ¾ cup sour cream
- ½ cup milk
- ½ cup dark rum
- ¼ cup butter of margarine, softened
- 1 cup finely chopped walnuts or pecans

Grease 10-inch Bundt pan. Microwave 1⅓ cups morsels in medium, microwave-safe bowl on medium-high (70%) power for 1 minute; stir. Microwave an additional 10 to 20 second intervals, stirring until smooth; cool to room temperature. Combine cake mix, eggs, sour cream, milk, rum, butter and melted morsels in large mixer bowl. Beat on low speed just until moistened. Beat on high speed for 2 minutes. Stir in 1 cup chopped nuts. Pour into prepared Bundt pan. Bake at 350° for 50 to 60 minutes or until pick comes out clean. Cool in pan on wire rack for 20 minutes. Invert onto wire rack to cool completely; transfer to serving platter.

GLAZE

- Remaining butterscotch morsels
- 1-2 Tablespoons milk
- Chopped walnuts or pecans (optional)

Microwave morsels and milk in small, microwave-safe bowl on medium-high power for 30 seconds; stir. Microwave at additional 10 to 20 second intervals, stirring until smooth. Cool for 5 to 10 minutes. Pour over cooled cake. Garnish with chopped nuts, if desired.

FRUIT, NUT AND BERRY POUND CAKES

EASY ALMOND POUND CAKE

Here's a quick and easy way to create an almond pound cake with a silky smooth texture.

> 1 (18.25 oz.) package deluxe white cake mix
> 1 (3.4 oz.) package vanilla instant pudding mix
> 4 eggs
> 1 cup water
> ⅓ cup vegetable oil
> 1 Tablespoon almond extract
> ¾ cup sliced, toasted and chopped almonds (See note below)
> Confectioners' sugar for garnish

Note: To toast almonds, spread in a single layer on a baking sheet. Toast at 350° for 4 to 6 minutes or until golden and fragrant. Cool completely before chopping.

Combine cake mix, pudding mix, eggs, water, oil and almond extract in large bowl. Beat at low speed with electric mixer until moistened. Beat at medium speed for 2 minutes. Stir in almonds. Pour into greased and floured Bundt pan. Bake at 350° for 40-45 minutes or until toothpick inserted into center comes out clean. Cool in pan 25 minutes. Invert onto wire rack to cool completely. Dust with confectioners' sugar.

APPLE CINNAMON POUND CAKE

This traditional-flavored cake is quick and easy to make. It uses pre-packaged cake mix and instant pudding to create a cake that's good with or without topping.

> 1 package (two-layer) apple cinnamon deluxe cake mix
> 1 package (4½ oz.) vanilla instant pudding mix (small)
> ½ cup vegetable oil
> 1 cup water
> 4 eggs

Blend all ingredients in large bowl and beat at medium speed for 2 minutes. Pour into a greased and floured 10-inch tube pan. Bake at 350° for 45 to 55 minutes or until center springs back when lightly touched. Cool right side up 25 minutes, then remove from pan and place on serving plate.

Glaze

> 1 cup confectioners' sugar
> 2 Tablespoons milk

Blend ingredients together and drizzle over cake.

APRICOT LEMON POUND CAKE

This quick and easy recipe uses pre-packaged cake mix and instant pudding. Apricot nectar is used as the liquid.

> 1 box lemon supreme cake mix
> 1 package (4½ oz.) instant vanilla pudding
> 1 cup apricot nectar
> ½ cup sugar
> ⅔ cup oil
> 4 eggs

Mix all ingredients well. Pour into greased and floured 10-inch tube pan. Bake at 325° for 45 minutes or until cake tests done. Let cool 10 minutes in pan; remove from pan and cool completely on wire rack.

Glaze

> 1 cup 4-X powdered sugar
> juice of 2 lemons

Stir together and pour over cake.

BANANA POUND CAKE

Another quick and easy recipe – add a cup of chopped nuts for the taste of banana nut bread.

    1 package yellow cake mix
    4 eggs
    ⅓ cup oil
    ½ cup water
    1⅓ cups mashed bananas (about 4 medium)
    1 package (3¾ ounces) instant vanilla pudding
    ½ teaspoon cinnamon
    ½ teaspoon nutmeg
    1 teaspoon vanilla flavoring

Combine all ingredients in large mixer bowl. Mix until blended, and then beat at medium speed for 4 minutes. Turn batter into greased and lightly floured 10-inch tube pan. Bake at 350° for 1 hour or until cake tests done. If desired, dust with confectioner's sugar before serving.

CHERRY CHOCOLATE CHIP POUND CAKE

A delicious cake that will disappear fast. This is an easy cake to make, good for holiday gift giving (recipe will make 2 loaf cakes or one tube cake).

- 1 (18.25 oz.) box cherry-chocolate chip cake mix
- 1 (3.4 oz.) box vanilla pudding mix
- 1 cup plain yogurt or sour cream
- 4 eggs
- 1/3 cup vegetable oil
- 1 cup finely chopped pecans
- 1/2 cup mini-chocolate chips
- 1/4 cup sugar
- 1/4 cup chopped pecans
- 1 teaspoon ground cinnamon

Combine cake mix, pudding mix, oil, eggs and yogurt (or sour cream) in large mixing bowl. With mixer at low speed, blend just to moisten, scraping sides of bowl often. Then beat at medium speed for 4 minutes. Stir in miniature chocolate chips and 1 cup pecans. Pour batter into greased and sugared (substitute sugar for flour) 10-inch tube pan. Combine 1/4 cup sugar, 1/4 cup pecans and 1 teaspoon cinnamon; sprinkle evenly on batter. Bake at 350° for 1 hour or until cake tests done. Cool in pan on wire rack for 15 minutes. Remove from pan and cool completely on wire rack.

LEMON CURD POUND CAKE

This quick and easy recipe has the rich taste of lemon and walnuts.

- 1 package yellow cake mix with pudding in the mix
- 1 11½ oz jar lemon curd (about 1 cup)
- 1 cup walnuts, coarsely chopped (optional)

Grease a 10-inch tube pan. Prepare cake mix as directed, but add lemon curd and use ¼ cup less water than directions specify. Stir in chopped walnuts, if using. Pour batter evenly into pan. Bake at 350° for 45 to 50 minutes or until tooth pick inserted near center comes out clean. Cool cake in pan for 25 minutes; remove from pan; cool cake on rack.

Glaze

- 1 medium size lemon
- 1 cup confectioners' sugar

Grate lemon peel and squeeze juice from lemon. In small bowl, with spoon, mix confectioners' sugar and 4½ teaspoons lemon juice until smooth and of easy spreading consistency, adding more juice if necessary. Spoon glaze over cooled cake.

EASY LEMON POUND CAKE

This is a quick and easy recipe that uses pre-packaged cake mix and instant pudding mix. For an even richer taste, substitute 1 cup sour cream for the water.

> 1 package Duncan Hines Moist Deluxe Lemon Supreme cake mix
> 1 package (4 serving size) instant lemon pudding mix
> 4 eggs
> 1 cup water
> 1/3 cup vegetable oil
> 2 teaspoons lemon rind

Preheat oven to 350°F. Grease and flour 10-inch Bundt pan or tube pan. Combine cake mix, pudding mix, eggs, water, oil and lemon rind in large bowl. Beat at medium speed for 2 minutes. Pour into prepared pan. Bake at 350° for 50 to 60 minutes or until cake tests done. If you have one of those very heavy Bundt pans, take the cake out a little sooner than you would with a light aluminum tube pan – it continues baking. Try not to over bake to ensure a moist cake. Cool in pan 20 minutes. Invert onto serving plate. Cool completely.

Icing

> 2 cups sifted confectioners' sugar
> 1/2 cup lemon juice

Heat powdered sugar and lemon juice until boiling. Use fork to prick holes in cake and pour hot icing over cake.

PEACH POUND CAKE

Here's an easy and flavorful pound cake that will bring to mind the luscious peaches of summertime in the south.

    1 box yellow cake mix
    1 cup oil
    4 eggs
    1 small box peach gelatin
    1 Tablespoon lemon juice plus water to equal ½ cup liquid
    ½ cup mashed peaches (canned)

Mix all together and bake at 325° for 45 minutes.

Icing

    2 cups powered sugar
    ½ cup mashed peaches
    1 Tablespoon lemon juice

Mix all together and pour over cake while still warm. (not hot)

BUTTER PECAN POUND CAKE

Delicious & easy to make. You may substitute Coconut Pecan Frosting for the Butter Pecan Frosting if desired.

> 1 box Butter Pecan cake mix
> 1 can Butter Pecan frosting
> ½ cup pecans
> 4 eggs
> ¾ cup oil
> 1 cup water
> 3 Tablespoons powdered sugar
> ¼ cup pecans

Beat eggs, oil, water and dry cake mix together. Fold in frosting and chopped pecans. Spray tube pan with cooking spray and sprinkle with powdered sugar and chopped pecans. Pour batter into small tube pan and bake 350° for 40 minutes. DO NOT OVERBAKE. Turn cake out onto wire rack to cool.

PINEAPPLE-ORANGE POUND CAKE

This recipe is fruity and flavorful. It's an easy-to-make recipe, using pre-packaged cake mix as its starting point.

- 1 (18.25 oz.) package deluxe pineapple supreme cake mix
- 1 (3.4 oz.) package instant vanilla pudding mix
- 4 eggs
- 1 cup orange juice
- ⅓ cup vegetable oil
- 1 Tablespoon grated orange peel

Combine all ingredients in a large bowl. Beat at medium speed with electric mixer for 2 minutes. Pour into a greased and floured Bundt pan or 10-inch tube pan. Bake at 350° for 50 to 60 minutes or until cake tests done. Cool 25 minutes in pan. Invert onto serving plate.

Glaze

- ⅓ cup sugar
- ¼ cup orange juice

Combine sugar and orange juice in small saucepan. Simmer 3 minutes. Brush warm glaze on cake.

RASPBERRY POUND CAKE

This is a quick and easy recipe, using a cake mix and gelatin. Raspberry yogurt and cranberry-raspberry fruit relish give it an unusual taste for a pound cake.

    1 (18 oz.) box white or yellow cake mix
    1 (3 oz.) package peach, apricot or orange gelatin
    3 eggs
    1 (8 oz.) container raspberry yogurt
    ½ cup cranberry-raspberry fruit relish for turkey
    1 cup water

Combine cake mix and gelatin in large bowl. Add eggs, one at a time, beating after each addition. Add remaining ingredients and mix well. Pour batter into a greased and floured 10-inch tube pan. Bake at 350 for 60 minutes or until cake tests done. Cool for 10 minutes in pan; remove from pan and cool completely on wire rack.

STRAWBERRY DELIGHT POUND CAKE

This is another quick and easy recipe, using pre-packaged cake mix and flavored gelatin. Just mix it up and pour it in the pan. It calls for frozen strawberries in the cake batter, but fresh ones will work; cut them up and cover with sugar for one hour before using to create a little juice to use in the glaze.

> 1 package (2-layer) white cake mix
> 1 package (3 oz.) strawberry gelatin
> 4 eggs
> 1 cup cooking oil
> 1 pint frozen strawberries

Thaw, drain and save juice from strawberries. Mash strawberries. Put cake mix, gelatin, eggs, oil and strawberries in a mixing bowl. Mix well for 2 minutes at medium speed. Pour batter into a greased and floured 10-inch tube pan. Bake at 325° for 1 hour, or until cake tests done. Let cake cool and turn out of pan.

Glaze

> 2 teaspoons margarine
> 1 cup powdered sugar
> strawberry juice

Melt margarine. Add powdered sugar and mix. Add enough strawberry juice to spread over cake.

STRAWBERRY SUPREME POUND CAKE

Another quick and easy recipe, again using prepackaged cake mix and flavored gelatin. It has strawberries in the frosting.

- 1 package (2-layer) yellow cake mix
- 1 package (3 oz.) strawberry gelatin
- 4 eggs
- ¾ cup water
- ¾ cup cooking oil
- 1 teaspoon vanilla extract

Combine all ingredients in large bowl. Beat 2 minutes. Pour into a greased and floured 10-inch tube pan. Bake at 350° for one hour, or until cake tests done. Cool 10 minutes in pan; remove from pan and cool completely on wire rack.

FROSTING

- 2 teaspoons softened margarine
- 2 cups powdered sugar
- 1 10-oz. package frozen strawberries, thawed

Mix margarine, strawberries and powdered sugar and pour over warm cake.

HONEY-WALNUT POUND CAKE

This is a warm and buttery nut cake that's a snap to make.

- 1 package butter recipe yellow cake mix
- 1 cup water
- ½ cup chopped walnuts
- ⅓ cup butter or margarine, softened
- ¼ cup honey
- 3 eggs
- ½ cup butter cream ready-to-spread frosting

Grease and flour a 9-inch tube pan or 2 loaf pans. Beat cake mix (dry) and remaining ingredients except frosting in large bowl on low speed for 30 seconds. Beat on medium speed 2 minutes. Pour into pans. Bake at 350° for about 50 minutes, or until toothpick inserted in center comes out clean. Cool 10 minutes; remove from pan. Cool completely, about 1 hour. Place frosting in microwave-safe bowl. Microwave uncovered on Medium for 15 seconds. Spread frosting over top of cake, allowing some to drizzle down sides.

SPIRIT POUND CAKES

SHERRY POUND CAKE

Here's a cake with the elegant taste of sherry the quick and easy way. This one uses a cake mix and instant pudding, so it's a snap to put it together.

    1 package (two-layer) yellow cake mix
    1 package (4½ oz.) instant vanilla pudding
    4 eggs
    ¾ cup cooking oil
    ¾ cup dry sherry
    1 teaspoon grated nutmeg

In large mixing bowl, combine cake mix and pudding. Add eggs, oil, sherry, and nutmeg; beat together until well blended. Pour into a greased and floured 10-inch tube pan or large ring mold. Bake at 350° for 30-40 minutes or until cake tests done. Cool 10 minutes in pan. Remove from pan and cool completely on a wire rack before slicing.

QUICK AND EASY RUM POUND CAKE

Like other quick and easy recipes using a packaged cake mix and instant pudding, this one gives most of the benefits with less of the work. Try a buttery rum glaze from Chapter 6.

- 1 cup chopped pecans
- 1 Duncan Hines (2-layer) butter cake mix
- 1 package (4½ oz.) instant vanilla pudding
- ½ cup light rum
- ½ cup water
- ½ cup vegetable oil
- 4 eggs

Grease and flour a 10-inch tube pan and sprinkle the chopped nuts on bottom. Combine cake mix and pudding mix in large mixing bowl. Add remaining ingredients and mix well. Pour batter over nuts in pan. Bake at 325° for 55 minutes or until cake tests done. Cool for 5 minutes in pan, then invert onto serving dish for glazing.

EASY APRICOT BRANDY POUND CAKE

Here's an easy recipe that is rich, delicious and easy. This cake freezes well.

> 1 (18.25 oz.) box yellow cake mix
> 1 (3.5 oz.) vanilla instant pudding
> 1 cup sour cream
> ½ cup apricot brandy
> 1 teaspoon vanilla extract
> ½ teaspoon orange extract
> ½ teaspoon lemon extract
> ½ teaspoon almond extract
> 4 eggs

In a large bowl, beat cake mix, pudding mix and eggs until smooth. Mix brandy and flavorings in sour cream and add to egg mixture. Beat at least 2 minutes on medium speed. Pour batter into a greased and floured Bundt pan or 10-inch tube pan. Bake at 350° for 50 to 55 minutes or until cake tests done. Cool in pan on wire rack for 20 minutes. Remove from pan and cool completely on wire rack.

SPICY POUND CAKES

CINNAMON POUND CAKE

This warm cake has a great aroma when baking and tastes even better. It's good warm with a big glass of cold milk, but tastes even better the next day.

- 1 box yellow cake mix (2-layer size)
- 1 small box vanilla instant pudding
- ½ cup vegetable oil
- 1 cup buttermilk
- 2 teaspoons imitation butter flavoring
- 1 teaspoon vanilla flavoring
- 4 eggs
- 4 teaspoons cinnamon-sugar
- (3 Tablespoons sugar, ½ teaspoon cinnamon)

Mix all ingredients just until blended; the batter will be very thick. Spoon half of the batter into greased and floured 10-inch tube pan; sprinkle with cinnamon-sugar. Add remaining batter. Bake at 350° about 40 minutes or until cake tests done.

Icing:

- 1 cup powdered sugar
- 2 teaspoons milk
- 2 teaspoons light corn syrup
- 1 teaspoon vanilla

Mix all ingredients and spread on cooled cake. The icing will dry to a hard shiny finish.

CROCKPOT STREUSEL POUND CAKE

Pound cake from the crock-pot? You bet, and it's easy because you use a packaged cake mix as well!

> 1 package (16 oz) pound cake mix
> ¼ cup packed brown sugar
> 1 Tablespoon flour
> ¼ cup finely chopped nuts
> 1 teaspoon cinnamon

Mix cake mix according to package directions. Pour batter into well-greased and floured 2 pound coffee tin. Combine, sugar, flour, nuts, cinnamon and sprinkle over cake batter. Place can inside crock-pot. Cover top of can with 8 layers of paper towels. Cover pot and bake on high for 3 to 4 hours.

PASTEL POUND CAKE

Pick the flavor/color gelatin of your choice and create a colorful pound cake for any theme, any time. Party on....

　　1 package yellow or white cake mix
　　1 (3 oz.) package any flavor fruit gelatin
　　¾ cup water
　　½ cup vegetable oil
　　4 eggs

Combine the cake mix, gelatin mix, water, oil and eggs. Beat for 3 minutes or until smooth and creamy. Pour into a greased and floured 10-inch tube pan. Bake at 350° for 50 to 55 minutes or until cake tests done. Cool in the pan for 15 minutes, then remove and cool completely on wire rack. Sprinkle with powdered sugar if desired.

Made in the USA
Lexington, KY
04 August 2015